In the Shadow of the Holocaust

In the Shadow of the
Holocaust

Nazi Persecution of
Jewish-Christian Germans

James F. Tent

UNIVERSITY PRESS OF KANSAS

Published by the University Press of Kansas (Lawrence, Kansas 66049), which was organized by the Kansas Board of Regents and is operated and funded by Emporia State University, Fort Hays State University, Kansas State University, Pittsburg State University, the University of Kansas, and Wichita State University

Library of Congress Cataloging-in-Publication Data

Tent, James F.

In the shadow of the Holocaust : Nazi persecution of Jewish-Christian Germans / James F. Tent.

p. cm. — (Modern war studies)

Includes bibliographical references and index.

ISBN 0-7006-1228-9 (cloth : alk. paper)

1. Jewish Christians — Nazi persecution — Germany.   2. Holocaust, Jewish (1939–1945) — Germany.   3. Oral history.   I. Title.   II. Series

D804.5.J48 T46 2003

940.53'18'088204 — dc21   2002013627

British Library Cataloguing in Publication Data is available.

Printed in the United States of America

10 9 8 7 6 5 4 3 2 1

The paper used in this publication meets the minimum requirements of the American National Standard for Permanence of Paper for Printed Library Materials Z39.48-1984.

To Werner Jentsch

and to all the other men and women

who suffered persecution as so-called *Mischlinge*

under German National Socialism

CONTENTS

This study began informally in the summer of 1978, when I, a young assistant professor of history, was riding on a long-distance train through the German Democratic Republic (GDR). During a part of that trip, I found myself in a compartment opposite an older man and a woman. We were the sole occupants of that compartment, and, as travelers often do, we fell into conversation. It transpired that my traveling companions were Professor Werner Jentsch and his sister. He revealed that he was a retired mathematician at the Martin Luther University in Halle an der Saale. She demurred (i.e., she said virtually nothing). As a GDR *Rentner* (retiree), Jentsch was allowed to travel abroad (mostly at his own expense). He and his sister were traveling by rail, he to Sweden to visit relatives and to hike in its mountains, she to her own undisclosed destination. Jentsch's trip was a special privilege, one accorded only to GDR citizens who had reached retirement age and who had relatives abroad who could bear the bulk of their visitors' expenses. I never learned his sister's name — she was most reluctant to speak with strangers, an understandable reaction by a GDR citizen in those Cold War times. However, for reasons that are unclear to me, her brother, Werner, was in a mood to converse. Starting slowly, he shed his inhibitions — this despite his sister's worried glances — and in a fascinating conversation lasting several hours, Professor Jentsch poured out his life's story. It was when we shook hands and were going our separate ways that I decided that if ever I could, I should write about Jentsch and about the persons who had shared his chilling, and as far as I knew largely unknown, experiences. Inadvertently, he became a spokesman for thousands of Germans of his generation.

What Werner Jentsch told me was that he was a *Halbjude* (so-called half-Jew) in Hitler's Germany. He told of the terrors life had held for him under National Socialism. After the war his racial status had, of course, not been a crime in East Germany. However, he also assured me that the persecution he had suffered from 1933 to 1945 was mortifying to his fellow citizens in the GDR, a topic the authorities especially would prefer not to hear about. Now, decades later and in the presence of a perfect stranger, he felt compelled to explain what being half-Jewish had really meant. After all, it was now one generation since the end of the war. Surely someone must be interested in what he had endured.

I confess that I was stunned as he patiently explained to me what had befallen people like him in Hitler's Third Reich. Half-Jews, he stated, had been called *Mischlinge*. These were persons deemed by the Nazis to have had two Jewish grandparents. Like full Jews they had become social pariahs in 1933, but they were pariahs whose abominable status only became apparent in German society several years after the full Jews' suffering really began. Jentsch elaborated. In the early years of National Socialism, he explained, *Mischlinge* had fallen into a separate legal category from their fully Jewish relatives and thus had not suffered the same fate as the latter during the most intense phase of Nazi genocide against full Jews. Full Jews had been ostracized from the first, excluded from the civil service in 1933, persecuted by the Nuremberg race laws of 1935 and the pogrom of November 1938, a process culminating in the Final Solution of 1942. However, Jentsch assured me, Germany's *Mischlinge* had also suffered persecution, albeit neither as immediate nor as severe as that of full Jews. At first, the Nazis had held them, the so-called *Mischlinge,* in a kind of legal limbo, allowing them to at least coexist in society and to hold marginal jobs. Yet, the same laws had restricted them from marrying Aryans or leading normal social lives. Some *Mischlinge,* Jentsch included, even served as soldiers in the war until sent home in disgrace. However, a net had begun to close in on half-Jews too, he said, so that by the end of the war, Germany's *Mischlinge* knew that they, too, were the next victims designated for slaughter. It was only late-war chaos that saved them, said Jentsch, and *Mischlinge* like him largely remained in Germany after 1945, soon-to-be-forgotten victims of the Holocaust, embarrassing leftovers from the trauma of Hitler's Germany.

During that memorable train journey of 1978, Jentsch assured me repeatedly that GDR officialdom had not displayed the slightest interest in his life's story. Now at last he had an impartial witness to whom he could impart what had happened a generation earlier. The conversation was not entirely congenial. Periodically, Werner's sister darted nervous glances at me and at her brother as he poured out his story. Finally, it dawned on me. She, too, was a former *Mischling* and was distraught that her brother had revealed such sensitive information to a total stranger. I resolved simply to listen.

Finally, the train arrived at my destination and wheezed to a halt. I gathered my bags and tried to make cheerful good-byes. Shaken by what I had heard, I hardly noticed the postal address that Werner Jentsch had pressed into my hand as I stumbled out of the train. I do remember waving as their coach pulled out from the station, and of seeing him and his worried sister through the compartment window. Quickly, their coach moved on toward the Baltic coast and their respective destinations. I never saw them again.

I entered Jentsch's address into my pocket calendar, telling myself I would write to him soon, very soon. However, upon my return to the United States, I learned from knowledgeable friends that GDR citizens who received private correspondence from the West would encounter difficulties. Stifling my urge to retain contact with a gentleman who had impressed me so greatly, I resolved not to write to Werner Jentsch.

A decade passed. By 1989 the Cold War was coming to its end. At that stage I had completed several other historical projects, the most recent of which was a history of the Free University (FU) of Berlin since 1948, a joint undertaking of German students and the American occupation authorities. The FU had compiled a fascinating history during its brief existence from its founding to 1988. Even cursory research showed that it had been, briefly, the central cultural focus of the Cold War between the United States and the Soviets in 1948. During the course of my investigations of the FU's history, I discovered, coincidentally, that several of that university's first students were survivors of the Holocaust. Like Werner Jentsch, they told me, obliquely at first then openly, that they, too, had been categorized as *Mischlinge*. Here was that term *Mischlinge* once again!

Following completion of my history of the Free University, I became involved in other projects. However, my resolve to write a history of Germany's half-Jewish citizens under National Socialism continued. I spoke candidly to those persons who had helped me to prepare my history of the Free University and who had once suffered because of their Jewish heritage. With their encouragement and help, I have compiled the history that follows. My investigation makes no pretense of being a comprehensive, definitive study of this aspect of the Holocaust, replete with exhaustive analysis of the Nazis' motives or of their internal bureaucratic discussions. Other historians have already done much of that important footwork. What struck me so force-

fully was the fact that so few personal accounts and case histories exist, especially in the English language, about such persons. Therefore, I determined
that I would try to provide a history that showed how people of partial Jewish
ancestry coped with conditions on a day-to-day basis from the time the Nazis
seized power until they were vanquished, and then to show how the legacy
of that anti-Semitic hatred has lingered in the minds of the victims ever since.

A brief description of the methodology employed in preparing this history is necessary. Given the limitations on the resources and the amount of
time available to me for interviews and for research, I decided early in my
study to conduct my interviews by taking down extensive notes while the
eyewitnesses recounted their experiences in German and answered the questions I posed or else interjected in the course of the interview. I did not use a
tape recorder, since verbatim quotations from the subjects were not envisaged, and the accounts of their experiences were intended to be read above
all by an English-speaking audience. As soon as possible after the conclusion
of the interview, I wrote up the notes in the form of a detailed protocol in
English and then mailed it to the person just interviewed with a request to
make corrections, amendments, additions, or deletions as he or she saw fit.
Those interviewed then sent their corrected protocols back to me. I entered
their corrections into new drafts of the protocols and returned them to each
person for further review. Sometimes this took two or three rounds after the
production of the original protocol before we could agree on the final reading. Most of those persons interviewed felt at ease in working with the English
language. In one or two instances where this was not the case, the person
interviewed was aided by family members, other relatives, or trusted friends
who could help in making the corrections. Undoubtedly, some historians,
especially specialists in oral history, would prefer verbatim transcripts taken
down in the original language from tape recordings of the interview. Lacking any technical or clerical support for this project, I decided upon the above
method. Another obvious bias in this form of oral history is that it cannot
take into account persons who were full adults or older citizens when the Nazis
seized power in 1933. Virtually all of them have died, normal human life spans
being what they are. On the other end of the age spectrum, children of Jewish-
Christian families who were born in the later years of Nazism could have only
vague impressions of what was happening, since they perceived the world
around them as infants or small children. One of the other frustrations I

encountered in this project was the fact that I could not utilize large portions of each eyewitness's interview (many of which ran dozens of pages in length) in order to limit the manuscript to an acceptable length and to avoid duplication of eyewitness experiences that might have become tiresome to the reader. Those interviews, several of which require strict confidentiality, will be deposited with a major archive once this history is published and will come under a lengthy closure rule until the eyewitnesses who have invoked confidentiality are no longer alive.

A final point about the interviews is also necessary. I took down the eyewitnesses' statements as accurately as I could, and with their help repeated their accounts in my narrative as faithfully as I could. As is well known, oral histories, although valuable, are hardly perfect instruments for recounting the historical record. Ideally, such accounts should be combined with parallel archival records or other original documents and accounts that can corroborate the eyewitnesses' statements. Often that was not possible in the interviews I conducted. I gained access to valuable archival collections of persecuted persons in Greater Hesse plus a few isolated documents in the Landesarchiv in Berlin. The Gestapo document collection in North Rhine–Westphalia also was extremely useful. However, none of the persons whom I interviewed was from those regions — half were from Berlin. Therefore, it was not possible to examine, for example, specific postwar restitution documents, filed by the very persons who later agreed to allow me interviews a half-century later. Yet, there are certain correctives to this imperfect process. First, especially among the Berlin residents whom I interviewed, there are informal but long-standing communication links. They have known each other and heard each other's descriptions of persecution and survival ever since the wartime period or at least since the postwar period. Therefore, what each individual Berlin eyewitness related to me was often confirmed by other friends and colleagues among that recognized social circle. In other instances, the persons referred to me who eventually granted interviews were well known beforehand to professional historians and to other social scientists, colleagues of my acquaintance in places as diverse as Munich, Hamburg, and Frankfurt, as well as Berliners who referred me to persons living elsewhere in Germany (I list their names below). Therefore, in only one instance did I interview a person who had not specifically been referred to me by either a part of the Berlin circle, with whom I have been acquainted over nearly two decades, or by other trusted scholarly colleagues in the social sciences. With respect to the one exception in this group, I can say that the eyewitness who came forward had responded to an article about my project after it had appeared in a respected newspaper in the Rhine–Main area in 1994 at the encouragement of Herr Hans-Georg Ruppel, archivist for the city of Offenbach am Main, and a veteran of historical research, including oral history interviews. Archivist Ruppel undertook to be the liaison between the respondent and me. That eyewitness, Helmut Langer (not his real name), was one of those persons who invoked strict confidentiality and whose conduct during the interview process struck me as utterly genuine. Therefore, it stretches the bonds of credulity for me to suspect that he is not the person whom he says he is or that he described persecutions he had not experienced. Archivist Ruppel entertains no doubts about Helmut Langer's legitimacy either, having conducted many interviews himself. Nevertheless, it is an undeniable fact that I have not specifically correlated the twenty eyewitness accounts used in this history with archival documents that refer to them alone. On the other hand, those extensive archival sources that I did consult (I had to treat the victims named therein anonymously), be they postwar Hessian restitution files, the two Berlin files, or the extensive Gestapo files from North Rhine–Westphalia, only confirm the experiences that the twenty individuals whom I have interviewed had undergone. For example, there were instances when eyewitness accounts and archival documents agreed exactly on details concerning specifically named forced-labor camps or other minutiae connected to persecution. Thus, it must be left to the reader to accept or reject the authenticity of the accounts presented to me by the eyewitnesses who aided me in my investigation.

That said, my gratitude to the following persons is enormous. Horst Hartwich, the long-serving director of the Free University of Berlin's International Affairs Office, recently deceased, was tireless in relating to me his experiences as a *Mischling* during the years I served under him while writing my history of the FU. Horst also introduced me to a number of his friends and acquaintances, fellow Berliners who had endured similar persecutions. With their valuable help, I was able to build a network of contributors whose eyewitness accounts played a vital role in the preparation of this history. The names of those eyewitnesses appear at the end of this history.

Professor Stanislaw Karol Kubicki of the Free University was also extremely helpful in enlarging my circle of contacts in Berlin and elsewhere, as was

Professor Johann Gerlach, formerly the president of the FU. Other valued supporters of this history include Dr. Beate Meyer of Hamburg, who, showing true professional courtesy, offered me the benefits of her decade-long experience in interviewing persons who had suffered Nazi persecution. It is no exaggeration to point out that Dr. Meyer is the world's leading expert on this subject. Fellow historian Dr. Ursula Huber in Munich enabled me to meet several other crucially important eyewitnesses. As already noted, Stadtarchivar Hans Ruppel of the City Archives of Offenbach am Main located another valuable eyewitness. Dr. Volker Eichler of the Hessian Hauptstaatsarchiv in Wiesbaden opened valuable collections of postwar restitution files. Dr. Jürgen Wetzel and Dr. Klaus Dettmer at the Landesarchiv in Berlin opened their collection to the very best of their ability, too. Dr. Black-Veltrup and Dr. Anselm Faust at the North Rhine–Westphalian Hauptstaatsarchiv in Düsseldorf did the same for the much larger collection of Gestapo records. Librarian Charles Milford granted me a valuable personal interview of his experiences and then provided me with the benefits of his superb bibliographical skills. Professor Kurt Shell in Frankfurt am Main kindly placed me in touch with Dr. Rudolf Klein in Vienna. Fellow Frankfurt citizen Dr. Elisabeth Rohr generously helped me with compiling the recollections of her mother, Martha Rohr. Erika Waldegger of Memmingen in Bavaria, referred to me by Dr. Huber and her associates at the University of Munich, recounted in great detail the persecution that her father, Emil Steiner in Kempten, had suffered. Bernd Rebensburg revealed to me from his schoolboy experiences at the Evangelisches Pädagogium (Otto-Kühne-Schule) that the bizarre world forced upon *Mischlinge* by the Nazis had been shared by other ethnic groups besides the German-Jewish *Mischlinge*. Hans-Werner and Ingrid Koeppel arranged a crucial meeting with that school's former director, Klaus Otto Kühne, who confirmed the accuracy of Rebensburg's statements. Sabine and Christian Koch provided invaluable support in Berlin.

Four wise and incisive readers of the manuscript are also to be thanked: Hans A. Schmitt, Joyce Seltzer, Gerhard L. Weinberg, and David S. Wyman. Each saved me from many pitfalls, be they matters of organizational, literary, or historical nature.

Last, and with eternal thanks, I recognize Margaret Wyman Tent for helping me shepherd this arduous project through to its conclusion. When the work seemed endless, and when the accumulated material seemed especially depressing, she steadied me and helped me find the way to keep writing. I am most grateful for her support. This study is the most difficult work I have ever attempted. Research and writing were not the main challenge. The real challenge lay in the fact that I had to confront on a daily basis true evil committed against decent human beings. There are few happy endings here.

Another point of clarification is necessary. Legally speaking, the countries and territories militarily occupied by Hitler's Gross Deutsches Reich (Greater German Reich) came under the rubric of "German," meaning "German-controlled," territory. In terms of diplomacy and international law at that time, the governing nation was Germany, no matter what title the Nazis chose to use. It is important to note, however, that National Socialist policy, especially its racial policy, reigned supreme in all of those territories—hence the term commonly used by historians ever after and also used in this text: "Nazi-occupied."

As in all my histories, any errors or omissions herein are exclusively my responsibility.

INTRODUCTION

Benefiting from eyewitness accounts by Germany's partially Jewish citizens in the period between 1933 and 1945, this study uses individual case histories to explore the lengths to which Hitler and his National Socialists were prepared to go in order to eliminate the last vestiges of Judaism in Europe. The Jewish Holocaust holds a unique place in our memories and in historical writings because of genocide, the Nazis' attempt to murder an entire segment of society by reason of race. Jews had always been the central focus of Hitler's hatred from the moment he entered politics to the moment he killed himself. His true believers felt the same, although a historical debate continues over when their permanent desire to remove Jews from Germany transformed itself into the decision to murder all Jews.[1] Ongoing investigations into that terrible crime have disclosed other dimensions and other victims of Nazi hatred as well. Their irrational notions of race were part of a pattern of intolerance, and they persecuted large numbers of victims not only on the basis of race, but also on the basis of ideology, religion, sexual orientation, and mental capacity, to mention only the most obvious examples. Thus, Europe's Gypsies (Roma and Sinti) suffered terribly, as did homosexuals, who perished by the thousands. Hitler's euthanasia program killed thousands of the mentally and physically handicapped. The Jehovah's Witnesses were luckless victims, as were untold thousands of Communists and Social Democrats. It is a futile exercise to compare the degree of suffering of one group of Holocaust victims with the others, although it is still important to note that Jews formed by far the largest and most prominent ethnic group targeted for complete extinction. Suffice it to say that National Socialism was brutally exclusionary and racist. It persecuted any minority groups or persons whom the Nazis considered to be undesirable.[2]

This study seeks to expose the sufferings of a category of victims that has largely gone unnoticed in investigations of the Holocaust: Jewish-Christian *Mischlinge* (i.e., German citizens who were categorized as *Halbjuden* — half- Jews — by that generation of Germans). It also includes, to a lesser extent, those citizens categorized as quarter-Jews. Terminology in this study was challenging because no one today would refer to persons as half-Jews any more than they would call them half-Christians. Yet, that generation used such terms (or far worse), and so, in order to establish categories of convenience, this study employs the most obvious terms.

The historical record shows clearly that Germans of partial Jewish heritage, especially half-Jews, ultimately became targets of Nazi genocide, but because of the peculiar legal status that Hitler and his minions erected around them, the *Mischlinge* mostly survived — if only by a slim margin. Their accounts reveal much about the dynamics as well as the arbitrariness of the Nazi movement. After all, it was a regime that, though threatened by impending military defeat, nevertheless expended much of its remaining energy and resources on eradicating the sad remnants of Judaism, including the hitherto legally protected full Jews married to Aryans in so-called mixed marriages (or if there were children, then they were designated as "privileged mixed marriages"). The Nazi hierarchy was also making preparations to murder the half-Jewish children of those marriages: the *Mischlinge* first degree. The best that quarter-Jews could hope for was forced sterilization followed by low-end jobs until they, too, died, presumably the last of their "racial" lineage. Interviews with eyewitnesses to such persecution, most of whom are now reaching the end of their normal life spans, in combination with recently opened archival sources, are what enabled this author to investigate the fate of those so-called *Mischlinge* a half-century after the defeat of National Socialism. The circumstances they once faced were so daunting that they, too, deserve compassion for the persecution they suffered and recognition for the fortitude they showed in overcoming adversity in a world where their suffering went unnoticed and where most of them coped as best they could, usually in isolation. Since so many of the victims in this little-known category were children who came of age under the Nazis, their situation is particularly poignant, given their naïveté and vulnerability.

The term *Mischling* applied only to German citizens (as distinct from partially Jewish citizens of other nations occupied by the Nazis). Therefore, it refers to a distinctive and limited number of persons. The best estimate is that the Nazis placed approximately seventy-two thousand German citizens into the category of half-Jews according to their census for Greater Germany in 1939. The quarter-Jews totaled perhaps forty thousand people.[3] The German-language term *Mischling* (a person of mixed religious or ethnic background) is a nineteenth-century creation, referring at first to children of marriages of mixed religion, such as a Catholic-Protestant union. Later in that same century, the term came to denote mixed "racial" or ethnic backgrounds. For example, children of German soldiers and African women in the time of Imperial Germany's colonial ventures were called *Mischlinge*. When French Senegalese occupation troops (after World War I) and American soldiers of African-American ancestry (after World War II) and German women produced children, their offspring (the first-mentioned group having already been sterilized in 1937) were also called *Mischlinge*.[4] The generations that have followed World War II have come to realize that this term carries distinctly racist overtones, and it is no longer acceptable. Yet, it was the term employed by the Nazis and was widely used by other contemporaries in its historical context. That is why the author sometimes precedes it with the qualifier "so-called." In the context of this study, a *Mischling* (singular) or *Mischlinge* (plural) refer to German citizens of half-Jewish and quarter-Jewish ancestry unless otherwise indicated. As noted, the terms half-Jew and quarter-Jew do not receive quotation marks in this study, in order to relieve the reader of cumbersome grammatical markings. Those were the most benign terms employed in that generation.

As the previous paragraph indicates, there were two main categories of *Mischlinge* as established by Nazi racial laws in 1935. A person with two grandparents deemed to have been Jewish by the Nazis (usually on the basis of his or her ancestors' associations to Jewish *religious* communities, despite Nazi claims of using "race" as the deciding factor; besides, religious community records from preceding generations were easiest to access) were labeled as *Mischling ersten Grades,* literally, a *Mischling* of the first degree. This was distinct from the second category in which the Nazi authorities decreed that there was one Jewish grandparent, consigning the victim to the status of *Mischling zweiten Grades* (i.e., a *Mischling* of the second degree). Generally, *Mischlinge zweiten Grades* did not suffer persecution to the same extent as half-Jews (to say nothing of what full Jews experienced), although they too felt some effects from Nazi racism, such as a sharp cap on higher education or professional advancement. Nevertheless, their chances of leading normal lives steadily diminished under the Nazis, and the best estimates are that quarter-Jews would have faced involuntary sterilization if Hitler's regime had remained in power. In fact, if Nazi fanatics like Himmler and Heydrich had had their way, the quarter-Jews would have been murdered, too. Often, the two *Mischling* variants received a shorthand version in historical documentation:

"*Mischling* first degree" and "*Mischling* second degree." Even so, as noted, the general public usually referred to them as *Halbjuden* (half-Jews) or, less frequently, as *Vierteljuden* (quarter-Jews). One other subcategory for the half-Jewish category is significant. Most *Mischlinge* came from secular households, although frequently their parents had them baptized or confirmed as Protestants or, less frequently, as Catholics (approximately 90 percent of the category). If a half-Jewish German citizen declared himself or herself to have accepted Judaism as the religion of choice or had remained on the records of a local Jewish community in the Nazi era, that person, even though a half-Jew and technically a *Mischling* first degree, was entered into a special category called a *Geltungsjude*. This meant that the Nazis considered that kind of *Mischling* to be "equivalent to a Jew." In consequence, the victim suffered persecution on the same scale as the indignities suffered by full Jews in mixed marriages. The Nazis arrayed approximately eight thousand *Mischlinge* first degree into this harshly treated group, all of whom were required from 1941 onward to wear the Star of David along with full Jews. Many *Geltungsjuden* died or were imprisoned during the twelve years of National Socialist rule. The Nazis treated sixty-four thousand persons as normal *Mischlinge* first degree, most of whom survived.

Even by Nazi standards, a *Mischling* first degree was half Aryan. Therefore, a question arises. Why did such persons become targets of so much internal discussion in the ranks of government and party officials in Hitler's Germany? Simply stated, from the early days of their movement, the Nazis had found such persons of partially Jewish heritage almost as abhorrent. Hitler had stated this explicitly in his condemnation of Jews and their progeny in *Mein Kampf*. "Nature likes bastards only little," he wrote in 1923–24. Borrowing from the racist theories of Houston Stewart Chamberlain, among others, he railed at length against "bastardization" and what he called crossbreeding and racial mixing. "If, for example," Hitler continued, "a single individual of a certain race were to enter into a union with a racially lower individual, the result would be, first, a lowering of the standard itself." He devoted several passages in his rambling account to the deleterious effects as he saw it of "crossbreeding" and how the future German State should put an end to intermarriages.[5] He returned to the subject often in public speeches, repetitious monologues, and internal party discussions. His true believers did the same.

[handwritten: [Did the "true believers" implement the laws?]]

Thus, in addition to full Jews, Germany's half-Jews also became prime targets once the Nazis seized power in 1933.

Internal party and government discussions during the creation of the crucially important Nuremberg race decrees of 1935 included an extraordinary statement by one of the primary architects of those discriminatory laws, Ministerialrat (Ministry Counselor) Bernhard Lösener of the Reich Ministry of the Interior. He manned the Ministry's desk for racial affairs. "In principle," he stated, "the half-Jew should be regarded as a more serious enemy than the full Jew because, in addition to Jewish characteristics, he possesses so many Germanic ones which the full Jew lacks."[6] On the face of it, Lösener sounded as ardently anti-Semitic as any other senior Nazi. Yet, upon closer examination, his convoluted reasoning reveals other aspects of his approach. Lösener was, with the backing of his superior, Staatsekretär (State Secretary) Wilhelm Stuckart, the key official who was responsible for racial affairs at the Interior Ministry. Despite his ominous-sounding assignment, Lösener and the largely unnamed civil servants under him were destined to become unlikely allies of the *Mischlinge*. True, Lösener had joined Hitler's National Sozialistische Deutsche Arbeiter-Partei (NSDAP) even before the Seizure of Power in 1933, a party notorious for its blatant anti-Semitism. Yet, as a senior civil servant and a believer in orderliness in government and its legal system, Lösener found himself over time cast in the — for him — unlikely role as protector of citizens who were not only half-Jewish but also half-Aryan, even by the Nazis' warped reckoning. Moreover, the *Mischlinge* often were members of families that in happier times had comprised part of the ranks of civil servants. They also had many fully Aryan relatives whom the Nazis were reluctant to alienate completely. It was in 1935 at the time that Hitler was promulgating his race laws that Lösener wrote a memorandum that aimed to prevent some Party members from equating half-Jews with full Jews. He had to couch his arguments in terms that sounded anything but compassionate. Otherwise, he would have lost any standing whatsoever in the senior circles of government, to say nothing of the ardently racist inner core of the NSDAP. To be sure, those Germans who were true believers in the National Socialist movement were not interested in any subtleties in Lösener's arguments, and they continued to view Germany's *Mischlinge* as legitimate targets of persecution on a par with full Jews. Therefore, Lösener and his subordinates adopted a low-profile but effective campaign to separate half-Jews from full Jews during crucial periods of lawmaking in 1935, 1938, and again in 1942. In effect, he mounted a delaying campaign that netted the *Mischlinge* several crucial years of relative grace. Citing practicalities and claims of tactical need, Stuckart, the de facto spokesman at the Interior Ministry, used Lösener's arguments to play on Hitler's fears as a politician. The latter did not wish to alienate large numbers of Aryan relatives, especially in the first decade of the regime's existence. Furthermore, Hitler, an ardent believer in the 1919 "stab-in-the-back" theory that disintegrating civilian morale had caused Germany's defeat in World War I, was, along with his propaganda minister, Josef Goebbels, sensitive to the attitudes of Aryans in Jewish-Christian marriages during the next war. Thus, Lösener, as the driving force at the Interior Ministry, could play upon those anxieties in blunting the fanatics' attempts at lumping half-Jews together with full Jews. Otherwise, they would surely have joined the full Jews, first in the ghettoes and then in the transports to the east that began in 1941 (i.e., they, too, would have disappeared into the Holocaust as full-fledged victims). Instead, the *Mischlinge* survived, uneasily, as a separate legal category under National Socialism. This hardly meant that the Nazis forgot about the half-Jews. During the war, the party's self-appointed guardians of racial purity demonstrated repeatedly that they were determined to finish "unfinished business." And in the end, the racial fanatics nearly had their way in the murder of Germany's half-Jews, too.

Yet, because Germany's half-Jews largely survived the war, most studies of the Holocaust generally have included Jewish-Christian *Mischlinge* fleetingly, if at all. Despite the frightful experiences *Mischlinge* endured, there is admittedly some justification for this neglect in major studies of the Holocaust. In terms of the sheer number of victims involved, the *Mischlinge* were a relatively small category. Yet, survive though most of them did, they suffered terribly, and by any normal standard, they would be singled out today as having been horribly mistreated, many of them victims of cruelties that today social workers might compare in their traumatic effect only to such criminal acts as gross cruelty to children, if not outright child abuse. In addition, those *Mischlinge* who were lucky enough to emerge alive in 1945 knew without any doubt that they were the next category of victims to be fed into the maw of the Nazi killing machine. In this respect the historical record is clear. Therefore, survivors, historians, and other interested parties have finally begun to address the experiences of former *Mischlinge* in the age of National Socialism with greater attention and sympathy.

The once slender bibliographical record regarding *Mischlinge* has begun to grow. One of the seminal writers on the Holocaust and an expert on the German bureaucracy that conducted the Holocaust, Raul Hilberg, provided much useful information about *Mischlinge* in the context of the Holocaust in his magisterial *The Destruction of the European Jews*, which appeared in 1961 (revised periodically thereafter). He also noted the internal bureaucratic haggling between the Reich Ministry of the Interior and the hard-line anti-Semitic elements in the government and in the Party, but by and large, the *Mischlinge* were a modest component in his comprehensive study. Then, in 1989, British historian Jeremy Noakes produced a more detailed contribution that appeared in Yearbook 34 of the Leo Baeck Institute under the title "The Development of Nazi Policy towards the German-Jewish '*Mischlinge*,' 1933–1945."[7] In it, the author eschewed individual accounts by survivors, concentrating instead on those critically important legal developments within the State–Party apparatus that so profoundly affected partially Jewish citizens. Besides some autobiographical accounts, other scholarly studies have also appeared in recent years. Hamburg historian Beate Meyer has produced the most authoritative examination of former *Mischlinge*. She has worked for more than a decade on various publicly and privately supported historical projects related to the persecution of Jews and *Mischlinge*, first and foremost in Hamburg in an oral history project, "Hamburger Lebensläufe — Werkstatt der Erinnerung" (Hamburg Lives — Workshop for Remembrance), later in Berlin, and most recently at Yad Vashem in Israel, gathering interviews from hundreds of eyewitnesses and canvasing state and local archives for written accounts. Her doctoral dissertation, published as *Jüdische Mischlinge* in 1999, is perhaps the most authoritative account available on the lives of German-Jewish *Mischlinge* and of the bureaucratic web that surrounded them both in the National Socialist era and in the period since 1945.[8] An American historian, Nathan Stoltzfus, has examined the status of "privileged mixed marriages" between Germans and Jews in National Socialist Germany whose children were, after all, the *Mischlinge* in question. His study, *Resistance of the Heart: Intermarriage and the Rosenstrasse Protest in Nazi Germany*, uses the courageous protest actions of Berlin women in February 1943 against the transporting of their Jewish husbands as the central focus of his pioneering

study.[9] His work also shows how worried the Nazis were in wartime about alienating Aryan relatives and thereby damaging civilian morale. In fact, that may have been the key factor that delayed Nazi persecution of partially Jewish citizens just long enough for them to avoid the fate of Europe's full Jews. Bryan Mark Rigg recently completed a doctoral dissertation at Cambridge University about Jews, *Mischlinge,* and other non-Aryans who served in the German armed forces under National Socialism.[10] His pioneering study was published in the spring of 2002 under the title *Hitler's Jewish Soldiers: The Untold Story of Nazi Racial Laws and Men of Jewish Descent in the German Military.* Other German scholars are contributing impressive scholarship on this subject, too. Gerhard Lindemann's lengthy study, *"Typisch jüdisch"* (Typically Jewish), which appeared in 1998, examines the treatment of Jews, half-Jews, and Judaism in general from the Weimar Republic to the early years of the Federal Republic, using the Protestant Church in Hannover and its relationship to Jewish-Christian parishioners as his focal point. Aleksandar-Saša Vuletić's *Christen jüdischer Herkunft* (Christians of Jewish Descent), published in 1999, meticulously examines the terms that defined *Mischlinge* and contains important material on how they tried to organize self-help groups under the Nazis up to the beginning of World War II.[11] Nevertheless, it was Noakes who established the basic framework to explain how National Socialism dealt bureaucratically with the issue of *Mischlinge* and to explain why at the very end they mostly survived when Germany's full Jews did not. He provided valuable details about how the faceless war of the bureaucrats was carried out where a few professional civil servants, mostly in the Reich Ministry of the Interior, but also, at certain times, in other agencies such as economics and labor, formed a — by Nazi standards — temporizing pole of opinion in opposition to hard-core party racists. Thus, it fell to Ministerialrat Lösener and his boss, Stuckart, to play the role of "moderates," urging the treatment of *Mischlinge* in an orderly, bureaucratic fashion. This was not a struggle of equals. The other more dominant pole consisted of the truly fanatical elements in Nazi leadership, such as Heinrich Himmler, Reinhard Heydrich, and the apparatus of the Schutzstaffel (SS), whose offices included the Reichssicherheitshauptamt or RSHA (Reich Central Security Office), the Sicherheitsdienst or SD (Security Service), and the Gestapo. Also influential were officials within the party, especially in the Party Chancellery, known as the Kanzlei des Führers des NSDAP (also called KdF, but not to be confused with the recreational organization Kraft durch Freude). Philipp Bouhler, an ardent anti-Semite, led this "Führer Chancellery."[12] Martin Bormann, Hitler's adjutant, played an increasingly influential role, as did other extremists such as Gauleiter Julius Streicher, publisher of the notoriously anti-Semitic and semipornographic weekly, *Der Stürmer.* The fanatics' beliefs combined well with Hitler's long-held extreme views. However, Hitler, the politician, felt he had to exercise caution, and it was bureaucrats like Lösener and his reluctant ministry chief, Stuckart, who skillfully played on those instincts. Thus, especially in peacetime, Hitler held himself somewhat in check out of the need to show at least some discretion toward Aryan citizens related to Jews and *Mischlinge.* To be sure, those inhibitions eroded under the constant pressure of the hard-liners, slowly in peacetime but with gathering momentum in wartime.

Noakes shows that this sinister tug-of-war took place in considerable secrecy, firmly tucked behind the Nazis' bureaucratic veil. Furthermore, Hitler's true role in policy making stems only from second-hand sources — he never committed himself to paper on this or on many other sinister developments in National Socialist policy. In consequence of that internal debate, the legal status of *Mischlinge,* and the degree to which they were persecuted, varied significantly from time to time and from place to place. It depended upon the momentary ascendancy of cautionary counsel by the "moderates" or tactical victory in behind-the-scenes maneuvering by the fanatics.

Arbitrary treatment of *Mischlinge* was hardly the exclusive prerogative of the Nazi hierarchy in Berlin. The victims' fates also depended in part upon the degree of racial fanaticism exhibited by local officials and their bureaucracies. Individual personalities among subordinate orders of Nazi officialdom in ascending order from Ortsgruppenleiter (local leader), to Kreisleiter (regional leader), to Gauleiter (district leader) show considerable variations in the enthusiasm or efficiency with which they engaged in persecution. Local police authorities, regional Gestapo officials, criminal police, and the like often played critical roles, too, as did the general population's degree of readiness to display anti-Semitism and to engage in acts of denunciation. However, the most visible effect of the senior hierarchy's internal debate with state bureaucrats was that laws, decrees, and directives concerning *Mischlinge* progressed in an irregular pattern, especially in peacetime. Nevertheless, despite these disparities, the long-term trend was unmistakable: ultimately Germany's half-

Jewish citizens were to be rounded up and murdered. This was so despite various exemptions granted, however reluctantly, by the Party or by Hitler to a few *Mischlinge* with respect to the Nazis' discriminatory laws and decrees.

It is worthwhile to take a glance at the stages of Nazi decision making with respect to "race," a concept that constantly preoccupied National Socialists from their origins to their defeat.[13] The sheer arbitrariness and disorderliness of Nazi laws surfaced immediately after the Seizure of Power in 1933. While Jews remained the foremost target of choice, *Mischlinge* also figured prominently in the Nazis' first broad-brush attempt at legislating who was Aryan and who was Jewish. Their Law for the Restoration of a Professional Civil Service, promulgated in April 1933 on the basis of the Enabling Act, contained a so-called Aryan paragraph. Anyone with even so much as one Jewish grandparent was, according to that paragraph, a Jew and therefore subject to dismissal from any and all government jobs. The civil service in Germany encompassed teachers, nurses, police and emergency services, postal, telephone, and railroad personnel, and many other service-oriented categories of employees in addition to the upper levels held by lawyers and other professionals. Thus, hundreds of thousands of employees were considered to be civil servants, from the highest levels to the lowest. For that reason alone, the Aryan paragraph proved, in combination with boycotts of Jewish businesses and attempted purges of Jews and partial Jews in the private sector, to be impracticable. Reluctantly, the Nazis had to backtrack somewhat simply to avoid economic chaos. They did not wish to impede the newly begun economic recovery for which they were seeking full credit. Some of them, especially in the Foreign and Economics ministries and those circles of industrialists worried about Germany's export economy, also had to take increasingly hostile international reactions toward the National Socialists' anti-Semitic campaign into account.

However, restraint on the part of the anti-Semitic true believers was only temporary. Two years later and without fear of economic depression now that the economy was on the upswing, they were eagerly engaged in helping Hitler formulate the 1935 Nuremberg decrees, later known as the Nuremberg race laws. The haphazard way in which those laws and decrees were announced says much about the Nazi regime. In 1935, Hitler, knowing that another party-induced anti-Semitic wave was well in progress, announced on 13 September at the Nuremberg Party Rally that new laws would be promulgated within two days. In the meantime, his specialist medical adviser, Dr. Gerhard Wagner, had caught his ear about the dangers of sexual relations between Jews or partial Jews with *Deutschblütige* (i.e., citizens of "German blood"). Playing upon this highly emotional issue among Nazi true believers, Wagner had already proclaimed publicly at the same Nuremberg rally that the Nazi leadership was moving to protect German blood, an utterance designed to force even Hitler's hand. His remarks were also indicative of the attitude on race that was overtaking the German medical profession. Thus, the issuance of such decrees, or at least the public announcement of their impending declaration, took place in an emotionally charged atmosphere. What is noteworthy here is the fact that the Interior Ministry representative Lösener, backed by his boss, Stuckart, attempted to insert into the proposed laws the following phrase: "This law applies only to full Jews." Hitler did not buy it. He crossed out the phrase shortly before it was presented to his rubber-stamp Reichstag. Yet, he insisted simultaneously that the same phrase be retained in the text of public announcements. These contradictory acts demonstrate Hitler's continuing ambivalence toward *Mischlinge*.[14]

Details of the two Nuremberg decrees warrant closer scrutiny. The citizenship decree as instituted on 14 November 1935 stripped full Jews of citizenship and forbade them to marry or to have relations with citizens of "German blood." Yet, it accorded so-called *Mischlinge* "provisional" citizenship status, meaning that their citizenship could be revoked at a later time. The second decree on protecting so-called German blood, which was instituted on the same day as the citizenship decree, barred both Jews and half-Jews from marrying citizens of German blood. However, it did not specifically ban relationships, including sexual relationships, between *Mischlinge* and German citizens outright. In effect, the two decrees held the fate of *Mischlinge* in limbo. This was a crucial distinction. Had the 1935 decrees included *Mischlinge* among the full Jews, they probably would have met the same fate as the full Jews seven years later, namely mass murder in the extermination camps. Yet, because of bureaucratic dissension and because of Hitler's equivocation, the *Mischlinge* were not placed in the same category as full Jews in 1935.[15] They became a quasi "third race." After promulgation of the Nuremberg laws, other decrees and directives followed. For example, they narrowed educational opportunities for *Mischlinge* drastically, first in higher education, and then in all other areas of education and training. In the private business sector, various organizations and employers' associations began to discrimi-nate openly against *Mischlinge* in the same way they had discriminated against full Jews several years earlier. Then, after the pogrom of 9 November 1938 *(Kristallnacht)*, the Nazis began to ghettoize full Jews. However, *Mischlinge* and Jews married to Aryan Germans were exempted from the ghettoization process. This, too, was another fateful decision that probably saved the *Mischlinge* once the authorities began to physically "relocate" Germany's full Jews to the east, preparatory to their murder two years later. The anomalies continued. The same *Mischlinge* who in the late 1930s were facing increased discrimination in schools, social organizations, and jobs were nevertheless subject to, of all things, military service in the German armed forces. This held true until Hitler reversed himself again in April 1940.

This tug-of-war produced curious twists. Looking ahead for a moment, it is worth looking at exceptions to the status of select Jews and *Mischlinge*. Following promulgation of the 1935 Nuremberg race decrees, Nazi authorities established elaborate mechanisms of appeal for persons seeking to be "pro-moted" from Jewish to *Mischling* first degree, or from that status to *Mischling* second degree or even to being Aryanized. Perhaps the most prominent case in the latter instance was that of Luftwaffe officer Erhard Milch, later a field marshal. Göring interceded with Hitler to have Milch changed from half-Jew to Aryan ("I decide who is Jewish," stated Göring in a famous aside). Obvi-ously, Milch enjoyed a highly unusual and favorable situation. Normally, appeals could only be made through two bureaucratic paths, either through the Reich Ministry of the Interior or through the Party. In practice the latter proved to be a virtual dead end, since Party leaders like Rudolf Hess were adamantly opposed to the entire concept, convinced as they were that there should be no further mixing of German blood with the blood of Jews or half-Jews or, for that matter, quarter-Jews. Those seeking change obviously wanted to escape persecution, but the bulk of the 9,636 applications sent to the Inte-rior Ministry and on to Hitler were for persons seeking permission to marry and therefore to waive the decree for the protection of German blood. The Nazis developed a labyrinthine application process, demanding sets of photo-graphs of the applicant as well as the submission of detailed questionnaires. The process aimed to establish the applicant's physical appearance (i.e., "racial" characteristics), detailed family background, "Jewish" characteristics if any, agreeableness of personality (also highly arbitrary), career achievements, prior military service, and so on. In cases where the parentage of the Jew or *Mischling* was unclear, physical characteristics became especially important, and sometimes Nazi medical anthropologists and physicians were consulted on "difficult" cases. Needless to say, Nazi authorities were inclined to be highly suspicious of all such applications. Indicative of the fairness of the process is the fact that from 1935 to May 1941, Hitler approved only 263 applications for persons seeking to be recognized as *Mischlinge* first degree as opposed to full Jews. Then, exasperated by the entire process and growing less tolerant of *Mischlinge* anyway, he virtually ceased to approve any more, especially in the civilian sector, effectively terminating the appeals process by 1941. His decision to stop considering further applications occurred about the same time that the *Mischlinge* became even more stigmatized. Within the context of the Holocaust, it is instructive to note that within a few months of the de facto termination of this already shaky appeals procedure, full Jews were being transported eastward for "resettlement" — and soon after to their deaths. In parallel with this drastically increased intolerance, the full Jews' *Mischling* relatives were beginning to feel the circle close around them, too.[16]

As the closing off of the appeals process shows, it was in the war years that the tempo of persecution quickened and the Party fanatics began to gain ascendancy. When the war became a "world" war in December 1941, the downward spiral became more obvious as the Party's most radical anti-Semites steadily eroded whatever inhibitions Hitler might have had with respect to persons of partial Jewish ancestry. Virtually all *Mischlinge* were reduced to the status of common laborers by midwar. About the same time, *Mischlinge* became a central subject of the highly secret debates among Nazi officials meeting in the Berlin suburb of Wannsee in January 1942, when Hitler's paladins, led foremost by Reinhard Heydrich, settled upon their notorious Final Solution for full Jews. It was there that, crucially, the arguments of Lösener as presented by Stuckart once again played upon Hitler's fear of negative political consequences if significant numbers of Aryan relatives should become alienated from the regime, were their *Mischling* relatives to be sent to their deaths along with full Jews. Even though sorely tempted by the fanatics to adopt a hard line, Hitler and his chief propagandist, Goebbels, nevertheless worried about the home front because of their memories of the collapse of German civilian morale at the end of World War I. Lösener and Stuckart were able to play upon those fears to their advantage in the internal debates.

Even so, after the Wannsee Conference of 20 January 1942 that put the final stamp on the Nazis' decision to murder all of Europe's Jews and that left the status of *Mischlinge* once more in limbo, the pace of persecution against half-Jews accelerated in parallel with the murder of all of Europe's Jews. Following rumors in the late summer of 1942 that Himmler was preparing to order his Gestapo to round up *Mischlinge* for transport to extermination camps anyway, the Interior Ministry's Lösener–Stuckart duo combined once more. They sent a letter to Himmler outlining yet again the reasons why it was expedient that *Mischlinge* be spared, at least for the duration of the war, and hinting that if necessary they would alert Hitler to the negative political consequences of any precipitous action on the part of the Gestapo. This move probably saved the *Mischlinge* from death once more, but even then the Party fanatics refused to give up. As Nathan Stoltzfus has demonstrated in his *Resistance of the Heart: Intermarriage and the Rosenstrasse Protest in Nazi Germany* (noted earlier), in February 1943, the Gestapo attempted to transport Berlin's last Jews (i.e., persons married to Christians), despite many of the victims' "privileged mixed marriage" status, a move seconded by Goebbels in his capacity as Berlin's Gauleiter. The ensuing public protests by mostly women succeeded — just barely — in forcing the regime to back down in the light of negative public reaction, a reaction Goebbels as propaganda minister (in contrast to his role as Gauleiter) had to take into account. However, one isolated protest (which the Nazis did their best to cover up) hardly meant a full reprieve for persons in mixed Jewish-Christian marriages. As the introduction of chapter 4 of this study shows, following several preparatory steps, including public condemnation of the *Mischlinge* as military shirkers, the Gestapo began a systematic roundup of all male *Mischlinge* in 1944. They were to become forced laborers in special camps, presumably as part of the total war effort. This had been decided in late 1943 and was set in operation the following spring. In consequence, thousands of young and not-so-young Germans, some of them military veterans of 1914–18 and other veterans of early campaigns in World War II, wound up in forced-labor camps that were only slightly less degrading than concentration camps. Female *Mischlinge* were treated only marginally better. The only concession to the women in that category was that they were to perform forced labor while living at home. Then, by early 1945, the gloves really came off. Under the auspices of the Gestapo, systematic roundups of all remaining *Mischlinge* and of Jews married to Gentiles, so-called *Mischehen* or mixed marriages, or, if they had children, "privileged mixed marriages," ensued. Isolated transports of *Mischlinge* to destinations like Theresienstadt began in the period from November 1944 through approximately March 1945. Besides, the Gestapo itself was personally engaged in the mass roundups in early 1945, a task that not only kept its rank and file busy but also kept those generally able-bodied men away from the front lines as Allied armies entered the "Thousand-Year Reich" from East and West. The timing for this final phase of Nazi persecution was critical. It was only the "chaos" of war's end (as noted, the rear-echelon fanatics were creating artificial make-work tasks for themselves while treating their prisoners with deliberate cruelty) and military defeat that prevented the deportation and slaughter of most *Mischlinge* in 1945, a fate they keenly understood, having been informed privately of the deaths of Jewish family members and other relatives from 1942 onward.

Heavily demoralizing for the *Mischlinge* was the fact that while all of this was happening, they largely suffered alone as isolated individuals. Starting in 1933, a number of Jewish organizations had been trying frantically to help Jews in Germany and then Jews in the rest of occupied Europe. Yet, their resources were woefully inadequate, and no foreign governments were willing to intervene. Jewish family members of mixed marriages quickly discovered that their emigration meant the sundering of family ties, since with few exceptions only the Jewish member could receive aid to emigrate. This policy decision was logical, since Jewish family members were so immediately threatened while partial Jewish offspring were not — yet. Overwhelmed by the tide of human misery that confronted them, the Jewish relief and emigration organizations could hardly spare their limited resources and efforts for German citizens who were not under such an immediate threat as the full Jews palpably were. Consequently, only a few *Mischlinge* obtained help in moving abroad. The rest were stranded.

Meanwhile, a few minuscule organizations such as a "Reichsverband" or "Reich Organization of Christian-German Citizens of Non-Aryan and Not Purely Aryan Descent" existed for a few years, but the Nazis suppressed it and other feeble organizations in the late 1930s.[17] True, there were small, mostly informal support associations within the state-sponsored Protestant Church and the Catholic Church, but they were the initiatives of individual pastors or priests and were exceedingly few. The British and American Quakers supported a small Berlin Center, whose director, Corder Catchpool, a British pacifist, offered assistance to politically and racially persecuted Germans. However, the center was a minuscule affair, and despite heroic efforts by its small staff, it could offer only limited aid — plus moral support — to Jews and *Mischlinge* and even then almost exclusively in Berlin.[18] Thus, it is no exaggeration to state that Germany's *Mischlinge* were for all practical purposes abandoned to their fate. They had to face steadily increasing persecution, mostly alone in society and mostly isolated from each other. They could only pray for the war to end before they shared the same fate as their Jewish relatives.

Therein lies the vast gulf between the Jews and the Jewish-Christian *Mischlinge*. Despite the deepening persecution in the late-war years, most *Mischlinge* outlived Nazism, and most full Jews did not. The few survivors among the latter emigrated after the war. The *Mischlinge* faced the same cross-roads in May 1945. Should they stay in Germany or should they follow the full Jews into exile? After the war, many of the surviving *Geltungsjuden* emigrated elsewhere — in distinct contrast to the "normal" so-called *Mischlinge* first degree. The latter chose overwhelmingly to remain in Germany, as did the *Mischlinge* second degree. They felt they had good reason to do so. Even by the irrational estimates of the Nazis, those self-same half-Jewish citizens were also half-Aryans, to use another National Socialist pseudo-category. Yet, because the citizens once categorized as half-Jews (or at least most of them) chose to reassimilate into German society, they rapidly became an invisible group (i.e., they were ignored after 1945 by the Germans and largely forgotten by everyone else). Mostly, the former *Mischling* victims feared further social ostracism. As a survival mechanism under National Socialism, most *Mischlinge* had chosen to adopt the lowest possible profile in the years 1933 to 1945, and they learned this attitude as children. They took humdrum jobs and sought to appear cooperative, friendly, and subservient to their supervisors, coworkers, and neighbors. Above all, they tried to draw as little attention to themselves as possible. Having survived the war, they decided, consciously or unconsciously, that this was also to be their survival strategy ever after. Expedience played the dominant role here. They quickly discovered in postwar society that societal reactions to their plight were usually anything but sympathetic. First, anti-Semitism, although officially forbidden, continued under the surface. Second, the former *Mischlinge* knew, and acquaintances were not bashful about reminding them, that their persecution had not been as severe as that experienced by full Jews. Besides, most *Mischlinge* were well aware that they had never received religious education as Jews anyway — nine-tenths of them had been baptized in the Protestant and Catholic churches. Given such reactions, it is no surprise that, with few exceptions, surviving *Mischlinge* pulled down a curtain of silence over what had befallen them between 1933 and 1945. That is also why many, although by no means all, half-Jewish German citizens and other citizens of partially Jewish ancestry either refused to seek compensation from postwar restitution authorities or else soon gave up the attempt. Such applications served only to draw unwelcome attention upon them. Above all, they were disinclined to write or speak publicly about their experiences. To do so was to invite even more public scrutiny and to expose their status as onetime pariahs within society. Thus, there are remarkably few memoirs or first-person accounts by survivors. It is no mystery that among the public today so few remember them or are aware of their cruel predicament.

This study does not attempt to deal systematically with the decrees, directives, and laws that the Nazis erected against *Mischlinge*. Scholars such as Raul Hilberg, Jeremy Noakes, Beate Meyer, Sigrid Lekebusch, Gerhard Lindemann, Bryan Mark Rigg, Nathan Stoltzfus, and Aleksandar-Saša Vuletić, among others, have already compiled a comprehensive legal and historical framework of persecution. In that sense this study is not a history of organizations or bureaucracies. Rather, it describes the lives and fates of a representative group of individual victims drawn from both genders and from all walks of life. Each of their profiles adds understanding to what persecution under the Nazis meant on a practical, daily level during the course of Nazi domination. While National Socialist legalisms enter into this work, they do so only insofar as they altered the status of Germany's *Mischlinge* during their long descent into near-fatal persecution. Thus, in contrast to Noakes's pioneering contribution on a racially motivated downward trend in the bureaucratic German State, this study examines instead the personal experiences of people who were mature adults, young adults, and children coming of age under National Socialism. Geographically, the sketches in this study cover much of the former Greater German Reich as well as the differing experiences of persons who were inhabitants of large cities as well as rural areas. It benefits from interviews with eyewitnesses, but it also incorporates information from official reports (both National Socialist and postwar documents), depositions, and legal evidence which post-1945 survivors or relatives of the deceased accumulated to demonstrate the degree of persecution to which they had been subjected. This study makes no claims of being comprehensive — too few eyewitnesses were available to this author to allow for statistical treatment of victims. However, it offers a social palette of young and old, men and women, urbanites and rustics, strong and weak, civilians and soldiers, survivors — and nonsurvivors. While this last category of murdered victims is not large relative to the total human cost of the Holocaust, the scars of persecution for the forgotten *Mischlinge* remain, and their accounts demonstrate what that persecution really meant. After all, the victims carried those scars with them for the rest of their lives.

This study contains one significant bias that fundamentally affects its structure. It places special emphasis on the lives of persons who experienced Nazi rule as teenagers or as young adults. It was at this stage that their lives and livelihoods were particularly vulnerable to persecution. One reason for this age bias is the fact that the number of mixed marriages between Jews and Christians, a relatively uncommon phenomenon in nineteenth-century Germany, mushroomed in the decade surrounding World War I and throughout the 1920s. To be sure, those mixed marriages ceased soon after the Nazi Seizure of Power in 1933. Thus, the majority of persons relegated to *Mischling* status under National Socialism were victims who were born in the period 1910 to 1933.[19] They endured persecution through several crucial stages in their lives. That is why the following chapters concentrate on their advances in the stages of life such as childhood and school days, vocational experiences, youthful ostracism in society, late-war persecution, end-of-war survival, and life in Germany after National Socialism. Accordingly, the chapters in this study reflect primarily the experiences of persons who actually went through those stages of development and neglect to some extent the experiences of persons who were significantly older or younger than those who came of age under the Nazis. Sadly, it should come as no surprise to readers that this study examines only the lives of persons sufficiently articulate and educated that they somehow imparted a written (or oral) record of what happened. Many — in fact, by far the great majority of victims — were not so favored.

Recognition of the persecution of citizens who were German-Jewish *Misch-* *linge* has come much too late to have any meaningful ameliorating effects upon the victims. Material compensation means little to them now. It is too late for survivors to experience liberation from the anxieties that have pursued them all their lives starting with the persecutions of 1933–45. However, this history, in parallel with other studies about the Holocaust, seeks to reveal to a greater extent the effects of Nazi persecution upon all of its victims. It hopes to demonstrate to readers today the human costs surrounding the persecution of individuals on the basis of a perceived — or induced — "abnormality" in a minority. National Socialists, using ethnic identity, political ideology, religion or other arbitrary associations, produced long-term social trauma for their victims. It is no exaggeration to state that *Mischling* survivors live with demons similar to those of persons who suffered severe trauma in childhood. Their common reaction was: Keep silent. Such persecution haunts both victims and perpetrators alike. Germany's former *Mischlinge* had been forced to lead their lives intimately intermingled in their own society as it grew increasingly hostile to and detached from them, although only a short time before 1933 they had been considered perfectly normal. Yet, after twelve years of Nazism, those same persons chose to reassimilate into the very society that had spurned them and that had acquiesced in the murder of its full Jews and that, in the final analysis, was prepared to condemn them to the same fate. The *Mischlinge* had to bear one more burden peculiar to them. Except for their own immediate families — where all the family knew that their Jewish members were being systematically murdered — the former *Mischlinge* came to realize that they lived in a world without friends and without allies. There was no one looking out for them.

Readers may well wonder why most former *Mischlinge* continue their pattern of distrust toward strangers and toward society in general now that racial persecution is widely condemned. At least part of the answer can be found by reading the following eyewitness accounts and archival evidence. Even so, for every account that appears in this investigation or in other studies, there are scores — probably hundreds — of personal memories that remain buried in the hearts and minds of survivors who cannot bear to reveal them today, two generations later.

1

Innocents in Classrooms

The demographics in Germany were such that the bulk of marriages between Jews and Christians took place in the decade surrounding the First World War and with growing frequency in the years of the Weimar Republic. Thus, the sons and daughters of those marriages were mostly children or teenagers coming of age when Hitler and the Nazis seized power in 1933. Even as the Nazis, after some hesitation, labeled the Jewish-Christian parents' marriages *privilegierte Mischehen* (privileged mixed marriages), they reduced the children of those marriages to the status of *Mischlinge*, either as half-Jews or as quarter-Jews. As noted in the introduction, the term was highly pejorative, but it was the universal term in Nazi parlance. Most families relegated to these inferior statuses suffered financially as the breadwinners (primarily men in that generation) steadily lost jobs and scrambled for other, less rewarding work. As noted in the introduction, the Nazis, immediately upon seizing power, boycotted Jewish businesses and imposed discriminatory laws that cast a wide net. In 1933, for example, the Aryan paragraph of their Law for the Restoration of a Professional Civil Service served as a legalism that enabled them to eliminate all Jews, including so-called half-Jews and quarter-Jews, from the civil service. Then there were the 1935 Nuremberg decrees, two race laws that stripped full Jews of citizenship and banned marriages between Jews and persons of "German blood." So-called *Mischlinge* received only "provisional citizenship" status, and they, too, were banned from marrying so-called Aryan Germans and eventually from having any relations with those selfsame Aryans. Harsh though those laws and boycotts were, they meant little to the *Mischling* children at first. To be sure, their parents knew better. The accumulated effect of such discrimination led to a steady impoverishment of Jews and their families despite the fact that many of them were urban, middle-class, and well educated. Typically, what attracted the children's notice was not financial decline. Rather, it was a family move to another, usually poorer neighborhood and to smaller accommodations. Even that experience was not always obvious to the little ones. For *Mischlinge* as children growing up under the Nazis, the first real engagement with Nazi persecution usually occurred in school.

Therefore, it is instructive to see how National Socialism directed its anti-Semitic efforts at education. Nazi lawmaking was inevitably chaotic, since the new regime was trying to transmit its irrational racial prejudices into a legal system that had been, for the most part, rational. During the old Kaiserreich, anti-Semites in the Reichstag had refrained from introducing discriminatory legislation once it became evident that proving who was or was not Jewish was almost impossible.[1] In 1933, the Nazis felt no such inhibitions, and they cared less about the consequences — at first. For example, the 1933 law's Aryan paragraph, if implemented rigorously, would have eliminated so many citizens from public jobs that, in combination with boycotts and other dismissals in the private sector, it would have produced chaos. Economic dislocations were counterproductive to the Nazis' aims of reviving the economy and ending unemployment rapidly. Therefore, cooler heads in various Reich ministries such as the Interior and Economics ministries urged caution. In education, the Law against the Overcrowding of German Schools and Colleges, enacted on 25 April 1933, also contained the Aryan paragraph, but in a supplementary decree it permitted *Mischlinge,* both quarter-Jews and half-Jews, to remain in public schools for the time being. In September 1935, Bernhard Rust, the Reich education minister, announced his intention of creating separate Volksschulen (elementary schools) for Jews and half-Jews by 1936. Quarter-Jews were to remain in the Aryan public schools. However, those plans were shelved, awaiting the outcome of the impending Nuremberg decrees. Then, in July 1937, Rust renewed his call for separate schools for full Jews. This time he made a small but crucial adjustment. *Mischlinge* first degree would still be permitted to attend Aryan public schools, although these half-Jewish children could transfer to the Jewish schools if they so chose. The *Mischlinge* second degree did not have that option. They were required to stay in the Aryan schools. This was another early indication of discrimination by degree, namely a sharp divide the Nazis were seeking to impose, this time between half-Jews and quarter-Jews. The distinction proved that the former were being grouped more and more with full Jews, the latter with Aryans, a gulf that would grow with time. Options in higher education narrowed perceptibly, too. None of the *Mischlinge* could become teachers, and various directives of the Ministry of Education of the late 1930s indicated that non-Aryans would not be permitted to study for professional careers in a large number of other professions besides teaching. They cited medicine and pharmacy as examples. In fact, high school graduates, recipients of the *Abitur* or secondary school leaving degree, soon discovered that de facto, most universities would not admit *Mischlinge* to any field of study. Finally, as the Nazis' anti-Semitic campaign intensified during wartime, the regime decreed that *Mischlinge* first degree were to be removed from all secondary schools in the spring of 1942, although occasionally individual pupils were able to find a few loopholes. Worse followed. In a final effort to stop education for any half-Jew, all *Mischlinge* first degree were removed from the elementary schools by the summer of 1944.[2] Thus, in its last throes, Hitler's Germany had, in effect, banned half-Jews from all public education. This pattern echoed what had befallen full Jews in public education several years earlier.

The children who attended school in the early years of Nazi control were generally oblivious to these laws and directives at first. Although experiences differed enormously from person to person, certain generalities about school life do emerge. Yes, traumatic political events might intervene in their lives in the 1930s. For example, the children often felt fear and uncertainty at home during memorable events such as Hitler's appointment as chancellor on 30 January 1933 or *Kristallnacht* on 9 November 1938. However, most of them did not personally feel the effects — unless brownshirted SA (Sturm Abteilung) rioters actually entered their parents' homes, as sometimes happened. Instead, they empathized with their parents, who had been their shield against social discrimination. On day one of their formal education, that protective shielding from family and home ended abruptly. There is an irony here. *Der erste Schultag* (the first school day) was traditionally a time of celebration for proud parents and pupils alike, with the latter receiving festive paper cones brimming with sweets and decorations in a celebratory atmosphere. After 1933, Germany's Jewish children and Germany's *Mischlinge* came to realize that that once happy day now carried dark undertones.

In this context, it should be noted that it was the attitude of the individual teachers toward their pupils that was critical in determining what kind of atmosphere Jewish pupils and pupils of mixed Jewish-Christian ancestry would encounter. If the teacher accepted National Socialist values, especially its racist thinking, then the young *Mischlinge* were almost certain to have problems with other teachers, classmates, youth groups, school administrators, and school life in general. If, on the other hand, the teacher was not a National Socialist or was only a nominal Party member who turned a blind eye toward the Nazis' racist principles, the other pupils were far likelier to accept the *Mischlinge* on equal terms. In short, the role of the teacher was critical to the fortunes of the children. In this respect, it is worth noting that the teacher was the first authority figure (outside the family) whom a child met. Moreover, Herr or Frau *Lehrer* (teacher) was the first symbol of state authority, since most teachers were civil servants. The German teacher was usually a respected and often an intimidating force in the life of a German community. In this respect it is also worth noting that children in Jewish and partially Jewish households were brought up like most Germans to respect authority to an astonishing degree. It is generally accepted that Germany's urban, middle-class families were, on average, extremely law-abiding and accepting of authority, and most Jewish or mixed Jewish-Christian families were solidly in that category. Consequently, if the state's authority figure, in this case a teacher, displayed hostility to the new pupil, the effects could be devastating.

Many German boys and girls of mixed religious heritage, however, enjoyed the tacit support of their teachers. Generalizations can be misleading, but as a rule, teachers in large city schools tended to be, politically speaking, slightly left of center. Up to 1933, they had been members of or at least supporters of the more moderate wings of the conservatives, or the democratic parties or possibly even the Social Democrats. Obviously, there were major exceptions to this generalization, but it was roughly applicable to the hundreds of elementary and secondary schools and thousands of teachers in large urban areas like Berlin, Hamburg, Frankfurt am Main, and Cologne, and, later, Vienna. In rural areas the tendency may have run the other way with conservative, nationalistic elements predominating among the teachers. The *Lehrer* were one of Germany's more respected professions, although there was a sharp differentiation between elementary school teachers and secondary Gymnasium teachers. The latter held university degrees, were paid more, and were accorded higher social standing. They tended, as a rule, to be more conservative and nationalistic than the elementary school teachers. However, they, too, felt themselves to be members of a respected profession, and their professionalism tended to blunt somewhat the effects of Nazi discrimination against minority groups such as Jews and *Mischlinge* — at least for a time.

Of course, the previous observations are generalizations. With time, the number of National Socialist teachers entering the profession increased, even as the proportion of more politically neutral educators fell. Nazi pressure was relentless. By 1936 over 97 percent of all teachers had enrolled in the National-sozialistiche Lehrerbund, the Nazi teachers' association. Worse, nearly one-third of all teachers had joined the National Socialist Party by 1936. Then, by the late 1930s, most teachers had passed through the Party's monthlong summer camps that stressed indoctrination and physical fitness. Those subjects assumed great prominence in schools, and the Nazis stressed more extreme sports such as boxing. National Socialism permeated the curriculum in other ways. The Nazis stressed history, especially German history with an emphasis on nationalistic themes. They upgraded biology but perverted it, allocating special emphasis to race and heredity. As an especially egregious example of racism, the teachers in this new field taught their pupils to place particular emphasis upon the measuring of their own and their classmates' skulls. They were instructed minutely in the identification of racial types. Thus the impact of National Socialism in German schools became increasingly noticeable, much to the detriment of Jewish children and of their *Mischling* schoolmates as the years passed.[3]

CASE HISTORIES

Berliner Eva Heilmann, the eldest daughter of Ernst Heilmann and Magdalene Heilmann née Müller, was born in 1920. Her father was a Social Democrat and president of the Prussian Landtag in the late Weimar Republic. Ernst was Jewish and Magdalene Christian, and both came from literate, hardworking families. The Heilmanns had four children (unusually large for an urban, middle-class family of mixed religion). Besides Eva, there were Peter, Ernst Ludwig, and Beate. The two boys joined their sister, Eva, in two-year intervals after her — Peter in 1922, Ernst Ludwig in 1924. The youngest, Beate, followed in 1927. All four Heilmann children experienced their early and middling childhood in the years of the Weimar Republic. They were a happy, well-adjusted, and politically prominent family in the bustling Berlin of the 1920s. Religion played almost no role in their lives. The family's true passion was politics. Specifically, they embraced the cause of German Social Democracy (SPD). The children really only confronted the issue of religious identity when they began entering elementary school and were supposed to declare a religious affiliation. There were four choices under the Weimar Republic: Protestant, Catholic, Jewish, or Dissident. The Heilmanns chose the last category. The four siblings started their public education by attending the neighborhood Volkschule (elementary school) in Kreuzberg, a heavily working-class district. It was a typical boisterous, inner-city school. However, it was at home that learning really began for the children.[4]

As a senior figure in the German SPD, Ernst Heilmann successfully campaigned for the Prussian Landtag elections in 1930 and headed the Socialist delegation until 1933. Magdalene, who was often by his side in the tumultuous political campaigns, concentrated on social welfare issues for working-class Germans, making frequent visits to inner-city areas and helping the socially disadvantaged. Both parents imparted a commitment to social and political issues to their children. Another important influence was the children's aunt Klara. Klara Heilmann was the elder sister of Ernst and a formidable, yet warm, personality. She, too, was highly intelligent and well read, and she taught French and German at a nearby school for Jewish girls. "Tante Kärla," as they called her, read fascinating stories to the Heilmann boys and girls, who listened spellbound to her own stories and to translations of children's stories from French and English literature. For example, she read them the tales of *Winnie-the-Pooh* by A. A. Milne, of whom almost no other German children were aware, since no authorized translation was yet available in German. Eva, Peter, and their younger siblings were often excited by Aunt Klara's stories, but during the dinner hour they listened as the adults passionately discussed politics. Growing up among such talented parents and relatives, the Heilmann children inevitably received a truly international and cosmopolitan education before they entered elementary school.[5]

Normal schooling came to an end for the Heilmanns in 1933. Inevitably, it was the elder siblings, Eva and Peter, who were fated to confront Nazi persecution first, although the younger siblings were also horribly scarred by it. A gifted child, Eva had entered the Viktoria Lyzeum, a Mädchen Oberschule or college preparatory girls' school, at age ten in 1930. Eva's first years there were happy under its highly competent principal, Frau Dr. Engelmann. However, the Nazi Seizure of Power put a pall over the school and placed an especially dark cloud over the Heilmann family. In May 1933, the Nazis dissolved all other political parties, then arrested Ernst Heilmann a month later and incarcerated him in their new concentration camp in Oranienburg, north of Berlin. Mercifully unaware of her husband's ultimate fate, Magdalene took the children with her several times for brief, strained visits. Ultimately, Ernst Heilmann was murdered at Buchenwald in 1940. Other members of his gifted family, such as his sister, the children's beloved Tante Kärla, were also destined to die in the Holocaust. From an early age, the Heilmann children became aware of what could befall Jewish citizens and their progeny.[6]

Meanwhile the children's education continued, if somewhat shakily. Following the announcement of Hitler's Nuremberg decrees in 1935, Eva's education began to unravel. The first warning sign was the sudden dismissal of Eva's popular principal. Although Dr. Engelmann was a practicing Protestant, she came from a Jewish family and was a convert — not that conversion did her any good in 1936. A wave of consternation swept through the Viktoria Lyzeum, but worse followed. Eva's homeroom teacher, Herr Warncke, had seemed innocuous at first. However, following the Seizure of Power, he began to appear at the school in his SA (storm trooper) uniform. Then, one day, soon after Dr. Engelmann's departure, Warncke pulled Heilmann aside and told the thirteen-year-old that soon the Viktoria Lyzeum would become *judenfrei* (i.e., rid of Jews). He actually tried to inform her in benevolent fashion, implying that she should become baptized (although that had not helped the school's principal). Eva Heilmann was nonplussed. The Heilmann forebears had been devout Jews, the Müllers devout Christians. Yet, her household was distinctly secular. Eva felt that a Christian baptism under such circumstances would be a betrayal to the religious convictions of her forebears and her immediate family. She immediately began looking for another school, and with some difficulty finally transferred to the Uhlandschule. In the meantime, at the advice of the family's lawyer, Magdalene had the other children baptized. Soon, Peter, the second oldest child, began receiving religious instruction from a well-meaning Protestant minister. Even so, he admitted privately that his heart was never really in it. Religion was simply not a central part of the lives of the Heilmann children.[7]

In the meantime, Eva began to discover firsthand what racial discrimination really meant. Hitherto, she had been popular, mixing easily among her classmates. Then one day it dawned on her that some of her friends were no longer sitting next to her. Looking around the classroom, she realized that the seating changes were not accidental. All of the Jewish and half-Jewish children were experiencing similar snubs. True, not all the girls were joining in; one of Eva's schoolmates, a pretty and popular Gentile girl, made a point of socializing with her. Many years later, the same girl migrated to Israel.

The Uhland Schule was a Mädchen Gymnasium (girls' college preparatory school). Its principal, Anna Schönborn, was a personally engaging but enigmatic figure to the Heilmanns, since she was a member of the Nazi Party! Yet, further investigation among Frau Heilmann's contacts had alleged that Schönborn had joined the NSDAP expressly for the purpose of remaining in her post and undermining Party policies. The teachers were competent, and Eva's fellow pupils were apt learners and congenial company. Yet, despite the positive atmosphere, unpleasantness sometimes surfaced without warning. Eva liked foreign languages and enjoyed her French teacher, whom she found competent. Then, one day, during Eva's recitation the teacher turned on her and shouted: "Shut your mouth, Heilmann. Your Hebraic accent is painful to hear!" Eva was devastated. At first she was not sure she had heard her teacher right, but a glance at his face told her otherwise. "Hebraic?" she asked herself. "Why Hebraic?" Eva had never heard Hebrew spoken in her life. Why would an adult, a hitherto respected teacher, say such a thing? She closed her book and sat down. Fortunately, this experience was not typical. Most of her teachers, she recalled, were decent, caring individuals. Eva Heilmann received her coveted *Abitur* in 1939, the mark of an educated German. Now she was ready for university life and a career.[8] Or so she thought.

Peter Heilmann also completed his *Abitur,* two years later, in May 1941, the last year that *Mischlinge* were allowed to finish secondary education. Within another year the younger Heilmann siblings, Ernst Ludwig and Beate, were banned from secondary schools altogether and were unable to obtain any diploma until after the war. Their family experience showed that persecution of *Mischling* schoolchildren intensified as long as the Nazis remained in power. Peter turned eighteen in 1940. Like Eva, Peter discovered that social discrimination against *Mischlinge* had become bolder in the classroom, but as a young male, he had to be particularly careful not to be caught being friendly with so-called Aryan girls. As a baptized Protestant, he joined his church's evangelical youth group, whose membership included both men and women, several of whom were *Mischlinge* like Peter. They met in the homes of members, drank tea, and read Shakespeare or other serious literature to each other. However, the pastor soon banned mixed-gender gatherings without direct supervision, a policy that had not existed before *Mischlinge* were members. Insulted by the church leader's obvious distrust, Peter quit the youth group and the church. Yet, that hardly helped matters. He recalled afterward that one of the striking features about life for him, as a schoolboy, was the sheer isolation imposed by his status as a *Mischling*. Not only could he not date Aryan girls, he was also supposed to avoid public theaters, concerts, the cinema, and particularly public dances. When he could, Peter took in cultural activities anyway — and kept a low profile.[9]

The school days experienced by the Heilmann siblings proved typical of what National Socialists had in store for Germany's underage *Mischlinge*. As they would do throughout society, the Nazis sought from the day they seized power to isolate, and then eliminate, every vestige of Judaism from German society. Obviously, full Jews were their primary targets. However, Germany's quarter- and half-Jewish citizens experienced the same waves of discrimination, too, if not always to the same degree. For the cohort of *Mischlinge* who entered or were entering the educational system, school days became steadily more harrowing, a descending spiral that accelerated until the last day of World War II. As the Heilmanns discovered, it was in the classrooms that Germany's *Mischlinge* began to encounter social isolation firsthand — along with their hapless Jewish classmates. Like Eva Heilmann, all of them looked around sooner or later, only to find that the chairs next to them were for the most part empty.

All across Germany similar scenes were taking place. Lore M., a *Mischling* schoolgirl in Krefeld, encountered a slight variation of such ostracism. Her teachers forced her to sit in the front row of each class. It was from this vantage that she finally swiveled around to stare at empty seats before swiveling back. Unlike Eva Heilmann, Lore M. did not have the good fortune of a Gentile girl or boy breaking ranks and befriending her. In the midst of a bustling school life, Lore M. had become a pariah. Her father, an electrician with a modest income and no contacts, could afford no other school for his daugh-ter. A pattern of social exclusion for *Mischlinge* was emerging all over Ger-many as National Socialism permeated the educational system.[10]

So-called quarter-Jews were by no means immune to this isolation. Like the Heilmanns, Hans-Joachim Boehm was also a Berliner. His family was neither politically prominent nor well connected. As noted earlier, Nazi official-dom began to differentiate more and more between persons who were half-Jewish and those who were one-quarter Jewish, so that the distinction became a kind of racial dividing line between those who were capable of being as-similated into German society — or at least its fringes — and those who were not. Even so, the fate of a *Mischling* second degree was hardly enviable, as Boehm's experiences demonstrate. One of his grandparents was Jewish, but neither his parents nor Hans-Joachim thought much about that fact — at first. Hans-Joachim received his elementary and secondary education in Friedenau, a downtown district of Berlin. A bright pupil, he performed well in elementary school and won admission to the Friedenau Gymnasium. Mean-time his father died in 1928, and his mother, also plagued by ill health and unable to keep adequate employment, was destitute. Following her husband's death, Frau Boehm had had to submit many bureaucratic forms for social aid, and the questionnaires required identification of religious and ethnic origin. Thus, it became known that one of the grandparents of her children bore the name Samuel. This had not been burdensome during the Weimar years, but it caused severe problems for Hans-Joachim Boehm after 1933. For the Nazis, Samuel was a red flag. Later, they required all Germans of Jewish origin to sign official papers with a middle name that they (the Nazis) con-sidered to be quintessentially Jewish. For men it was Israel. For women it was Sara. As far as the Nazis were concerned, Samuel was equivalent to Israel or Sara.[11]

In some respects, Hans-Joachim was lucky at his new Friedenau Gymna-sium. The principal was no Nazi. Herr Rektor was, in reality, an old-line Ger-man nationalist who found the Nazis to be uncouth. Sadly, his disdain caught up with him, and he was soon replaced with a principal sympathetic to Na-tional Socialism. Until then Hans-Joachim enjoyed Herr Rektor's tacit pro-tection, he recalled, and the teaching staff proved to be equally impartial. He received a solid secondary education from able teachers. Although pupils often took their cue from the teaching staff, this was not always to be the case.

Hans-Joachim suffered from another "liability" for those times. His facial appearance was considered by many to be "Jewish," and several of his class-mates taunted him. Sneeringly, they called him "Itzig," and baited him. A few other classmates suffered the same abuse. They soon banded together and formed their own circle of friendship.[12]

Other complications arose. Within a short time Hans-Joachim's school-mates would be old enough to join the Hitler Youth. During the Weimar Republic, youth groups had grown in popularity. Girl Scout and Boy Scout organizations, religious youth groups, and other specialized youth organiza-tions had sprung up. Starting in 1933, the Nazis banned them. The only group that counted now was the Hitler Jugend (HJ) and the girls' equivalent, the Bund deutscher Mädel (BDM). Children aged ten to thirteen joined the Jungvolk (the general youth movement). Then, at age fourteen, they gradu-ated into the more senior HJ and BDM, respectively. It is difficult today to comprehend their attractiveness to youth. In the 1930s, the Nazis apportioned such lavish support on the HJ/BDM as to constitute a youth movement of a different kind. "Youth leads youth," their banners proclaimed. Poor families expended precious incomes to buy uniforms for their sons and daughters. National days of celebration featured them in parades in all of Germany's cities. The HJ developed its own esprit, producing its own rituals, songs, and myths. By 1939, virtually all of Germany's children were members. It had become a national phenomenon.

In 1933 Hans-Joachim wanted to join, too, seduced by the HJ's youthful dynamism. Then reality intervened. A year after the Nazi takeover, when he was old enough to join the Jungvolk, Hans-Joachim hesitated. Cruel encoun-ters with schoolmates who were already in the HJ had given him pause. He feared (rightly) that the other boys' racism in school would be even more pronounced in the HJ. Moreover, it was also becoming apparent that the HJ prided itself on its military appearance. This, too, struck a discordant note with Hans-Joachim and his family. Therefore, he did not join in 1934. Time was not on his side, however. By 1936, the bureaucracy decreed that all school-children of the requisite age must join, and Hans-Joachim received what amounted to an induction notice on 20 April 1936, a birthday present from the Führer. Ignoring the notice would have been too dangerous, he recalled, so he reported to the HJ office to initiate his application. Then an inspiration struck him as he returned home with the requisite forms. Four weeks later, in conformity with an HJ deadline, he returned to the office and informed the local youth official that as of the end of the school year, he was moving to Hamburg. If they were to place his induction papers in his own care, he would deliver them personally, so eager was he to join. Impressed by his enthusiasm, the HJ official agreed. Hans-Joachim's willingness to serve as courier would save him paperwork. Hans-Joachim returned home after dumping the forms in a litter barrel. Later generations, whose lives have been monitored by computerized bureaucracies, can only marvel at such a ruse. But it worked for Hans-Joachim Boehm in 1936.[13]

If it was anything, Nazi prejudice was arbitrary, especially to partially Jewish citizens. To be sure, its anti-Semitism was utterly consistent. However, the fate that awaited Hans-Joachim's brother, Erich Boehm, bears out the arbitrariness. Erich, his brother recalled, was an enthusiastic joiner. He bore the physical characteristics of a "true" German in contrast to Hans-Joachim, and because of this stereotypical outward appearance, Erich's classmates readily accepted him. He joined the HJ promptly, blossomed, and even graduated to a special component, the Marine HJ (i.e., sea scouts). They wore splendid blue uniforms and felt themselves to be part of a new elite. Later still, Erich transferred to another vanguard group, the Motorized HJ in Berlin. No one bothered to inquire why Erich was so easily accepted into such National Socialist organizations when his older brother was not. The difference was simple. Hans-Joachim suffered the stigma of looking "Jewish." That was the first red flag. The second was when curious bureaucrats invariably discovered that he had a grandparent whose given name was Samuel. With Erich they never bothered to look. Superficialities counted for much in Hitler's Germany, adding significantly to the arbitrariness with which they dealt with individuals.[14]

Like Hans-Joachim Boehm, Ernst Benda had one Jewish grandparent, making him a *Mischling* second degree. The Benda family lived in Siemensstadt in the north of Berlin, where his half-Jewish father was an engineer at the large electrical firm of Siemens and Halske. In 1932 Ernst had attended his grandfather's birthday party. Ministerialrat Benda was a ministerial counselor for the Reichswehr and a distinguished veteran who had served on the German General Staff in World War I. As a mark of respect, a two-man honor guard in full ceremonial uniform paraded in front of Grandfather Benda's house on his birthday. Then Hitler came to power. Ernst was almost eight years old on 30 January 1933. "We were all sitting together in the kitchen, . . ." he recalled. "Then, over the radio an announcement came, reporting about the gigantic torchlight parade [under Hitler's window]. At that moment, my father turned to us and said: 'This means war!'"[15] He spoke true. The Nazis immediately dismissed Grandfather Benda from the civil service. Meanwhile Herr Barzin, the new Ortsgruppenleiter in Siemensstadt, singled out the Bendas, publicly declaiming that he had forbidden his children to play with those "Jewish Benda children!" That incident taught schoolboy Ernst that his whole family was being targeted. In 1938 his beloved uncle Klemens informed the Bendas that he had seen enough. He was departing immediately for a professorship in psychiatry at Harvard University. Even more vivid was the aftermath of 9 November 1938, when Ernst saw firsthand the results of *Kristallnacht,* when mobs destroyed a synagogue in nearby Spandau. Glass still littered the streets in front of looted Jewish-owned shops.[16]

Despite those dark incidents, Ernst had better luck in school. His elementary and secondary school teachers were pleasant and competent. Even so, signs of discrimination surfaced. Ernst and his older brother, Hans-Jochen, could not join the Hitler Youth. When they began attending the nearby Kant Gymnasium, it also became apparent that even though they might earn the *Abitur* (both were gifted pupils), they would never be permitted to attend a university. Their Gymnasium teachers remained friendly, although Ernst's English teacher was a Party member and prone to nationalistic outbursts. The boys dismissed him as a *Quatschkopf* (windbag). Ernst's German teacher was also a member of the NSDAP, but he was decent to Ernst and the other boys. He was impressed with Ernst's language talent.

The Kant Gymnasium's principal, Herr Krüger, specialized in ancient Greek and Latin and ignored the Nazis as much as possible. His traditional values permeated the faculty. Ernst recalled that his equally gifted brother, Hans-Jochen, had won the school's literary prize with an essay that strongly criticized the Nazis. Herr Krüger invited Hans-Jochen into his office for a chat, then screamed in a stage voice that the essay was unacceptable. Hans-Jochen had never seen the principal act in such a manner. The principal quietly withdrew the prize. However, the essay incident faded from view with no political repercussions for Hans-Jochen. Herr Krüger walked a tightrope, educating his pupils and paying minimal obeisance to the Nazis.[17]

Another incident at home revealed chilling deeds that were taking place under the Nazis. The warning came in the form of an evening knock at the door in the fall of 1941. The unexpected visitor was a young Wehrmacht soldier who asked the Benda boys if he might speak to Frau Benda. She remembered him as their furnace repairman in peacetime and bade him sit. Frau Benda and the family had made a most agreeable impression upon him, the soldier said, so now on his leave, he wanted to speak. Distraught, the young soldier told his listeners that he had just returned from the eastern front, where in addition to horrible battle experiences, he had witnessed atrocities committed against civilians by his own army. Stunned, Frau Benda interrupted the young man at this point and asked who the victims had been. "They were mostly Jews," he replied, adding that some may have also been non-Jewish members of the captive population. He learned from soldiers that some of the victims were said to have been intellectuals. "Even so," he added, "most were Jews." The Bendas offered their guest hospitality, but given his agitated condition, he soon took his leave, never to return. Now they knew what was really happening to the Jews in the East. Ernst dared not share such information with classmates or teachers. The chances of being denounced for spreading malicious gossip were too great, and life in Berlin at this stage of the war was sufficiently normal that others might react with disbelief.[18]

Ernst enjoyed his German teacher despite the latter's childish faith in National Socialism. When faced with wartime reverses, the teacher would offer such platitudes as: "If only the Führer had known about this!" Then he would remind his pupils that National Socialism was producing a new society. Besides, the Führer was too busy to concern himself with every detail. As a lover of German poetry, he would invite his boys to his apartment on Tuesday evenings to listen to radio recitations of the poet Hölderlin. On the evening of 3 February 1943, the teacher's face was a study in concentration as a skilled commentator recited verse. Then, suddenly, a strange voice interrupted the broadcast to announce that an entire German army had been annihilated at Stalingrad. At that moment Ernst Benda watched as his German teacher's world crumbled. "I saw it in front of my very own eyes," he recalled many years later. Nine weeks later Benda finished school. Even though a quarter-Jew, he was now accorded the privilege of serving in Hitler's armed forces.[19]

Teacher again

Fellow Berliner Horst Hartwich, son of a Jewish pharmacist and an Aryan mother, had been an excellent pupil and a good athlete. Nevertheless, *Mischling* status had complicated his education from elementary school, through commercial school, and finally to the Lessing Gymnasium. Some of his teachers were kindly and treated him fairly. Others were hardly so benign, and the latter exhibited their prejudices ever more boldly when German armies were triumphant. In 1940 when France fell, his civics teacher at the commercial school, Dr. Jacobi, announced a treat. He would show them photos from his collection of "criminal" personalities from the Weimar Republic. "They are all full, half, quarter, eighth Jews and similar riffraff," he assured them. Turning to Horst, he added: "Hartwich go somewhere else. You bother me when I am teaching." Stunned, the fifteen-year-old rose from his seat and slunk out of class.[20]

Two years later in the summer of 1942 at the Lessing Gymnasium (he had found a complicated way to avoid, at least temporarily, the Nazi restrictions against *Mischling* enrollment in secondary schools), Horst was explaining a finer point of a work by Goethe in literature class. Eager to please his teacher, Dr. Ratloff, Horst spoke too quickly and jumbled his words. Finally, his teacher interrupted and told him to slow down and not to proceed *"mit der jüdischen Hast"* (with Jewish hastiness). The expression was a common one for those times, and the teacher had not used it with intent to harm. In fact, Horst had not even noticed the phrase. Obeying the friendly tone of his teacher instead, he had slowed his delivery and made a strong finish. During the class break, Dr. Ratloff summoned Horst to him, an unusual gesture. Fearful of what would happen next, the boy approached his teacher. "Horst, I used an inappropriate expression towards you," Dr. Ratloff stated. "I forgot that your father is a non-Aryan and I wished in no way to hurt you." The teacher extended his hand and shook the surprised boy's hand firmly. Then he turned and reentered his classroom. Horst looked down at his hand and realized that his eyes had grown damp. Individual teachers could make a difference. However, that difference was not decisive. A few weeks later, his high school principal summoned him and another boy, Klaus Muehlfelder, to his office and told them that as *Mischlinge* they could no longer attend secondary school. Horst left the premises within the hour. So long as National Socialism reigned, his education was over.[21]

Margit Weinbaum also confronted hostile teachers, but unlike Hartwich, she did not have a robust nature or an intact household upon which she could depend. Margit was the only child of a humble couple living in Frankfurt am Main when her invalid Jewish father died in 1934. In dire economic straits, Margit's mother sent her twelve-year-old daughter to live with her aunt Jenny in Cologne. Margit entered a nearby girls' school, but Frau Wildschenck, her new teacher, was an enthusiastic Party member who quickly identified Margit as a *Mischling*. Margit's new classmates were not slow to observe their teacher's open hostility toward her new pupil. The other girls ostracized her then and there. Teacher Wildschenck forbade her from participating in school trips and excluded her from the class photo. As the school year came to an end, the girls submitted their best artwork for an exhibition. Margit was delighted when her work was chosen and felt that at last her talent would change matters. The exhibition opened, and to her delight Margit immediately saw her sketches. Then she looked closer. Although given places of prominence, each sketch was unsigned. Her teacher had erased her name from each and every piece. The first school year ended badly. The second year was no different. Finally, in the spring of 1936, Aunt Jenny removed Margit from school two months early and gave her home tutoring. That summer a distraught Margit returned to her widowed mother in Frankfurt.

Matters in Frankfurt had not improved either. Given her deceased father's name, Margit was automatically added by the state police to the list of Frankfurt's Jewish community. Her mother protested, since neither she nor her daughter had chosen a religion. Nevertheless, Margit received periodic summonses to appear before the Gestapo. Terrified by those visits, Margit grew ever more nervous. Finally, in 1940, out of sheer desperation, her mother sent her back to Aunt Jenny in Cologne, where she had no choice but to resume attendance in the girls' school. The Gestapo followed. Aunt Jenny reported later, "Even here they would not leave her alone. She received constant Gestapo subpoenas to appear before them, which caused her to shake and to cry." Margit finally finished school in 1942. However, by that time persecution at school and by the Gestapo had left her an emotional wreck.[22]

Margit Weinbaum's school experiences demonstrated that teachers could inflict terrible emotional damage on children. Since they formed the first outside authority figure in the life of a German child, educators had the ability to create an environment that was either nurturing or destructive. While many schoolteachers under National Socialism ignored or at least dampened the effects of Party persecution, many others eagerly embraced the new ideology's racist values. Furthermore, Nazi supporters did not have to form a majority of the teaching staff of a school in order to make an impact. With the weight of the regime behind them, and backed by daily propaganda, by youth organizations, and by a plethora of state authorities, teachers imbued with National Socialist values could exert influence far beyond their numbers. Moreover, the percentage of such enthusiasts for National Socialism only increased over time. Therefore, the status of children registered as *Mischlinge* in German schools deteriorated year by year.

Recognizing the importance of a healthy school environment, parents of *Mischling* children sought frantically to locate sympathetic schools. That goal was often illusory, as the experiences of Ursula Kühn indicate. Ursula was born in Hamburg in 1929, the younger of two daughters of Egon and Johanna Kühn. Her father was a physician, her mother a former bookseller from Giessen. Egon was Jewish and Johanna Christian, but religion was not a noticeable feature in the household environment. One of Ursula's first childhood memories came on the first of May 1933, when Nazi Brownshirts marched through Hamburg, leading the Labor Day celebrations. Despite the excitement, she could sense her parents' dread as the huge uniformed men marched past. That night, for the first time in her life, Ursula began to have nightmares. Other signs of stress surfaced. When their friends visited, her parents bundled her and her older sister off to bed, and intense adult discussions began. Yet, when Ursula or her sister entered the living room on some pretext, a hush fell and all eyes turned upon them. She knew from eavesdropping that her parents and friends were discussing the need to flee Germany.[23]

Other unsettling trends arose. Although her parents had numerous friendly acquaintances in their neighborhood, they never held private conversations with those neighbors. They avoided politics, she recalled, and never offered their opinions about the Nazis or about the status of Jews. Nor did they talk about emigration. She had one close girlfriend in the immediate neighborhood when they were toddlers, but Ursula came to realize that when the two families came together, her parents only exchanged outward pleasantries even if the neighborhood was abuzz over political events. Early childhood experiences taught Ursula to lead a two-tiered existence. She learned to observe her parents' relations with other adults carefully. She also learned to distrust any and all strangers. Those childhood experiences hardened into lifetime habits. Despite her extreme youth, Ursula noticed that the family circumstances had changed. In 1935, for reasons she did not understand, they moved to a much smaller apartment. After the pogrom of *Kristallnacht* of 9 November 1938, she realized that her father, hitherto a busy physician, was no longer busy. His patients had disappeared because he was a "Jewish" doctor — whatever that meant. Finally, in the autumn of 1938, Dr. Kühn lost the right to practice medicine altogether. Meantime another shocking image had left its imprint. Following *Kristallnacht,* she walked along shopping streets covered with glass. Ursula walked across a bridge spanning Hamburg's Binnen Alster, a body of water, and something in the lake caught her eye. Gazing down, she reeled backward. There were bodies floating everywhere, miniature bodies. A second look told her that they were not humans after all. They were dolls or mannequins. Looters had taken them from shop windows and thrown them into the lake. Child though she was, she knew that she was gazing upon evil. Her nightmares returned.[24]

Despite these bleak developments, Ursula's childhood was not uniformly dismal. In 1935 at age six, she began attending elementary school and met an influential teacher. Klaus Bröer was everything a parent — or child — could hope for in a schoolteacher. He was a cultured man, a gifted teacher, and a warm human being. Furthermore, Herr Bröer possessed many talents. He was a gifted musician and an active theatergoer, well acquainted with Hamburg's active cultural life. Better still, he shared it with his young charges. Best of all, he was anti-Nazi, as was his wife. In fact, Herr Bröer had deliberately chosen teaching in elementary schools over secondary schools as a strategy of survival. In the lower schools he could avoid Nazi pressure better. It was in the upper grades that the Party exercised the most influence. Most of his pupils were Aryan, but a few were *Mischlinge,* and three were fully Jewish. He treated them all the same — with skill and care. Against the odds, Ursula received an excellent start in school.[25]

It was otherwise at home. A few weeks after *Kristallnacht,* Ursula arrived home to find several large men in the family apartment. At first she thought they were movers because they were shoving furniture around. Then she noticed her parents standing in a corner, pale and tight-lipped. Instantly on guard, she said nothing. After the strange men left, she learned that the mysterious visitors were police officials conducting a search. Then, a few days later,

Egon Kühn received an affidavit from a cousin in the United States, offering to sponsor his emigration. The sad news was, the sponsorship applied only to Egon, the family's only Jewish member. Ursula, a high-strung child, promptly suffered a bout of nervous exhaustion, and her mother sent her to an aunt in Giessen, where it was quieter and the air was better. Ursula acquiesced but suspected that her parents did not want her to see them making preparations for her father's departure. True enough, a few months after moving in with her aunt, Ursula received a letter from her mother, stating that her father, with whom she had always had a close and loving relationship, had departed on 23 June 1939 for the United States. Ursula wept.[26]

War came two months later, by which time Ursula was back at home with her mother and sister. With the help of a medical excuse, she gained a few more months of time away from school, an interval her mother used to secure her admission in the Hansaschule, a girls' upper school in downtown Hamburg in 1940. The new principal, Dr. Lüth, who was also the English teacher, convened all the girls shortly after Ursula's arrival to hear his summation of the world situation now that the war was widening. He expressed pride that Germany was once again confronting a coalition of powers in a world war. Then, after a dramatic pause, he assured all of the girls that Germany's worst enemies were not foreign armies; they were right here at home. They were the Jews. Moreover, he stated, glancing around the assembly, the Hansaschule still had had several half-Jews in attendance. "We have no legal basis to get rid of them yet," he announced, but he assured his young listeners that those offensive pupils would soon be expelled. He also stated that there were rumors, valid rumors in his opinion, that half-Jewish schoolgirls had been inciting Aryan pupils to acts of vandalism. There were "enemies" at the Hansaschule, he assured them, and they would be eliminated. Then he dismissed the assembly. Ursula returned home in tears. Frau Kühn frantically searched for yet another school.[27]

With the help of Ursula's earlier teacher, Herr Bröer, Ursula's mother located another principal, who was known, tacitly, to be unenthusiastic about National Socialism. After listening to Bröer, the other principal agreed to accept Ursula and the next day informed Dr. Lüth of the change. The latter accepted the decision without demur, and so Ursula settled into a school without an ardent anti-Semite for a principal. She remained there for the next three years, obtaining as normal an education as a *Mischling* could expect in

National Socialist Germany. Meanwhile her older sister had finished her basic schooling and moved to a village near Stade, where she became a nanny for a forester's large family, leaving Ursula and her mother in their small apartment. They survived the terrible firestorm of July 1943, but their apartment was utterly destroyed. Frau Kühn was forced to hunt for temporary living accommodations for herself and her daughter, plus take jobs of any kind including domestic service.

Meanwhile Ursula's school routine was so disrupted that the authorities ordered a *Kinderlandverschickung* (child evacuation) for the entire school. Teachers and children moved en masse to Wittstock on the Baltic coast, where Ursula stayed until the summer of 1944. Despite homesickness, Ursula had some luck. She was quartered with a sympathetic elderly woman, Frau Rohrbach, the widow of a railroad engineer who had remained a Communist to the end of his life. Ursula was safe with Frau Rohrbach. Enjoying her new security, she wrote detailed letters home about school life, including humorous descriptions of Hitler Youth parades, full of noise and posturing — in the midst of mass evacuations and rumors of German defeat on all fronts. In June 1944, she completed her last year of elementary school and as a *Mischling* was denied any further education. Lacking any alternative, Ursula returned to her mother in Hamburg. By this time Frau Kühn could scarcely make ends meet. She also told Ursula of Jewish relatives who had been transported to the East and never heard from again. A revered uncle, Herr Rosenthal, who was married to an Aryan, still lived in the neighborhood, but he warned Ursula in secret that she must never greet him in public. One day soon after, in the company of other girls, she passed him on the street, down-at-heel and wearing his Star of David armband. It broke her heart, but she obeyed his warning and walked by in silence. Ursula was badly shaken by this and other events. The air raids continued, and Ursula's anxiety attacks increased. By this time Frau Kühn was in despair. In the autumn of 1944, she went to the local labor office yet again, looking for work of some kind for herself and help for her distraught daughter. Women married to Jews were not exactly objects of pity for National Socialist officials, especially by 1944. However, Frau Kühn received help that day. A large, heavily built official whom she had not met before heard her out, with Ursula shaking at her side. Rising from his chair after glancing at Ursula, he gave a startled Frau Kühn a firm handshake and then immediately set about arranging all the necessary forms for the girl's evacuation to relatives in Giessen. Ursula's school days were over. Now she would have to find a way to survive elsewhere as an adult at age fifteen.[28]

Born five years earlier than Ursula Kühn, Meta Alexander, a Berliner, also came from a middle-class background. Her father, Ernst, was Jewish, and her mother, Käte, was Roman Catholic. Both families could trace German ancestors many generations into the past. Ernst had been a cavalry lieutenant in World War I. Wounded three times, he proudly wore his Iron Cross on Armistice Day and on other patriotic occasions. He cofounded a laundry and linen service with his future wife's brother, a fellow Berliner. At first, Käte had functioned as secretary to the joint family concern. Then she and Ernst fell in love, and when they married in 1923, Ernst converted to Catholicism. If any German family could have been considered to be a model of ethnic and religious integration, it was the Alexanders. Meta's Jewish grandparents, Frieda and David, lived harmoniously in the same apartment as their children and grandchildren in Berlin's Bayerisches Viertel. That district had a prominent Jewish population that mixed freely and amicably with its Christian residents. The family laundry prospered; their apartment was comfortable; and they could even afford a maid and a car. The Alexanders traveled widely and had a large circle of friends in the exciting Berlin of the 1920s. Meta remembered her first eight years as a time of unmitigated pleasure.[29]

The first shock in Meta's life occurred in August 1932, on the day of Germany's presidential elections. The results showed a disturbingly strong showing for Hitler, whom the family despised, and Meta's grandfather, David, grew so angry that he suffered a heart attack and died. In 1933, conditions rapidly worsened for the Alexanders. Meta's father had to sell the laundry at a devastating loss. Ironically, his Aryan brother-in-law had sensed danger earlier, sold out his portion of the business, and left for America. Meta's father, a German patriot and decorated war veteran, could not bring himself to do the same. The Alexanders soon fell into poverty.

Meta's elementary schooling had begun well with competent teachers. Then, in April 1933, a new music teacher joined the staff. One day he appeared before them dressed in an SA storm trooper uniform, replete with glistening brown boots. In a stentorian voice that knocked the children back into their seats, the teacher announced that now they would learn new songs — songs that reflected the spirit of the new society! The uniformed teacher launched into the standby of the Nazi movement, the "Horst Wessel Lied." Then he gave loud renditions of soldiers' marches, ending with a bloodcurdling song used by the SS that included lyrics like "When the knife spurts Jewish blood, things run twice as well." At this point, Meta and many of the other pupils broke down and cried.[30]

It wasn't until the following year that Meta Alexander was able to transfer to the Saint Franziskus Oberlyzeum, a Catholic secondary school for girls of Berlin. The school's director was an unusual personality in that mainly Protestant capital. A priest who had made his mark as a fine educator in Westphalia, Father Alexander Coppenrath ran an excellent school in Berlin. Perhaps for that reason, he was known among the Nazis as *der westfälische Dickkopf* (the Westphalian stubborn mule). Numerous Berlin families, Catholic or otherwise, began sending their daughters there, and they were not disappointed. The school's sisters maintained quality teaching, dispensing much the same curriculum they had offered before 1933. Meta Alexander, now a *Mischling* first degree, profited too. No one seemed to take notice of her, and anonymity under current political circumstances was the best one could hope for.[31]

The Catholic Church was strong enough to retain its own youth programs such as the St. Matthias Gemeinde for a time. The girls wore distinctive green uniforms of which they were proud. They participated in many after-school activities and myriad weekend projects. Sometimes they went hiking in Berlin's Grunewald and occasionally undertook more ambitious camping trips to the Spreewald south of the capital or elsewhere in Brandenburg. Father Coppenrath understood the value of such activities and gave his school's youth group vigorous support. The National Socialists, especially their HJ and BDM leaders, did not welcome the priest's success. In 1938, they disbanded the St. Matthias Gemeinde and all other Catholic youth organizations. Soon after, the Nazis arrested Father Coppenrath for resistance to National Socialist ideals. For a time Meta and her friends continued to meet clandestinely, hoping to keep their group together. However, within a year even their clandestine meetings ceased. For German children, the only youth organization that counted was the Hitler Youth — except that non-Aryans like Meta were not welcome. With unstinting support from her teachers and administrators, Meta finished her *Abitur* in 1942, the last year *Mischlinge* could do so. By then it was obvious that university studies were out of the question for her. She and her parents pondered what was best for her in wartime Germany where Nazi-inspired anti-Semitism was growing worse.[32]

While the bulk of *Mischlinge* were born in the years of the Weimar Republic, several thousand citizens of mixed Jewish-Christian background were older. They had confronted Nazism either as late teenagers or as full adults starting in 1933. Among them were citizens stigmatized by the Nazis as *Geltungsjuden* (i.e., persons deemed equivalent to Jews). The sons of the Haurwitz family in Berlin were relegated to that category of German-Jewish *Mischlinge*. Hans Haurwitz was born in August 1918 in Berlin-Charlottenburg and was the youngest of two sons. His brother, ten years older, was single in 1933, and after gauging trends for a year or two, he migrated to South Africa. Educated and mobile, Hans's older brother fit the profile of German Jews who had made their measure of Hitler in timely fashion and had departed from Germany.

The youthful Hans did not have that option. Until 1933 Hans's father had been a successful businessman in an important technical field. He was co-owner of a Stettin-based firm that produced advanced surfacing materials for roofing, roads, conduits, and other industrial uses. Benefiting from the modest upswing in the German construction industry, the Haurwitz family moved to Berlin in the mid-1920s. Even the depression did not dampen business until 1933 when the Nazis forced Hans's father to sell his business. Overnight the family became poor. Hitherto, Hans had liked school and had performed well. Under normal circumstances, he would have completed his *Abitur* as a matter of course and then attended a university. His teachers had been competent, and he had not encountered unusual discrimination. Yet, in 1935 at age seventeen, Hans Haurwitz left his Gymnasium one year before he would normally have graduated. Following discussions with his family, he had decided that a practical education was imperative for survival, either in Germany or as a migrant to another country. Thereupon, Hans was apprenticed to a cosmetics firm, Scherek, a Jewish-owned business. The plan was a logical one in those dangerous times. The question was, would it succeed for a seventeen-year-old *Geltungsjude* for whom the Nazis were showing even less tolerance than for a *Mischling* first degree?[33]

Strictly speaking, Helmut Langer was not a German. Born in 1930 in a village near the industrial town of Gablonz in Czechoslovakia's Sudetenland, he, too, was a so-called *Mischling* first degree. It was his fate to have been born to a Sudeten German father of the Christian faith, and to a Sudeten German mother of Jewish heritage. Although not a particularly religious family, the parents saw to it that Helmut and his brother, Eckard, who was two years older, were raised as Catholics. Misfortune struck the Langer family early. Frau Langer died of complications during the birth of their third child in 1935. After a decent interval, their father married the family's serving girl who had worked for them for years. She continued to run the eggs and butter business the boys' mother had established, a valuable asset that stood the family in good stead during the depression. The same family business also paid dividends during the lean war years to come.

Helmut and his brother attended the nearby elementary school, and all was well at first. However, the Sudetenland was ceded to Germany in September 1938, and World War II began a year later. Misfortune soon fell upon the Langer family. First, the boys' father was drafted into the Wehrmacht and was mostly away from home thereafter. The boys experienced the burgeoning anti-Semitism in the Sudetenland, a district already known for its intolerance even in quieter times. Helmut's older brother was barely able to finish his elementary education and receive his school-leaving degree in 1942. Helmut was not that lucky. It was widely known in the village that the two boys were *Mischlinge* first degree. Perhaps Eckard might slip by, but timing worked against Helmut. Despite his solid performance in the classroom, he was terminated in 1944 at age thirteen. It was a bitter end to an education that had already been jarred by unpleasant incidents.

Besides being a good pupil, Helmut was also athletic, and he joined the Hitler Youth at age ten. Apparently word of restrictions against *Mischlinge* had not yet reached local HJ authorities, and his non-Aryan status was not widely known outside his village. Joining with youths from Gablonz proper and from other adjoining villages where he was not known, Helmut gained social acceptance. He wore his HJ uniform well, and the other boys admired him for his athletic skills and his friendly nature. Consequently, the Hitler Youth became a high point in his otherwise dreary life in the village where the stigma of being a *Mischling* clung to him. He went out on hikes, field exercises, camping trips, and all the other activities associated with the HJ. One of their favorite activities was a *Geländespiel*, held in the spring of 1943, a kind of jamboree with many competitive sporting events and maneuvers among the HJ units. Helmut joined in enthusiastically. He helped his group win top honors, engaging in nighttime games, athletic contests, and team exercises. He and his friends excelled at marching smartly, pitching tents, mastering the field compass, and demonstrating general all-around prowess. In short, Helmut and his chums had a wonderful time together. On the third and final day of the youth outing, all the boys came together for their closing ceremony. It should have been a crowning, emotional moment for all of them. However, a new youth leader, a half-German, half-Swiss of the name Spindler, seemed compelled to prove at the closing ceremony that he was the best German nationalist of them all. With the entire formation of HJ units drawn up in formal ranks, Herr Spindler called Helmut and one other HJ member forward. Helmut wondered if some special recognition was imminent. Then, under all the other boys' rapt gaze, Spindler dismissed them from the Hitler Youth immediately. "*Mischlinge* are not Germans!" he screamed. Helmut and the other boy obeyed Spindler's order to about-face and depart. Silently, with downward gaze, they walked past the ranks of boys. Once behind the tents and alone, Helmut broke down. He would never be just one of the boys, nor would he be a "real" German. His dismissal from school the following year only added further proof of this fact, if any were needed.[34]

Hanns-Peter Herz was among the younger German-Jewish *Mischlinge* who grew into full youth under National Socialism. Born in 1927 in Neuköln-Britz, a Berlin working-class district, he was raised in a strongly Social Democratic family. His father was Jewish but had converted to Protestantism. His mother was Christian. One of Hanns-Peter's early childhood memories occurred on the evening of 30 January 1933 when his parents began receiving unexpected guests. They were all Social Democrats. Hanns-Peter was not sure what it was all about, but he felt fear and foreboding in his parents, a new experience for him. Equally unsettling was the fact that all the adult visitors exhibited similar anxiety. Another unsettling experience came on 1 May 1933. When the family awakened on that traditional European Labor Day, they discovered that someone had crudely chalked a huge sign over their apartment building entrance: *Juden heraus!* (Jews get out!). Hanns-Peter was not sure what it meant. His father tried to explain what being Jewish meant in Nazi Germany, but the boy was confused. Soon after this, his parents arranged to have him baptized. Eventually, he was confirmed in the Evangelical-Protestant Church.

In September 1933, Hanns-Peter, now six, entered the local Britz elementary school. He was not aware of it, but already the Nazis had begun to curtail his educational opportunities. In normal times he would have entered a nearby special school for gifted boys and girls of working-class families, the highly respected Karl-Marx-Schule, founded after World War I by a Social Democratic educator, Fritz Karsen. Immediately upon seizing power in 1933, the Nazis had closed down Karsen's school, and its founder barely escaped Hitler's clutches. His departure left a gaping hole in elementary–secondary education in German society. Unaware of these larger developments, young Hanns-Peter found an agreeable learning environment in the Britz elementary school. Hanns-Peter liked most of his classmates. A few were Jewish, and a few others were *Mischlinge* like him. The children, of whatever religious persuasion, generally got along well with each other. A few children were openly anti-Semitic, and they baited Hanns-Peter and others. Fortunately for him, Hanns-Peter's father was a journalist. He and his equally articulate wife were deeply concerned about quality education and about potential racial bias, so they prepared special textbooks for Hanns-Peter in order that he would not be indoctrinated by Nazi propaganda.

Because Britz lies near the city center, a new population influx took place shortly after the Nazi Seizure of Power. The Party's SA storm troopers and its newly enlarged SS complement and their families needed affordable housing in the capital. Blue-collar Britz was attractive because of its favorable location. Suddenly, uniformed men were everywhere on the streets of Britz. Thus, for several years after 1933, Hanns-Peter's parents saw to it that he was never alone outdoors. Various neighbors, former SPD loyalists, constantly kept an eye on their young charge. As the influx of Nazis continued, Adolf Eichmann and his family moved into the neighborhood, and, by a strange twist, their eldest son, Klaus, began to attend the same school as Hanns-Peter. In retrospect it seems improbable, but to a surprising degree the local children and the children of the newly arrived National Socialist families got along with little rancor. In fact, the Eichmanns' little Klaus frequently played with Hanns-Peter. Sometimes, Hanns-Peter visited the Eichmann home. He found Frau Eichmann a nice mother. Thus, racism and personal relationships in Nazi Germany could work in strange ways and produce bizarre anomalies![35]

In 1938 Hanns-Peter finished his elementary education and, having demonstrated that he was a talented child, he qualified to enter the Kaiser Wilhelm Real-und-Reform Schule in Neukölln. Despite its involved title, it was a respected Gymnasium. However, the thrill of Hanns-Peter's success was marred on opening day by the school principal. "Your son will not have it easy here," he assured Hanns-Peter's parents. "However, our teachers will help him as best they can." The principal was as good as his word. Most of the teachers remained fair to their pupils despite increased anti-Semitism. They continued to act as true professionals, and they treated their children with courtesy and respect, he recalled. Nevertheless, even there patterns of persecution began to catch up with Hanns-Peter, as it did sooner or later with all of Germany's *Mischlinge*.

One of the boys in Hanns-Peter's Latin class was the son of a local Nazi official, Herr Lippert, an SA man and a Reichskommissar (Reich commissioner, although Hanns-Peter was not sure of his exact function). The Lippert youth was a bully, and unfortunately for Hanns-Peter, he singled out his smaller classmate for special attention. Lippert sat beside Hanns-Peter in Latin class and often taunted him with verbal barbs that the smaller boy tried to ignore. Interpreting passivity as acceptance, Lippert one day chalked a prominent Star of David on Hanns-Peter's chair and yet another one on his school jacket draped upon the chair. By an unfortunate coincidence, Hanns-Peter returned to his chair at the very moment class was to begin. It was too late to do anything about the hateful graffiti because the Latin teacher, Herr Paschowski, was entering the room. Hanns-Peter waited for class to begin. After all, Herr Paschowski was a Party member, and there was no use drawing attention to himself unnecessarily.

What happened next was as memorable as it was unexpected. Paschowski glanced at the graffiti. His face hardened, and he immediately strode over to Hanns-Peter. "Who did this?" he thundered. Obeying the creed of schoolboys and schoolgirls the world over, Hanns-Peter kept silent. However, another schoolmate (not a *Mischling*) steered his gaze toward Lippert. Without hesitation Lehrer Paschowski ordered the offending pupil to the front of the class. Smiling, Lippert came forward. As soon as the boy was in place, Paschowski ordered him to take the chalkboard sponge in hand and expunge the marks from Hanns-Peter's chair and jacket. Lippert walked over to the offending chair and did so. Paschowski then ordered the young offender back to the front of the class. There, under the full gaze of all the boys, he proclaimed loudly: "**Nicht** *noch einmal wird das bei mir passieren!* [That will **never** happen here again!]" Thereupon, he boxed young Lippert's ears. No one in the class ever misbehaved in such fashion again.[36]

True, Herr Paschowski was a member of the National Socialist Party. He had joined in order to keep his job and to lessen the effects of Nazi influence on the education of German children. It became a cliché after the war for former Nazis to claim that they had joined the NSDAP in order to subvert or at least to soften its effects from within the system. Often — too often — those claims were spurious. Yet, in this instance it really was the truth. In postwar trials, Hanns-Peter Herz and other schoolmates came to the defense of their respected Latin teacher. Such a positive experience, however, was quickly overshadowed by the more prevalent racism of National Socialism. Hanns-Peter discovered this when he finished school some months later and began to search for a way to make a living.[37]

One of the chilling facts of life in Nazi Germany was that anti-Semitism was often more pronounced in rural areas than in big cities. Woe to families who were Jewish or partially Jewish who lived in small, isolated villages as small minorities among a rustic, often intolerant citizenry. Jakob Kranz, of humble origins, was a metalworker by training who, making up for his impoverished youth, completed a secondary school education as an adult — no easy feat at any time. By 1930 his hard work and education finally paid off. Jakob became the manager of a coal mine outside Kassel. At the same time, following a three-year courtship, he married Helene Friedmann, a nurse who was Jewish. Their daughter, Frieda, was born the following year. Despite the depression, Jakob's firm remained solvent, and the Kranz family seemed at long last to have entered a happier phase in their lives. Living frugally and working hard, they had built their own house in a small village outside Kassel. Then, in 1933, the idyllic phase of their family life came to an end. Under Nazi law, Jakob, the Aryan spouse, and Helene, the Jewish mother, along with their *Mischling* daughter, enjoyed a *privilegierte Mischehe* (privileged mixed marriage). Theoretically protected, the Kranzes discovered that life for them in a village of sixteen hundred souls, all of whom seemed to be infected with anti-Semitism, had become a living hell. It transpired that there were simply no other Jewish Germans in the village or even in the Kreis (district). They alone were the targets of racial wrath. After the Seizure of Power, Helene constantly kept a wary eye out for fellow shoppers at the local market who, given the chance, dug her with their elbows or stepped on her feet. Sometimes, seemingly by accident, fellow villagers threw doors open in her path, and she learned to be ready for such "accidental" incidents. Appearing in public became humiliating and daunting. Yet, as an adult, she coped. Coping was not so easy for little Frieda, especially when she entered elementary school in the autumn of 1935.

Two years earlier, toddler Frieda had not been able to appear on a village street without a neighborhood child or even an adult shouting insults at her. From her first day at school, Herr Kranz had to escort her there and home again. There was one saving grace for little Frieda, however: the village teachers did not abuse her. Neither did they encourage abuse by her schoolmates. However, the general atmosphere in the village was such that most of the other schoolchildren viewed her as a natural target for scorn and abuse. During lunch recesses or play periods, she experienced constant harassment by classmates, including insults and slaps. Quick to learn, Frieda adopted a low profile. She began hovering in a corner of the schoolyard, trying to stay away from the more aggressive children. She did not dare to eat her lunch in public because another child would steal it. Repeatedly, other pupils would grab her school satchel with its books, pencils, paper, and other learning materials and scatter them in a gutter or in the village's ample piles of livestock manure. Elementary and secondary education for Frieda Kranz in that provincial setting from 1933 to 1945 was torture.[38]

Even in the spring 1945, when the war was drawing to a close, children continued to rip her dresses when she walked to church services. Village adults joined in the late-war harassment. Her father reported that only a few months before the defeat, an adult male had ripped Frieda's school notebooks out of her satchel, beat her over the head, and screamed racial epithets as she ran away. Even in her home the racial incidents continued despite the looming Nazi defeat. Because of the likelihood of violence, Frieda had mostly retreated to her own property, playing in the family garden behind a stout wooden fence. However, the fence was no guarantee of safety. Village children often lofted stones over it at her from the street. Once, a large boy, the butcher's son who had also abused her at school, vaulted the fence and snatched her hair. Then he jumped back before her parents could intervene. On another occasion, a second boy nearly blinded her with his rock throwing. Frieda scarcely dared to take public transportation because of harassment by other children, even in the presence of adults who always refused to intervene. Particularly distressing was the fact that village mothers, who in 1932 had coddled the infant Frieda, were now among those who abetted the discrimination. Baptized a Christian, she undertook rare public appearances in order to attend confirmation classes and finally received confirmation into the Protestant Church at age thirteen in late 1944. Even so, with the war turning down and Allied victory imminent, Frieda endured renewed abuse by her neighbors. Finally, in April 1945, American troops rolled into town. For Frieda, who had just turned fourteen, the advent of foreign troops was a wonderful birthday present. Her persecution should now have ended. Or had it? Even after the war, Frieda encountered subtler forms of persecution. A teacher who had defended Frieda in the Nazi era against the worst class heckler, the village butcher's son, suffered angry verbal attacks from the boy's father, resulting in the teacher's transfer out of the village school in the first postwar school year. The family Kranz from a small Hessian village, especially their daughter, Frieda, was permanently scarred by twelve years of National Socialist persecution, liberation notwithstanding.[39]

Ralf-Günther G. was a young *Mischling* whose circumstances removed him from Germany, only to place him in even greater danger. Toward the end of the Weimar Republic, Ralf's mother, Edith H., had married Walter G. in Berlin, and Ralf was born in September 1932. His father was Jewish and his mother was Christian. The marriage was not a success, and the couple divorced in 1936 with Edith taking formal custody of their son. She moved to the Netherlands a year later, temporarily leaving Ralf in the care of friends, and she married Richard W. in 1937. Like her first husband, Richard, too, was Jewish. A year later, six-year-old Ralf arrived in the Netherlands to be reunited with his mother and to meet his new stepfather. Elementary schooling for the boy was not easy because of his unfamiliarity with the Dutch language. However, those difficulties paled in comparison with what happened next. In August 1941, Adolf Eichmann of the Reichssicherheitshauptamt (RSHA), in agreement with a proposal by Reich commissioner for the Netherlands, Arthur Seyss-Inquart proposed that half-Jews in the Lowlands be considered equivalent to full Jews and thus subject to removal to the East. An official from the Reich Ministry of the Interior, Regierungsrat Dr. Werner Feldscher, who represented Bernhard Lösener, reported back to his colleagues that Eichmann and the others in the RSHA were trying a new gambit. They wanted to surround Germany with territories where the definition of who was Jewish was more stringent, thus forcing the Reich to include half-Jews in its deportation orders as well. Although this action set off an internal debate among Party members and government officials in Germany proper, it soon resulted in a harsher policy in the Netherlands.[40] Thus, in May 1942, the Nazi occupation authorities forced Edith's Jewish husband, Richard, and young Ralf to wear the yellow Star of David. Rightly fearing imminent deportation, Edith and Richard went underground with Ralf on 10 August 1942, taking refuge in a tiny room in an obscure location where the parents seldom ventured out and the boy remained virtually a prisoner. Ralf stayed in hiding with his parents until the Wehrmacht surrender of 5 May 1945. He had received little formal schooling before 1942 and none thereafter. To be sure, such an abnormal childhood and such a disrupted education might have produced lifelong repercussions. For Ralf it was a moot point anyway. A sickly boy under the best of circumstances, years of confinement, a poor diet marked by near starvation in the last half-year of the war, and a total lack of medical care contributed to Ralf-Günther G.'s death at age fifteen in 1946. German *Mischlinge* residing outside Hitler's Greater German Reich suffered the kind of peril known only to Europe's full Jews.[41]

Klaus Muehlfelder (later he changed his name to Charles Milford) was a Berliner, born in 1927 and raised in Reinickendorf, a northern district of Berlin. His father was a medical doctor from Thuringia, and Jewish. His mother was a Berliner and Christian. Although neither parent was religious, each sensed the temper of the times. Originally, their plan was to allow Klaus to make his own religious preference known when he came of age (1948). Following the Seizure of Power, they baptized him immediately. Thus, scarcely aware of the fact, little Klaus became a Christian. Later, he studied for his confirmation into the German Evangelical-Protestant Church and received it in 1941. Meanwhile, the Nazi regime had to acknowledge his parents' marriage as a *privilegierte Mischehe* (i.e., a privileged mixed marriage). In short, Klaus and his Jewish father came under the protection of their mother/wife who was, by Nazi standards, a *deutschblütige Ehefrau* (a wife of German blood).

Klaus's Volksschule (elementary school) was a good one, and for the first four years he encountered no problems. His recollection was that his schoolmates and his teachers were supportive. Then, upon entering the Gontard School, a Gymnasium, the atmosphere appeared to change. His first homeroom teacher sometimes wore his Party uniform to school, and rumors of bullying and intimidation flew among the *Mischling* children. However, as in the case of Hanns-Peter Herz, reality soon departed from anticipation. Rather than persecute his non-Aryan pupil, the teacher, whether brown-shirted or not, treated Klaus with the same civility that he showed to all the other pupils. In 1940, Klaus's school joined a civil defense exercise called *Kinderlandverschickung* (child evacuation) because of the likelihood of aerial raids upon Germany's cities. The Gontard School moved en masse in September 1940 to the Warthegau (occupied Poland). The exercise coincided with the first British air raids on Berlin. For Klaus and his schoolmates, the evacuation was an exciting adventure, an extended class trip. Moreover, it included everyone and was nondiscriminatory. As Klaus saw it, all children from his school, *Mischlinge* included, were treated equally in what the participants considered to be Germany's first war emergency. Even so, upon his return, Klaus discovered that his "class trip" had been an aberration. His formal schooling came to an abrupt end in the spring of 1942 when he was called from class to join fellow *Mischling* Horst Hartwich in the principal's office. The latter announced that a new directive from the Reich minister for education, Bernhard Rust, required that all *Mischlinge* first degree be removed from school immediately. All over Germany similar scenes were taking place in its secondary schools.[42]

Vienna-born Rudolf Klein, whose physician father, a German from Bohemia, and whose mother, a Czech nurse also from Bohemia, was born in 1920. His father was Jewish and his mother Christian, and they baptized Rudolf as a Catholic. Because Austria remained an independent republic until the Anschluss of 1938, Rudolf's elementary and secondary schooling was unhindered by Nazi persecution. Even so, homegrown Viennese anti-Semitism more than made up for it. His secondary school, the respected Piaristen Gymnasium, located in the prosperous Eighth District, was named after a religious order of monks, but the school atmosphere was secular and the teachers were mostly laymen. In fact, only the religion instructor was a Catholic priest. Six of Rudolf's classmates were from fully Jewish backgrounds, including his closest friend, Kurt Schell (later Shell). There were also several half-Jewish classmates as well.

The 1938 Nazi takeover changed matters immediately. First, Rudolf's six Jewish classmates were transferred within days to a school in Vienna's Second District (the Austrian capital had a number of well-defined city districts, akin to the *arondissements* of Paris). Vienna's Second District was known as the "Jewish District." All over Vienna, Jewish schoolchildren were being concentrated in the Second District. Wishing to show solidarity, Rudolf volunteered to join ranks with Kurt and the other transferees from the Piaristen Gymnasium, but his father intervened. The elder Klein observed that he, Rudolf, was within three months of receiving his coveted *Matura* (*Abitur* in Germany). It would be foolish for him to spoil his opportunity of graduating from one of Vienna's most respected secondary schools on the eve of graduation. Besides, Rudolf's isolated protest would achieve nothing. Reluctantly, Rudolf acquiesced and graduated three months later. Fortunately, Kurt Schell and his five other Jewish Piaristen school chums also graduated from their new school. Prudently, and with help from Rudolf's family, Kurt Schell migrated immediately to the United States. Rudolf, now a *Mischling* first degree, remained at home — for the time being.[43]

Although most *Mischlinge* were to be found in the largest cities such as Berlin, Hamburg, Frankfurt, and, after March 1938, Vienna, others were spread all over Central Europe. Martha Rohr, although born in Berlin, never really knew the city of her birth. She was born on 25 December 1916, what German society called a *Kristkind* (Christmas child). Alas, her parentage was informal even by the relaxed standards of the late-war Kaiserreich. Her father, Alfred Jonas, was a soldier of the Great War, temporarily on leave. Her mother, Elisabeth Müller, was a domestic servant. They enjoyed a brief wartime romance, then, all too soon, Jonas returned to the western front. Elisabeth, now pregnant, continued in domestic service until her delivery day. It was a difficult birth, and tragically Elizabeth died of complications several weeks later. Needless to say, Martha's father, a frontline soldier, was in no position to care for their newborn daughter. Besides, his prospects for survival were poor. Martha was placed in a foundling home and then, a couple of years later, given up for adoption.

Meanwhile, a childless family, Herr and Frau Knebel, residing in Wintersdorf, a small village near Trier on the Luxembourg border, sought to adopt a child. Hardworking farmers and innkeepers, the Knebels seemed to be an ideal choice as adoptive parents. Thus, the Knebels came to raise Martha as their own. Hitherto childless, they nevertheless produced three biological children, only one of whom survived to adulthood. In the meantime the Knebels adopted a second infant girl. All of the Knebel children attended Wintersdorf's elementary school.

Martha's new life was not marked by anonymity. Her "cute" Berlin accent set her apart, even as a winsome toddler. Besides, village gossip soon had it that Martha's birth father was Alfred Jonas, a Jew, and that her Christian mother, Elisabeth Müller, had died in childbirth. A transplanted Berliner of mixed religion, Martha was quickly typed as an exotic creature among the local citizenry. In 1923, Martha started elementary school. Because she was bright, Martha became popular with her teachers, and she was blessed with good looks and a pleasant personality. Thus, Martha Knebel, as she was now known, passed through Wintersdorf's elementary school with ease. No thought was given to her attending a college preparatory school, nor was she encouraged to attend a university. Such horizons did not exist for the Wintersdorfers in general and the Knebels in particular. They were peasants and proud of it.

Martha began at an early age to help out with the usual family chores. After her obligatory eight years of elementary school, Martha performed the usual village tasks, working in the fields by day and performing myriad other chores in the life of a small farming village. It should be noted that the Knebels had ignored Martha's birth father, Alfred Jonas, who, having survived the war, had finally located Martha. In fact, he had offered to pay for her attendance at a Gymnasium, an offer the Knebels refused. The Knebels minimized all contact between Martha and Alfred. They censored his mail and disallowed visits. Thus, at age fourteen, perky schoolgirl though she was, Martha found herself working full-time on the farm and at the family inn. She led the normal life of a village maiden in her rustic setting, planting, tending, and harvesting with other family members according to the rhythm of the seasons. In the evenings Martha, by now a pretty teenager, waited tables at the Knebels' local inn, the Gasthof am Bahnhof. Thus, by 1930 Martha was leading a lifestyle not unlike that of a country girl of the nineteenth century. Perhaps so, but even in far-off Wintersdorf the year 1933 duly arrived, and with it the Nazi Seizure of Power. Eventually, Hitler and his movement would change Martha's seemingly idyllic existence. Like Jews and *Mischlinge* throughout Germany, she, too, eventually discovered that tolerance of non-Aryans was anathema to the self-appointed guardians of Germany's *Herrenvolk*.[44]

Martha Rohr was somewhat unusual as a *Mischling* in that she led such a rustic existence. For many other bright young German women — Jewish, Gentile, or whatever — the twentieth century had brought great promise in higher education — until 1933. Between the Seizure of Power and the out-break of war in 1939, total university enrollment had declined by almost three-fifths, a reliable indicator of the respect the Nazis held for intellectual attainment. Within Germany's secondary schools (Gymnasiums and other college preparatory schools), the proportion of girls fell from about 35 per-cent to 30 percent. In 1934, the first full year under the Nazi dictatorship, ten thousand young women earned the *Abitur*. However, only fifteen hundred were permitted to go on to a university even though the *Abitur* had, tradi-tionally, allowed all recipients a university education. Even then, the discrimi-nation did not end. Incoming university women in Hitler's Reich were almost always channeled into home economics or languages, academic dead ends by the standards of the time. Suffice it to say, the Nazis had little use for women with intellectual potential. However harsh their policies were toward women in general, they were far harsher toward *Mischling* women in particular.[45]

Intelligence alone was not decisive. Bright though she might be, Martha Knebel was destined by circumstances to play the role of the peasant lass — until ensnared in the machinations of Nazi persecution later in Hitler's Reich. It was young women like Eva Heilmann, Meta Alexander, and Thekla Brandt who typified the big-city girl caught up in irrational, racially determined educational and career bottlenecks. Thekla Brandt was, like Martha Rohr, Prussian-born. However, unlike Martha, Thekla was born into a stable fam-ily environment after the Great War. She was one of four children born to a middle-class Brandenburg family. Both parents were physicians. Her father was a Christian. Her mother, born Ilse Teichmann, was Jewish. Thekla en-tered elementary school in 1930, three years before the Seizure of Power. She had enjoyed a happy childhood already, and school was a pleasurable experi-ence, too. Along with her siblings, Thekla found life good even as her par-ents were establishing a prosperous joint medical practice. In fact, by 1933 the elder Brandts had become a respected, even revered, social fixture in their working-class neighborhood in Neukölln.

Thekla's elementary schooling continued without incident into the early Nazi years. Then, in 1934, she moved to a respected secondary school, the Lyzeum Neukölln in eastern Berlin. To everyone's shock, the principal of her new school turned out to be a member of the NSDAP. Fearing the worst, the Brandts sent Thekla off to the Lyzeum on the first day. Thekla returned home smiling. Unbelievably, nothing happened. The principal had simply left the children alone, and normal school life resumed. One likely explanation was the fact that the teachers were mature adults. None was under the age of forty. They conformed, as she observed later, to the typical profile of the aging Prussian *Studienrat,* an aloof Prussian civil servant. They were neither kind nor unkind. Rather, they were indefinably distant. They were also, for the most part, neutral in respect to Nazi ideology. They never attempted to impose a National Socialist outlook. At the same time, they did nothing to prevent Nazi biases from arising. Thus, racial prejudice could and did surface. For example, in 1934, the children in Thekla's class were preparing their annual class trip. During one planning session, the teacher asked Thekla to please go find some chalk. She suggested that her young charge would find it in a remote part of the school. Implicitly trusting her teacher, Thekla rushed off to find the chalk. During her absence, the teacher quickly polled the other pupils, asking if they would allow their classmate to accompany them during the impending class trip. The girls answered in the negative. Informed of the decision upon her speedy return, Thekla felt deeply betrayed by this violation of trust by schoolmates and by her hitherto respected teacher.[46]

Thekla and her sister soon encountered other forms of discrimination. To the Brandt children's shock, they learned that their mother, being Jewish, was not permitted to practice medicine anymore. The daughters also discovered that they could not join the Bund deutscher Mädel (BDM) even as the Brandt family's two sons were banned from joining the Hitler Jugend (HJ). Being resourceful, they began to find ways to counter Nazi persecution. Their mother continued to aid the Brandts' medical practice — sub rosa to be sure — and the children found alternative youth groups. First, Thekla became involved with her Protestant church, but it was in another organization, the Verein für das Deutschtum im Ausland (VDA), that she and her siblings found real acceptance. Thekla became a standard-bearer in the VDA ceremonies. Meanwhile, her more athletic sister joined a local Turnverein (athletic club). Thus, the Brandts, adults and children alike, got by. Thekla completed her *Abitur* at the Lyzeum Neukölln in the spring of 1942; she was one of the last *Mischling* pupils in Hitler's Germany to do so. Although eminently qualified for higher education and a professional career, Thekla Brandt was about to discover, like so many other *Mischlinge* before her, that her prospects in National Socialist Germany were nil.[47]

While the term *Mischling* usually referred to half-Jewish German citizens, it was also a term that could be interpreted as "half-breed" and was highly deprecatory. Bernd Rebensburg, a private school pupil, experienced situations whereby not only *Mischlinge* but other schoolmates of mixed heritage did not fit neatly into Nazi racial stereotypes. Hitler was obsessed foremost by anti-Semitism, but National Socialists viewed all "foreigners" in their midst with suspicion. When asked by the author, Rebensburg stated: "Concerning the theme of *Mischlinge* in the Germany of 1933–45, I recall that I confronted it in 1933 and 1934 at the Evangelical [Protestant] Pädagogium in Bad Godesberg, now called the Otto-Kühne-Schule." The Pädagogium (now universally called the Päda) was a boarding school that included an international contingent of pupils, a few of whom were half-Jewish and quarter-Jewish, as well as a handful of pupils from other multiethnic backgrounds. "My classmate and fellow boarder [Hugo F.] was considered to be, racially speaking, an Abyssinian [Ethiopian]," Rebensburg recalled. "His complexion was dark; he had curly hair and thin lips. In approximately 1930, when he was a high-school junior, he was also the leader of the VDA." Hugo was enamored of life in Germany and was not fazed when the Nazis seized power. "At the beginning of the 'Thousand-Year Reich' in 1933, he even wore a swastika armband," Rebensburg recalled. However, the phenomenon of a half-African youth aspiring to join the German community was too much for the Nazis. Soon, local authorities forbade Hugo to wear such emblems. Then they found other ways to make his life unpleasant. Suffering increasing ostracism like so many other *Mischlinge*, Hugo F. came to realize that National Socialist Germany was no place for him. "Embittered, he left Germany and moved to Milan," Rebensburg recounted. "He survived the war there, but he refused ever after to resume further contact with us classmates."[48]

There were other pupils at Bernd's boarding school who did not fit readily into Nazi racial categories. "In our boarding school there were three Mexican *Mischlinge* of the name [Obermann]," Rebensburg recalled. "There were two girls and one boy; the boy [Herman] had a splendid physique." Physical appearance and prowess counted for much with the Nazis, as did attitude. Unlike Hugo F., Herman Obermann passed muster, based on their arbitrary standards. "He became a soldier for Germany," Rebensburg added. "The last time I saw him he was wearing the army uniform of an officer-candidate. He looked splendid, standing over six feet tall with sparkling eyes. But he was also of brown complexion and had prominent lips. It was obvious that he was of mixed race. I was informed that he died in the war." Racial discrimination in Nazi Germany was, if anything, arbitrary. Schoolboy Bernd encountered another *Mischling* whose fate showed a darker side to National Socialism.[49]

As an Aryan youth of proven leadership ability and intelligence, Rebensburg took over a local youth organization in Bad Godesberg at a time early enough that the Nazis had not yet assumed a monopoly over all youth groups. "I assumed control over the 'Freischar junger Nation' [Volunteer Corps of the Nation's Youth]. We comprised approximately eighteen boys, aged 12 to 17 years. Among the members of this group, following its transfer into the Hitler Youth, was a child of the Occupation [meaning the Allied Occupation of the Rhineland, 1918–23]. He was from Plittersdorf." Plittersdorf was a small village on the outskirts of Bad Godesberg where tradespeople, craftspeople, and day laborers serving the wealthier Godesbergers resided. It was while leading the youth group from this working community that Bernd met a *Mischling* of a different kind. The boy's father was a French-Senegalese soldier from the post–World War I occupation, Bernd recalled. A French military caserne or barracks had existed in Plittersdorf from 1919 to 1930, and some of its dwellers had been French colonial troops. "His mother was a German," Bernd noted. "We called him 'Askari' [Askari was the term applied to an African soldier in the service of Germany's African colonies until 1914–18]. He looked like an African. Then, in 1934, he simply disappeared." Neighbors and acquaintances, youth leader Rebensburg included, became concerned. Upon questioning local authorities, they were told that "Askari" had been recruited for a campaign in the former colonies. "At age fourteen?" Rebensburg asked this author in disbelief. He also indicated that the Kupfer family, Askari's nearest neighbors, knew far more about what had happened to the youth on that night. Freischar troop leader Rebensburg queried them soon afterward, knowing that they were not supporters of the Nazis. "It was apparent that they knew much more," he recalled, "but they refused to reveal anything to me because of their fear of the NSDAP." Soon after, Bernd finished school and joined the navy. He never learned anything more about Askari.[50] Rebensburg's school-age experiences with *Mischlinge* under the Nazis demonstrated that Nazi racial preferences were subjective and arbitrary. Hugo, the "half-Ethiopian," and Askari, the "half-Senegalese," were anathema to the Nazis, and they were driven out or made to disappear. Herman Obermann, the "half-Mexican," who had the good fortune to display a splendid physique, became an officer — and eventually paid with his life. Nevertheless, no matter how arbitrary Nazi standards became with respect to *Mischlinge* of any kind, Hitler and his minions showed special hostility toward certain groups, foremost toward Jews, then toward Germany's half-Jews, the hapless *Mischlinge.* When the issue turned to multiethnic minorities, as far as the Nazis were concerned, Germany's Jewish-Christian citizens had become by far the victims of choice in 1933.

CONCLUSION

Germany's partially Jewish citizens, labeled by the Nazis as *Mischlinge,* were a group of limited size, approximately seventy-two thousand persons as *Mischling* first degree and forty thousand persons as *Mischling* second degree. They were, for the most part, children or teenagers when the Nazis seized power in 1933. Therefore, they faced increasing social discrimination at a crucial time in their development, namely during their formative childhood years and in the educational system of the country of their birth. As a group, they were far too few in a population of over seventy million to form a sense of self-identity. In fact, this disparate collection of individuals, mostly composed of schoolchildren, teenagers, and young adults, never came close to attaining group identity. Many of them entered a highly developed educational system that, initially, provided a good, sometimes excellent, elementary–secondary education. However, there were other factors that worked against their chances at maintaining a normal existence. Most, if not all, children of mixed marriages suffered significant declines in their economic well-being as the Nazis removed their parents, especially the breadwinning family member who was often Jewish. Starting in 1933, it was first and foremost the Jews who were excluded from the professions and from normal business and commercial pursuits. True, the children probably did not perceive such impoverishment as seriously as their parents recognized it. If the little ones moved into poorer neighborhoods, smaller apartments, and shabbier surroundings, such changes were probably not as important to them as the loss of a favorite doll or playmates from their old neighborhoods. Even so, interviews with eyewitnesses indicate that moving to new neighborhoods could be and often was traumatic. The transplanted children had to find new friends and learn how to cope with their unfamiliar environment. Although children tend to be much more flexible than adults, there were no guarantees of happiness for Jewish or partially Jewish children in an increasingly intolerant society.

However, education remained the one socializing institution where Nazi persecution of school-age *Mischlinge* could make a profound difference. German elementary and secondary education may have been competent, at least as far as generalizations allow. Even so, the quality of that education was arbitrary. And as long as the Nazis remained in control, not only did the quality of German education decline, but its very curriculum underwent a downward spiral into racial separation and racial intolerance as the Nazi emphasis upon physical training, biased history, racial and biological indoctrination, and exclusionary nationalism demonstrated. Ultimately, it often came down to a matter of personalities. In the final analysis, the pupils were heavily dependent upon their teachers. If the teachers reacted in normal human fashion to their young charges, then the chances were good that all the pupils would fare well. Aryan classmates would take their cue from that first authority figure — the teacher — and behave. Non-Aryan pupils would fare well, too. If not, then the cascade into racial intolerance began. At higher levels the school administrators also played an ever more important role. Youth and church leaders came next.

This situation was not static. The longer the Nazis remained in power, the greater the likelihood grew that half-Jews and later quarter-Jews would be excluded from the educational process. This increasing exclusion of children from a normal social obligation by society was especially grave in the industrialized, technology-driven Germany of the 1930s. Especially in the war years, the process of discrimination in education increased. By the spring of 1942, *Mischlinge* first degree could no longer obtain the *Abitur* and were excluded from the secondary schools thereafter. By the summer of 1944, the Nazis passed decrees excluding *Mischlinge* first degree from the public schools altogether, although 1944–45, the final school year under Hitler's Reich, was so chaotic that public education was grinding to a halt anyway. Even so, by 1944 Germany's half-Jewish children had gone the same route that the fully Jewish children took in the late 1930s: they were effectively excluded from public education. Painful though it might have been, discrimination at school was merely a harbinger of darker things to come for Germany's *Mischlinge*. Soon, those same schoolchildren would have to find jobs, any jobs. After all, higher education and careers were out of the question as long as the Nazis remained in power. Worse, the persecution that had initially affected their schooling would grow to encompass all facets of their lives.

[Can't escape sense of lack of comp/contrast w/ other Jewish victims]

[Immanent threat – never realized]

nature of teacher → students.

Isolation.

[One by one] ¼ Jews became known from bureaucratic forms.

switching schools; frantic; traumatizing of children.

Assimilated

Total arbitrariness of enforcement. cf. 2 bros. – one makes it [illegible]

↓ 1942 – withdrawn
1944 – excluded from publ. schools.
[ca. 5–10 yrs behind policy of full Js]

Mischlinge Need Not Apply

From the outset, National Socialist laws concerning employment were drafted with the intention of excluding not only full Jews but also half-Jews from jobs and careers. The process started in the public sector but soon spread to the private sector. For example, the Nazis carried over the Aryan paragraph of their Law for the Restoration of a Professional Civil Service of 1933 into laws concerning admission of individuals into the legal and medical professions within months. An "Editors' Law" quickly followed, barring persons of Jewish heritage from all areas of journalism. Soon, other public and private associations began to adopt the requirement until finally the Reich Ministry of the Interior, fearing economic dislocation from too many dismissals too soon, informed various authorities not to extend the Aryan paragraph any further into the private sector. For example, the paragraph was not to apply to the Deutsche Arbeitsfront or DAF (German Labor Front). The DAF was the Nazi-absorbed association of labor unions and presided over a wide variety of mostly blue-collar jobs in the private sector. To be sure, the Interior Ministry's message displeased Nazi zealots, and the latter often ignored such restrictions. Thus, a year after passage of the 1935 Nuremberg decrees, the Reich economics minister had to remind his Reich economic chamber and assorted business associations that *Mischlinge* were still citizens, at least provisionally, and were not to be dismissed the way full Jews were being dismissed. The Reich labor minister felt compelled to issue a similar reminder in 1939. Those follow-up directives demonstrated that businesses in the private sector were continuing to discriminate against *Mischlinge* no matter what the Interior Ministry policy might be. Egged on by local and regional Party officials such as Ortsgruppenleiters, Kreisleiters, and *of laws → ↓ J's occup'as.*

Gauleiters, many employers refused outright to hire *Mischlinge* or to allow apprenticeships no matter what the Berlin-based ministries were ordaining. Other government agencies added to the discrimination. In 1938, Reich Education Minister Rust issued a directive barring a reduction of school fees for *Mischlinge* in large families. To be sure, large Aryan families would continue to enjoy reduced school fees. Inevitably, *Mischling* secondary school pupils in economically straitened families would have to drop out of school prematurely in order to seek employment.[1]

Mischling school graduates and dropouts alike soon encountered a maddening arbitrariness in hiring practices as they scrambled for jobs of any kind. However, one sector in which Nazi arbitrariness appeared in its most extreme form came when *Mischlinge* were called up for service in the armed forces. Following Hitler's announcement of open rearmament and the creation of the Wehrmacht in April 1935, followed by the Nuremberg decrees several months later, an intense debate developed among government ministries and the Party leadership about eligibility for military conscription. Efficiency-oriented "moderates" in the Reich Interior Ministry, seconded by General Werner von Blomberg, the Reich minister of war (dismissed in February 1938), wanted to add the thousands of able-bodied young male *Mischlinge* to their draft pool. Nazi fanatics such as Hitler's deputy, Martin Bormann, objected vociferously, fearing that those who fulfilled military service would qualify for full citizenship, an eventuality that was anathema to anti-Semites. As he often did, Hitler waffled on a final decision, with the result that when World War II began in September 1939, thousands of draft-age *Mischlinge* were inducted into the Wehrmacht. Then, in the spring of 1940, watchdogs in the Party Chancellery informed Hitler that *Mischlinge* on home leave were appearing in public in uniform, accompanying their fully Jewish parents. Horrified, Hitler promptly ordered a new Wehrmacht directive on 8 April 1940, excluding half-Jews and those married to Jews from military service. The directive affected a total of twenty-five thousand men already in military service or else subject to induction during the war years. However, events had already preempted Hitler. His military campaign in Norway began on the very day he issued the exclusionary directive, and the invasion of France followed one month later. Several thousand *Mischling* conscripts were already in uniform. As a result, those same conscripts served in the early campaigns of World War II. Then the Nazis set about weeding them out. The callousness and sheer ingratitude exhibited by Hitler and his minions toward Germany's *Mischling* soldiers defy description. For many of those young men, service in the armed forces was their first "career," and for those hundreds of unfortunates who did not survive, it was the only career they ever knew.[2]

To be sure, discrimination in employment against *Mischlinge* had already begun in 1933, and for six peacetime years, Germany's half-Jews had had to scramble for jobs. At the end of each school year, thousands of young people, many of them well educated, qualified, and intelligent, were seeking work of any kind. With time, as racial persecution intensified, the *Mischlinge* began altering their perceptions of what the best job should be. Most concluded that it was preferable to find a humdrum position that would permit a living wage and that would allow them to live a low-profile existence as far away as possible from the gaze of the Nazis and their sympathizers. Even that modest goal proved increasingly difficult to achieve. Furthermore, all German youth upon completion of their education were supposed to provide a *Pflichtjahr* (i.e., a year of free labor) in the Reichsarbeitsdienst (RAD), the National Labor Service. For the young men, RAD service meant quasi-military drill — with spades — before engaging in heavy labor, perhaps on a farm, in forestry, or some other physically demanding task. For the young women, it often meant functioning as an au pair for a family with many children, performing long hours of drudgery. After this "voluntary" year, the youths, at least the Aryans, would go on to the military, to vocational training, and to the universities. Initially, some *Mischlinge* participated in the *Pflichtjahr*. However, after a few years half-Jews were banned from the RAD, too. The screws continued to tighten so that by April 1944, all *Mischlinge* first degree were banned from membership in the Deutsche Arbeitsfront. This decree eliminated them from the entire labor market, since membership in the DAF was compulsory for most jobs, even in the private sector. Simultaneously, the Gestapo began issuing orders throughout Germany for *Mischlinge* first degree to report to forced-labor camps, thus ending any pretense that *Mischlinge* could work and function in society at all.[3]

CASE HISTORIES

As noted earlier, some *Mischlinge* were inducted into the military, cutting short any normal employment. However, those *Mischlinge* found one thin silver lining upon entering the Wehrmacht. They received a certain shielding from National Socialist laws because they operated under the Wehrmacht's own military justice system.[4] Werner Jentsch from Halle an der Saale was one of those *Mischlinge* who enjoyed that odd form of protection — until another twist of the rules by Hitler cast him out of the army. Jentsch had been a bright pupil with a gift for mathematics when the Nazis seized power. He completed his *Abitur* in 1936, and under normal circumstances would have begun university studies. However, as a *Mischling* first degree, Jentsch was relegated to the private sector and became a businessman-apprentice. Even that modest calling ended on 1 September 1939 when he donned a uniform and went off to war.

After rapid basic training, Jentsch was rushed to western Germany as part of the forces guarding against a possible French attack. Then, in May 1940, he participated in the campaign in France. His infantry division was one of many that helped enlarge the crucial breakthroughs made by the armored divisions that spring. Like so many other young German soldiers, he marched endless miles from 10 May to 21 June 1940 when France capitulated. For a few months, his division rested. Then, in March 1941, Jentsch joined in the campaign that conquered first Yugoslavia and then Greece. His division was one of many preparing for the German invasion of the Soviet Union the next month.

However, Werner Jentsch never participated in that fateful campaign. For him the war ended without warning in the Balkans. On a quiet day that spring, a few troops noticed a strange military security officer entering their divisional headquarters. Shortly afterward, all of the men in Werner's company were called together for *Appell*, the morning inspection, seemingly a normal event. This time, however, the company was paraded before the newly arrived security officer. He glared at the assembled troops and then barked a command: "All *Mischlinge* take one step forward!" Out of a company of over a hundred veteran soldiers, Jentsch and two comrades advanced. The same officer then announced to all and sundry that these *Mischlinge* were dismissed from military service forthwith. They were *wehrdienstunwürdig* (unworthy of military service). The *Appell* ended then and there. Immediately, they were separated from their comrades-in-arms and sent back to Germany with what amounted to a dishonorable discharge. Thus began a strange three-year interlude for Jentsch as he scrambled to find low-end labor suitable for a *Mischling* — if not necessarily for a veteran soldier.[5]

There were thousands of *Mischling* civilians like Werner Jentsch whom the Nazis thrust into uniform, sent out on campaign, and then unceremoniously ejected. Another example of such "careers deferred" is that of Otto Hess. He was a middle-aged Berliner when the war started. Otto's Christian mother died in 1921 when he was age ten. His Jewish father, a stockbroker, committed suicide within months of the Nazi takeover. Although the elder Hess had fought on the western front in World War I and received a rare battlefield officer's commission, it had counted for little by 1933 when he became "unemployed." By this time *Mischling* son Otto had earned his *Abitur,* but banned from any university, he worked for the Berlin firm Telefunken instead. Then, in January 1940, Hess was drafted into the Wehrmacht's newly formed 295th Division, which completed training just in time for the invasion of France in May 1940. Thus, Private Hess, at nearly thirty years of age, became a foot soldier.[6]

Ten years older than most inductees, Otto did his best in basic training, even though it was extremely arduous. Remembering his veteran father's advice, he tried to warn his young soldier-comrades that the French were formidable opponents and should not be underestimated. Even so, his company, as part of a spearhead division, eagerly advanced to the River Aisne, expecting an easy crossing. Although the French army was in retreat, it was not yet defeated, and it energetically contested the river line. Scores of Otto's comrades died, and many more were wounded. After France's defeat, Hess was stationed in Paris for a few weeks, and it was there that the Nazi dragnet of *Mischlinge* caught up with him. Citizen-soldiers like Jentsch and Hess, serving in newly minted formations, enjoyed no officer protection from Nazi depredations. Amorphous add-ons, they had had no time to build personal ties, and no one was looking out for them. There was one thin silver lining for Hess. Unlike his division, he soon found himself heading back to Germany albeit in disgrace. He never saw his comrades-in-arms again. They all went to Russia.[7]

Another *Mischling* who came to understand the dangers of military service was Hermann D., a native of Bochum, born in 1920. The fate of his Aryan father was unclear, but his Jewish mother, Helene D., raised him alone. With the advent of Hitler's Third Reich, the Gestapo in Düsseldorf observed that she was a full Jew without the protection of a "privileged mixed marriage," and in 1942, they began making plans to have her transported to a concentration camp. In the meantime, son Hermann had become an infantry soldier. He had participated in the invasion of the Soviet Union and fought on the eastern front for two years. Unlike Werner Jentsch or Otto Hess, Hermann D. had had luck of sorts. Either the authorities had overlooked his status as a *Mischling*, or his unit protected him. However, in the autumn of 1942, Hermann D. was badly wounded during fierce fighting in southern Russia, and surgeons amputated his legs. He returned home as an invalid in early 1943.

Aware of the fact that the Gestapo was threatening his mother with deportation, Hermann D. decided to pay a personal visit to Gestapo headquarters in Duisburg. Thus, in March of 1943, after donning his uniform and mounting a wheelchair, Hermann D. placed a document on the desk of the Gestapo officials. It was a letter from the OKW (Oberkommando der Wehrmacht, i.e., supreme headquarters of the Wehrmacht), dated 4 January 1943. In it, the OKW officially recognized that he, Hermann D., "has by order of the Führer of 17 December 1942 been placed in the category of *deutschblütig* persons and that this disposition will also apply to his offspring." Obviously, Hitler was still reviewing *Mischling* files — at least for soldiers. Even so, in Hermann D.'s case Hitler added a qualifier passed along by the OKW. The new status would apply, they stated, only "as long as the other partner [i.e., a future wife] does not contain alien blood. He and his offspring also have the right to declare themselves *deutschblütig*." Getting straight to the point, Hermann D. demanded his mother's release. Confronted by an order bearing Hitler's name, the Gestapo officials had no choice but to back down. On 23 March, a nameless Gestapo bureaucrat recorded that "the Jew [Helene] D. . . . has been removed from the evacuation because of the wounding of her only son." True, Hermann D. had forced the Gestapo to retreat, but he had paid a high price in order to achieve that victory. He and his mother returned home.[8]

Those citizens with one grandparent deemed to be Jewish by the Nazis, namely *Mischlinge* second degree (quarter-Jews), did not suffer persecution to the same degree as *Mischlinge* first degree. However, their status was not enviable, especially when as young adults they were confronted with sharply diminished career choices. For Berliner Hans-Joachim Boehm, finding a job was urgent. Although a gifted pupil who won entry to the nearby Friedenau Gymnasium, Hans-Joachim was a half-orphan (his father had died when he was only eight), and his widowed mother was in dire economic straits. Normally, the Boehm family would have qualified for aid for Hans-Joachim's schooling. However, a recent Nazi directive denied any such funding for *Mischlinge*. Determined to ease his mother's financial burden and intent upon finding a job, Hans-Joachim left the Gymnasium in 1937 before finishing his *Abitur*. He obtained an apprenticeship in a private firm as a *Kaufmann* (businessman) and found that he enjoyed the world of business and commerce. With his apprenticeship completed in August 1939, he looked forward to an increased income and the chance to help his mother and younger siblings. Conscription promptly ended that dream. First he completed basic training in the Reichsarbeitsdienst (RAD). Although Hans-Joachim had suffered harassment at school because he looked "Jewish" to some of his schoolmates and bore the middle name of Samuel, he fared better in the RAD. In fact, he excelled in basic military training. He was also well educated, not so common in the mass call-ups of the war, and the RAD gave him additional training as a Schreiberling (i.e., a military clerk). In fact, his performance was so good that upon his transfer to the Wehrmacht, officers at his training depot in Cottbus encouraged him to apply for officer training. Pleased by their encouragement, Hans-Joachim began filling out the necessary application.

Then reality intervened. The application form required him to list the names of his parents and grandparents, and the name Samuel surfaced again. Hans-Joachim never heard another word about officer training. Instead, he served as an enlisted man holding the dangerous job of forward artillery observer. Hans-Joachim also had the dubious distinction of serving on the eastern front from the day the Wehrmacht invaded the Soviet Union in 1941 until the last day of the war. He suffered two serious wounds, one of which spared him from being at Stalingrad in 1942, whereas the second evacuated him from Poland in 1944 just before another army was annihilated. Even so, during four years on the eastern front, Hans-Joachim remained a private. A *Mischling* second degree, bearing the name Samuel and lacking friends in higher places, could expect nothing more.[9]

Fellow Berliner Ernst Benda was also a *Mischling* second degree. A few years younger than Boehm, he finished his *Notabitur* (accelerated diploma) at the Kant Gymnasium in Spandau in January 1943. A civilian career in wartime was out of the question. Besides, Ernst had long dreamed of serving in the navy. After three months of RAD basic training in the Saarland, he took a battery of examinations, which included the possibility of serving in the navy. Benda achieved outstanding scores and soon found himself in occupied Denmark undergoing navy basic training. Unlike Hans-Joachim Boehm's grandfather who had borne the name Samuel, Ernst Benda's grandparents had non-Jewish names, so that his status as a *Mischling* second degree was not readily apparent among his shipmates or immediate superiors. Ernst had another advantage that Hans-Joachim, a high school dropout, did not have. Because of his *Abitur,* the Kriegsmarine had flagged Benda for special assignments. After basic training, he became a radioman, manning the Kriegsmarine's highly secret encryption device, the Enigma machine. Then Benda joined a training flotilla of Germany's highly advanced E-boats (high-speed motor torpedo boats) in the Baltic before serving in a regular flotilla in Norway. He endured all the usual hardships and dangers in a war zone and performed in exemplary fashion. The commander of his boat was so impressed that he recommended Benda for officer training. Then the recommendation went to Berlin. Like army private Hans-Joachim Boehm, sailor Ernst Benda never heard another word about officer training thereafter. He, too, was a *Mischling* second degree.[10]

In the spring of 1939, *Mischling* first degree Eva Heilmann, a Berliner like Hans-Joachim Boehm and Ernst Benda, completed her *Abitur.* Easily the best student in her class, she should have graduated with top honors. However, another Aryan classmate, tapped as a future leader but possessing only average grades, was in contention for top honors. The school authorities solved the problem by downgrading Eva's *Abitur* to average levels. This pairing allowed the racially favored BDM girl to win top honors in her graduating class. No appeal was possible. Eva Heilmann would also have to abandon any hope of entering a university.

Heilmann's next career move was to fulfill her *Pflichtjahr,* or year of public service. Under RAD auspices, she traveled to Neustadt an der Dosse, a small town in Brandenburg that contained an RAD camp. After several months of training, she joined other eighteen-year-olds in working four-week stints at various farms in northeastern Germany in need of seasonal labor, taking care of children, harvesting, or whatever. Occasionally, she and her new friends from the RAD were permitted to return home for short furloughs. Eva told her mother of her experiences in rural settings but also mentioned RAD orientation courses. One of them taught the girls *Rassenkunde* (i.e., racial sensitization). *Mischlinge sind Kretine* (*Mischlinge* are cretinous) and *Mischlinge sind dumme Kerle* (*Mischlinge* are stupid jerks) were a couple of observations issued by the Nazi instructors. Incredulous, Frau Heilmann asked her daughter to repeat the phrases, and when Eva did so, not noticing her mother's agitation, Frau Heilmann did something rare: she boxed her daughter's ears! How could Eva repeat such absurd slogans without comment and without more deliberate consideration? Supremely surprised, Eva never forgot her mother's outburst. Subdued, she quietly finished her state service.[11]

Later that summer Heilmann applied for a travel visa to Great Britain where she hoped to be a nanny. However, the Gestapo got wind of her application and spiked it. As the daughter of the incarcerated SPD Prussian Landtag deputy, Ernst Heilmann, she had the potential to embarrass the National Socialist regime. Instead, Eva, to her surprise, obtained a brief tourist visa to the Netherlands, now that she had fulfilled her RAD service. Then she applied for a nursing program, since medical school was no longer possible for *Mischlinge*. However, by this time requirements for nursing programs had stiffened. Eva learned that she would have to take a physical examination to determine if she was "racially" acceptable for nursing. She went to the local Gesundheitsamt or Public Health Office, but since her application form identified her as a *Mischling*, special personnel were there to greet her. Heilmann was forced to undergo a thoroughly demeaning physical examination. Despite her outward appearances as a "Gretchen"-style German maiden with long blond hair, the examiners concluded that she was racially "undesirable." Her earlobes were shaped in such a way that the examiners concluded that she had excessive "Jewish" genes. Her face, her head, and her general body shape added credence to their findings, they claimed. Her Aryan examiners concluded that her breasts were larger and more pendulous than would have been the case with Aryan (i.e., German) women. Having failed the Nazis' "scientific" physical examination, Eva Heilmann was denied entry into any nursing program. She spent the next six years performing such tasks as selling magazines or scrubbing floors.[12]

Peter Heilmann, Eva's younger brother, was also forced to engage in the most menial, degrading jobs. Peter found work with a pest control firm in Berlin. His job consisted of fumigating apartments and other structures, ridding them of rats, lice, insects, and vermin of all kinds. Its one virtue was that it was steady; nobody else wanted such a job. Therefore, even at a time when his former schoolmates were disappearing into the military, Peter held regular employment. The downside was that the work was not only dirty; it was potentially dangerous. Heilmann recalled that after sealing an apartment, he could employ a variety of pesticides for the fumigation phase. The most common chemical at their disposal was a product called Zyklon B. Inevitably, the strong smell of chemicals got into his clothing. He recalled that when he rode the Berlin subways from job to job, fellow passengers always gave him a wide berth. Besides being unpleasant and dangerous, the job was also tedious. Typically, Peter began work at 7:00 A.M. and finished around 5:00 P.M. He worked six days per week and received wretchedly low wages. In a real sense, the job was that of a forced laborer, since he could find no alternative. As it turned out, the Nazis ultimately did provide an alternative. In 1944, they rounded up Peter and other male *Mischlinge* and put them into forced-labor camps. Thus, even the most undesirable work ultimately proved to be too benign for *Mischlinge* in the eyes of the Nazis.[13]

In 1942 Meta Alexander, also a Berliner, finished her *Abitur,* but she quickly discovered, as had so many other *Mischlinge,* that university studies were unattainable.[14] Meta became a laboratory assistant instead, working for the Auergesellschaft, a private chemical firm in Berlin. To be sure, the job hardly challenged her, but it was safe, gave her regular work, and allowed her to lead a seminormal existence — for a time. Then, in the autumn of 1943, Berlin experienced heavy bombing raids, and Meta's firm evacuated most of its operations and personnel to far-off Konstanz on the Swiss border. Meta's grandmother, Otillie, and Otillie's sister had just been bombed out of their apartment. Therefore, Meta joined the exodus, freeing up quarters for her aged relatives. She worked in Konstanz for the next year, safe from Allied bombs. Besides, the Nazi authorities lost track of her and the local population appeared to be unenthusiastic about the war. They heard foreign broadcasts from the Swiss and were much more attuned to Germany's approaching defeat. Despite her relative safety, Meta Alexander worried constantly about her parents and about other family members in Berlin. Finally, in the autumn of 1944, she secured a transfer back to the capital to join the skeleton staff of the Auergesellschaft. Like so many, Alexander judged the war to be nearly over and assumed that she would return to Berlin at the moment of its capitulation. Alas, it was not to be. Employment of a different kind soon beckoned for Meta Alexander.[15]

Thekla Brandt, like Meta Alexander, had wanted to study medicine. Her parents were both medical doctors, even if her mother, who was Jewish, was barred by the Nazis from practicing — officially at least. Medicine was a family tradition for the Brandts, who had operated a respected family practice in Neukölln, one of Berlin's working-class districts. After finishing her *Abitur*, Thekla and her mother paid a call on Professor Johannes Stroux, dean of medicine at Berlin's world-renowned Friedrich-Wilhelms University. Dr. Brandt ate humble pie. She begged Stroux to admit her daughter. Stroux sympathized but declined. Since Thekla was a *Mischling* first degree, there was no way that he could admit her. Besides, he told his crestfallen visitors, even if admitted, she would never be able to take the crucial state medical examinations as long as the Nazis were in power.[16]

Rebuffed, Thekla Brandt directed her energies elsewhere. Talented in many ways, she thought that she might have a chance to become a foreign correspondent with news organizations. Consequently, she studied English and French, advanced her typing ability, and learned other correspondence skills at the Rackow Schule, a private professional school in Berlin. Then Thekla discovered in midwar that outside events were overtaking her private accomplishments. Germany's presence abroad was ebbing fast, and the need for persons with her skills was plummeting. Besides, the Nazis were not allowing *Mischlinge* into the world of journalism anyway. Slightly older and wiser, Thekla finally found an apprenticeship as an assistant chemist in a private chemical firm in Halle an der Saale. Immersed once again in a technical field allied to medicine, Thekla was able to pass a license examination in chemistry in Halle, no small accomplishment for a *Mischling* first degree in 1943. However, alarmed by the ever-worsening air raids on Berlin, she, like Meta Alexander, finally returned home. Thekla and her sister hoped in a time of medical shortages to work in their father's private practice in Neukölln (their Jewish mother continued to keep a low profile). However, like Meta Alexander, the Brandt daughters discovered that the Nazis had different employment plans for them.[17]

Ironically, Hilde B. might have crossed paths unknowingly with the Brandt daughters or Meta Alexander. This was because she moved in wartime from western Germany to the capital in order to find employment. Like the Berlin women she, too, was forced to find a job away from home. All three had been gifted high school students, and each had wanted to study medicine. To be sure, each had been thwarted. However, Hilde B.'s effort to find a career proved even more daunting than Meta Alexander's or Thekla Brandt's unhappy experiences. Born in 1915 in Berlin, Hilde B. and her parents moved immediately after World War I to Wiesbaden where she obtained her basic education. Hilde B. was bright and at age ten entered a Realgymnasium where she earned her *Abitur* in 1934, a year after the Nazi Seizure of Power. She wanted to study medicine but learned that she needed an *Ariernachweis* (proof of Aryan status) in order to be admitted to university studies. Since her father was Jewish, no such document was forthcoming. Therefore, university studies were out. She and her parents assessed her situation realistically and concluded that she should obtain a vocational education and wait for the Nazi aberration to pass.

Nearby Frankfurt and Offenbach comprised a center of the leather trade in Germany. Dexterous as well as intelligent, Hilde B. applied for and was admitted to a special trade school in Offenbach, the Meisterschule des Deutschen Handwerks (Advanced School for German Handicrafts), where she learned sophisticated leatherworking. The plan seemed to be a good one, and it worked — for a time. Unfortunately, as the ripple effect of Nazi racist policy spread, its effects caught up with Hilde B. again. Educational authorities in all areas, be they academic, technical, or vocational, had begun to discriminate against Jews and half-Jews, egged on by local Nazi officials. Determined to prove his anti-Semitic credentials, Gauleiter Sprenger in the Hesse-Nassau Gau (administrative district) began combing through trade school enrollees. Hilde B. and specifically her lack of the all-important *Ariernachweis* came to his unwelcome attention. Thus, upon Gauleiter Sprenger's personal order, the Meisterschule for leatherwork expelled Hilde B. in 1938 despite years of specialized training and proofs of her talent. An extraordinary appeal by the school's director won her a temporary reprieve, but it really was temporary. Lacking state approval, Hilde B. could not obtain a proper apprenticeship or receive the crucial letter of recommendation she needed from a master leatherworker. Thirteen years of Hilde's elementary–secondary education (culminating in an *Abitur*) had come to nothing. Now, five years of specialized vocational training had also led to a dead end.

Frustrated, Hilde B. was unsure what to do next. As a stopgap, she worked as a business manager for a private import–export firm in Frankfurt, a job she filled ably for two years. Then, in 1941, Hilde B. discovered that her low-profile existence was once again insufficient protection. Following Hitler's decision to invade the Soviet Union, a limited call-up of single women for the armaments industries ensued. Hilde B.'s name surfaced in the police files, and she received an order to work in an odious copper-smelting plant on the outskirts of Frankfurt in Heddernheim. Forewarned that the work was dangerous and unhealthy, Hilde B. settled upon a bold course. She decided that she would move to the very center of power of the political movement that had been dogging her for years. Without telling anyone, Hilde B. promptly bought a one-way ticket to Berlin.

Experienced in the business world by now, she quickly found a job in the giant department store firm of Karstadt and quietly went to work, trying to attract as little attention as possible. Reckoning that Karstadt's very size would offer her anonymity, Hilde B. took a low-level, poorly paid entry position. For a few months her marginal job seemed to produce the anonymity she sought. Nevertheless, factors beyond her control undid Hilde's survival plans. The personnel director for Karstadt in Berlin was a civilian but was also a "supporting member of the SS" (i.e., an ardent Nazi). He personally investigated Hilde's bona fides and, finding no authentication of her Aryan status, quickly ascertained that Hilde B. was a *Mischling* first degree. The personnel director goaded Hilde B.'s section head into action, and she suddenly realized that a job at Karstadt was not to be her salvation after all.

In the meantime she had made a number of friendly acquaintances in Berlin, and one of them, Dr. Ernst Seewald, an official in the Reichsvereinigung Eisen, a national consortium for ferrous metals, found a secretarial job for Hilde. Seewald had been impressed by Hilde B.'s abilities and was touched by her plight. Finally, her prospects appeared to be improving. The one problem with her newfound refuge was the fact that the Reichsvereinigung Eisen was, by its nature, connected to armaments-related industries. Even though she was now working as an entry-level secretary again, Hilde B. was required to produce her bona fides once more. Thus, the firm's Party liaison officer or Abschnittsleiter, Robert Kahlert, immediately alerted his superior, Kommerzienrat Hermann Röchling, who in turn alerted Ortsgruppenleiter Schulz, who promptly contacted Hitler's labor chief, DAF Leiter Robert Ley, about Hilde B. and her lack of an *Ariernachweis*. Anonymity for Hilde B. evaporated once again. In fact, outrage was now in full bloom as an aroused Robert Ley personally ordered Hilde B.'s dismissal. Thus, on an icy day at the end of December 1942, uniformed officials suddenly appeared at Hilde B.'s desk. Ley's instructions were unambiguous. They read that Hilde B. was to be "placed out on the street immediately." Threatened with arrest if she did not comply then and there, the diminutive Hilde B., under the gaze of dozens of fellow office workers, including her benefactor, was hustled out of the sacrosanct halls of the Reichsvereinigung Eisen and tossed out onto a Berlin street. The cumulative effects of long-term stress finally began to take their toll. Hilde B.'s eyesight, following years of detailed work in leather fashioning, started to fail. Her thyroid gland caused her increasing health problems, and despite her twenty-eight years, she began to experience increasing bouts of faintness from circulatory problems. Nevertheless, she coped. After her humiliating dismissal from the ferrous metals concern, Hilde B. found a part-time, poorly paid job in an obscure government agency handling the increasing flow of German refugees from Eastern Europe. Even this marginal position ultimately came into doubt. After all, Hilde B. had become a known presence in Berlin. By mid-1944, Hilde B. received word from well-meaning friends that her name was on a call-up notice for non-Aryan persons. Even as she had once disappeared from Wiesbaden overnight in 1941, so, too, in 1944, Hilde B. departed unobtrusively from Berlin on a night train. Bereft of friends and protectors, she had decided, reluctantly, to return to her widowed mother in Wiesbaden. Once a vigorous young woman, she conceded that the Nazis had finally worn her down, and she retreated to her parental home in broken health.

Thus began a juggling act. In the last six months of the war, Hilde B. hid out in her mother's house in Wiesbaden or, alternatively, in an old mill in outlying Wispertal as the Gestapo or local police officials called periodically for her to report for forced labor. Willy-nilly, Hilde B. survived — just barely. In fact, at war's end, she was a patient in a sanatorium in Königsstein, suffering not only from thyroid problems but from pronounced psychological problems as well. Hilde B. had somehow survived, but the cost had been high. Her odyssey showed that *Mischlinge* had no jobs and no future in Hitler's Germany.[18]

Hilde B. was a victim whose age had fit the profile for most half-Jews, but for older citizens dubbed *Mischling* by the Nazis, citizens already married with children, the economic consequences of persecution could be devastating for the whole family. They were fewer in number than the larger cohort of younger *Mischlinge*. Nevertheless, they were also present, and as with *Mischlinge* of other ages, their levels of persecution varied from region to region, depending on the actions of individual Nazi officials such as a Gauleiter, Kreisleiter, or Ortsgruppenleiter in the given locality. The sad life of Emil Steiner amply demonstrates this point. Born in 1900 to a brew master and his wife who settled in Kempten in Bavaria, Emil was half-Jewish. Hurrying to complete his *Notabitur* in 1917, he immediately volunteered for military service. Emil emerged from a year of fighting on the western front as a Fähnrich (sergeant; the term also implies officer-candidate) at age eighteen. After the war, he studied business, and once the German economy stabilized in 1924, he became an accountant for the Aral Oil Company in Kempten. He married a local woman, Eleanor. They produced two children, Erika and Rolf, and the Steiners led normal happy lives in Kempten — until the advent of National Socialism. Then their lives fell apart. The local Nazi official, Kreisleiter Brändle, was a fanatical anti-Semite, and since there were so few Jews in that section of Bavaria, he seemed particularly inclined to target *Mischlinge*. Brändle ordered Eleanor Steiner to appear at his office in 1933 and demanded that she divorce Emil. Outraged, Frau Steiner walked out on the red-faced Brändle. Her refusal to be intimidated infuriated him, and he began a twelve-year campaign of unrelenting harassment. Nazi officials made periodic house searches, confiscating family possessions that struck their fancy, such as fine dinnerware. In 1934, Aral fired Steiner despite his decade of outstanding service to the firm. Finally, after much searching, he secured a low-end job with a rural coal distribution company in Oberstdorf, many miles away. The local Nazi authorities specifically required that his salary not exceed two hundred Reichsmarks per month, and that his job should keep him apart from his family for long periods. For the next eleven years he mostly lived alone, often in primitive conditions in a temporary structure adjoining his place of work. Eleanor and the children stayed in their apartment in Kempten. As the years passed, they worried about his declining health. Emil developed stomach ulcers that worsened over time. Finally, gaunt and frail, he returned to Kempten in August 1944 and collapsed in front of his family, coughing up blood. The nearest physician, a Nazi, categorically refused to handle a *Mischling*. Fortunately, Eleanor, after frantic searching, found a retired surgeon, Dr. Madlener, who still had access to Kempten's only hospital. Dr. Madlener could see that the patient was in dire straits, and he operated immediately, removing a portion of Emil's stomach. Somehow Steiner survived, and his family carried him away from the hospital in a pitiable condition. Work for

Steiner was out of the question, but that became a moot point anyway. Less than four weeks after the operation, Emil was in a cattle car on his way to Theresienstadt, part of the roundup of all Kempten *Mischlinge* ordered by Kreisleiter Brändle, who wanted to be the first to have a Kreis that was truly *judenfrei*. Thus, Emil Steiner came to experience the kind of persecution that hitherto only full Jews had endured.[19]

Sometimes the persecution of *Mischlinge* in search of employment delved into unexpected areas. Elsa Helfricht (her stage name) was a singer. A native of Essen, Elsa R. demonstrated at an early age that she had a lovely voice. Later, she trained to sing opera and became a local sensation in the Lower Rhine region. Thus, it was logical that the Karneval Gesellschaft "Fidelio" (a local entertainment society in Ruhrstein) would invite her to sing as their lead soprano on 13 June 1936 for an evening gala of light opera that they listed as *Ein Abend lustig und fidel* (An Evening Cheerful and Merry). As expected, Elsa R. was a huge success with the crowd, many of whom were prominent local Nazis. The only problem was that Elsa "Helfricht" was a half-Jew, and recriminations were not long in coming.

A week later, Herr Gräwe, leader of the local chapter of the Reichsmusik-kammer or RMK (Reich Music Chamber), denounced her to the Gestapo in Essen. Herr Gräwe included a copy of the newspaper advertisement for the "Cheerful Evening." It showed Elsa to be the lead female singer. Nor was this her first transgression. "This half Jew engaged in a public concert last year during which she inveigled the Kreisleitung [district leadership] of the NSDAP into attending," he fumed. Thereupon, RMK leader Gräwe forbade her to participate in any further public appearances. "Yet, even today," he contin-ued, "she has the effrontery to maliciously deceive the German People, claim-ing that it was one of her remote ancestors from antediluvian times who was Jewish." He then invoked the Nuremberg decree that was supposed to pro-tect "German blood." However, RMK leader Gräwe elevated it to protection of the "German soul." No record exists as to how the Gestapo — not known for its religiosity — reacted to such an imperilment of (German-Christian) souls. However, music leader Gräwe was not finished: "I view the actions of this half Jew as a challenge against German Party Comrades and a degrada-tion of the holiest of our German cultural legacy." Thereupon, RMK Führer Gräwe demanded the institution of major legal proceedings against her. It was true, he added, that one conventional route of punishment remained, namely the imposition of a fine, as outlined in the RMK regulations of 1 November 1933. However, RMK Führer Gräwe would have none of that. "I find this to be simply inadequate in order to put this impudent half Jew in her place." After all, Gräwe admitted, he had already tried that approach, and it had failed.

For once the Gestapo must have found one of its informants to be ridiculous, even if he was fuming against a *Mischling*. The Gestapo's records ended at that point, indicating the likelihood that they either ignored the RMK music Führer, or else encouraged him to impose another one of his fearsome fines. And yet, it was not the done thing for a *Mischling* to be a public entertainer in Hitler's Third Reich. Elsa R. would have to wait for better times to find employment for her obvious talents. It was also true that she was lucky that she had committed her "transgressions" in 1935 and 1936 rather than a few years later, when the Nazis had become more fanatical. Having excluded full Jews from such venues, they began to systematically remove virtually all *Mischlinge* a few years later from the fine and performing arts.[20]

Gestapo actions could have more dire consequences for women in conventional employment. Single working mothers who were *Mischlinge*, far from receiving the benefit of the doubt, could suffer even worse persecution if they worked in a profession the Nazis were prone to guard jealously. Ernesta V., who resided in Wiesbaden, was such a case. Born to a Berlin publisher and his Jewish wife in 1902, Ernesta V., a baptized Protestant, chose nursing and social work as her career during the Weimar Republic and was well established in the medical profession by 1933. Married to an Aryan at the time of the Seizure of Power, Ernesta V. was an early victim of the Nazi purge of Jews and partial Jews from the civil service and the professions. Thereafter, she earned a sharply reduced income as a pieceworker in a tailor's shop making uniforms. Later still, she was reduced to distributing pharmaceutical products at an even lower wage. Simultaneously, her personal life went downhill, so that by 1939 Ernesta V. was divorced and living alone in Wiesbaden with her young son, Ernst, for whom she could barely provide. As if these woes were not enough, Ernesta V. became a target of the particularly aggressive Gestapo authorities in Wiesbaden, although the postwar sources do not reveal why. Suffice it to say, she came under unfriendly observation.

It was in April 1943 that two Gestapo men came for her. They bundled her off to their headquarters in Wiesbaden's Paulinenstrasse 9. Apparently she did not make a favorable impression on them. After placing her in a dank cell in the basement, they took turns beating her. Then, inexplicably, they released her, threatening to arrest her again if they so desired. Broken by the beatings and in despair, Ernesta V. decided that she might not be able to care for young Ernst if the Gestapo came for her again. Thereupon, she made a bitter choice as she later revealed to postwar authorities: "In June 1943, I gave my son . . . to the Frankesche Stiftung [a Protestant educational and philanthropic foundation] in Halle since I had to reckon with my impending arrest." Sanctuary for her son did not come free. Ernesta V. transferred the last of her inheritance to the foundation in order to secure her son's entry. Ernesta V. survived the war, but alone and in ill health. In 1946, surgeons had to remove her left breast, a result of the beatings she had received in the Gestapo cell. Later, in 1948, Ernesta V. applied for compensation for her lost income and injury. Friends and neighbors corroborated her story before the Hessian restitution authorities. The record does not disclose if she was ever reunited with her son.[21]

Some men fared no better. Hans Haurwitz was born in Berlin-Charlottenburg on 17 August 1918. His father was Jewish, his mother Christian. Although a *Mischling* first degree, Hans chose a difficult path. Raised as a Jew, he refused to renounce his faith, and unlike many other *Mischlinge*, he did not seek confirmation in either the Protestant or Catholic churches. Therefore, the Nazis placed him in the special category of *Geltungsjuden*, equivalent to Jews. This was no easy choice. Of the seventy-two thousand Germans categorized under the Nazis as *Mischlinge*, only about eight thousand suffered persecution as *Geltungsjuden*. During the war years, like his father, Hans had to wear a bright yellow Star of David on his outer clothing with the word *Jude* (Jew) boldly inscribed upon it. His schooling was rudimentary. There was no thought of his entering a secondary school or going on to a university. His ration card was also stamped with the word *Jude*, so that he was ineligible to purchase items that Aryan Germans could obtain, such as butter, eggs, and fats. The Haurwitz men, senior and junior, mostly subsisted on potatoes and cabbage. And even those staples were often rejects, vegetables that had become frozen and were considered inedible for the general population. "Every night I went to bed hungry," he recalled of those terrible war years. One of the few sources of relief that helped to keep father and son alive was their wife and mother's sharing of her normal ration. She, as an Aryan, was entitled to purchase the usual quantities of foodstuffs, although it was a struggle to find the means to pay for them, considering the strenuous work and meager pay the men in her family had to accept.[22]

Ordinary jobs in the civilian sector were out of the question for the Haurwitz men. They became forced laborers instead. At first, they were sent to Westhafen, one of Berlin's two inland waterway depots served by barge traffic. Along with other Jews, father and son had to off-load bulk coal into trucks and then distribute it to Berlin's residential buildings and businesses. The coal haulers carried large panniers weighing 100 to 150 pounds to the various storage facilities. Hans observed afterward that he was lucky to be young and fit in 1939. He had been an enthusiastic athlete in school, but even he was scarcely prepared for such arduous labor. He pitied the older men in his group, and they made informal arrangements whereby Hans slipped in to perform some of the most physically demanding chores.[23]

After a year of hauling coal, Hans and his father transferred to the unloading of bulk rail shipments of empty wine bottles and other discarded glass from occupied France. They had to separate bottles by color and shape, then haul the cargo to other sites for recycling. Working in musty, confined railroad cars amid filth, flies, and vermin — to say nothing of jagged, broken glass — they labored day in and day out at the unpleasant task. Its only virtue was that it was not so physically demanding as hauling coal. Eventually, even that job ended as the supply of bulk items from France and other occupied areas diminished. Then, Hans and his father transferred to a long-haul transport company that moved heavy merchandise and equipment from city to city. Fortunately, they could stay in Berlin because their job was to manhandle heavy equipment from warehouses to railcars in Berlin's rail depots. This proved every bit as exhausting as hauling coal, and Hans had to take over many of the heavy-lift jobs that the older men could not perform.[24]

Hans and his father continued their backbreaking labor virtually to the last days of the Third Reich. However, it was their good fortune to live in a down-at-heel apartment building in Berlin-Charlottenburg that survived the air raids when sturdier buildings all around them turned into rubble. The sixteen families counted themselves lucky to be alive, and they tried to help less fortunate neighbors. Even the Haurwitz family was able to provide shelter to a neighboring Jewish family when their apartment was destroyed. Neighbors generally helped out under these appalling conditions. Hans recalls that the two pro-Nazi families in his building did not object when all of the occupants congregated together in the building's air-raid shelter — not the case for all citizens. Thus, the Haurwitz family finished the war with a roof over their heads, in reasonable health, and "employed." For a Jewish husband, a *Geltungs-jude*, as son, and Aryan wife and mother in a despised *privilegierte Mischehe*, that was no small feat.[25]

Most so-called *Mischlinge* did not develop the commitment to Judaism that Hans Haurwitz exhibited, not surprising in an increasingly secular society. Hanns-Peter Herz from the Neukölln District of Berlin was more representative of approximately sixty-four thousand *Mischlinge* first degree in the Nazi years in that he was baptized at birth into one of the two main Christian faiths (in his case the Evangelical-Protestant Church, the church in which the majority of *Mischlinge* were baptized) and confirmed at age thirteen. His religious preference did him little good. Despite his excellent school record, he was forced to leave the Kaiser-Wilhelm Gymnasium. Yet, before that happened, Hanns-Peter had already gained work experience of a kind. As a part of the Nazi Party's Kriegseinsatz für Oberschüler (War Service for High School Seniors), he volunteered for war-related part-time duties. He was assigned to work in the baggage claim office of the Reichsbahn (National Railroad) at Berlin's Friedrichstrasse Station. Upon reporting in, he encountered three full-time railroad workers. Two were common laborers, but the third was a former train guard who had been demoted for telling an anti-Nazi joke. They looked puzzled when Hanns-Peter presented himself. "Why no HJ [Hitler Youth] uniform?" they asked. Hanns-Peter looked them over while he contemplated his answer. He concluded that they looked decidedly like the former SPD Party members he had known in early childhood. Taking a chance, he told them that he was a *Mischling*, and his gamble paid off. The three adults glanced at each other — and smiled. Hanns-Peter was accepted immediately into their group, and they formed a miniature, if low-key, anti-Nazi workforce in one of Germany's key rail centers. They enjoyed inflicting damage, secretly to be sure, on packages and luggage belonging to Party officials or to rear-echelon military officers, especially if they were convinced that the contents were black market items. In such instances, they knew that the claimants were unlikely to make a fuss about damaged or destroyed goods.[26]

However, once the Nazis removed him from school, Hanns-Peter Herz had to find more permanent work — no easy task for a *Mischling*. Fortunately, his father, an old-time SPD member, and Otto Dibelius, a celebrated Protestant theologian, helped him to find a low-profile job. Dibelius had already tutored Hanns-Peter for his church confirmation, and as a leading "confessing" Christian, Dibelius was bitterly opposed to Nazi-oriented "German" Christians. Using his many contacts, Dibelius steered Hanns-Peter to the offices of the Ostdeutscher Schrotthandel, a firm that processed scrap metal all across eastern Germany and Eastern Europe. Unobtrusively, the company had become a safe haven for a few racially and politically persecuted persons. Hanns-Peter became one of four apprentices, three of whom were *Mischlinge*. The fourth was the son of a prominent Communist. Yet another employee was a young Polish woman. Hanns-Peter found them congenial, and they worked together well, supporting each other. Hanns-Peter remembered that the employees had erected a large map of Europe in one of the central offices. Ostensibly, it showed the advances of the Wehrmacht with bold markers. In reality, it disclosed Allied positions with more subtle markers. Thus, they knew when Goebbels's propaganda machine was lying. Then in August 1944, just as Hanns-Peter and his coworkers noted the dramatic breakout of Allied forces in France, his life changed again, and not for the better. Nazi officialdom had not really forgotten him. It invaded his safe haven, and Hanns-Peter Herz, like virtually all other men who were *Mischlinge* first degree, received official notification that he was to report for induction into a forced-labor unit of the Organisation Todt. The Nazi dragnet dispelled any notions he might have entertained that people like him could hold jobs, even menial jobs.[27]

Like Hanns-Peter, Martin F. was also a Berlin *Mischling*, born in 1920. Unlike Hanns-Peter, Martin F. was one of those *Mischlinge* who, like Hans Haurwitz, was persecuted as a *Geltungsjude*. He had finished his elementary schooling in 1934 and prudently opted for a low-profile apprenticeship in sales with a private firm. He had just completed his three-year training when in November 1938 he was rounded up by the authorities and, along with full Jews, was placed in a forced-labor camp. Martin F. never worked a normal job thereafter. In November 1943 the Gestapo removed him from the camp and confined him for several weeks in their prison complex in Berlin. They charged him with resistance against the state and with preparing to commit high treason, unlikely crimes for a person who had been under tight military security for five years. Nevertheless, the Gestapo found him guilty as charged and committed him to a concentration camp. He survived several of those camps and was finally liberated by the Americans on 8 May 1945. Although he survived the ordeal, Martin F. never regained his health, and after eking out a precarious existence in a haulage firm in East Berlin, he finally fled to West Berlin after the June uprising of 1953 in the East. The more compassionate (and wealthier) authorities in West Berlin finally acknowledged the shabby treatment he had received as a *Geltungsjude* and offered him some compensation plus a disability allowance. His sad life demonstrated that for *Mischlinge* who were also *Geltungsjuden,* the notion of making a career, even a private one, was nearly impossible in National Socialist Germany.[28]

Although the majority of *Mischlinge,* who were negatively affected by Nazi discrimination, were young people entering the job market after school, this was not always the case. Karl R. was already an established, successful architect in Mönchen-Gladbach on the Lower Rhine when the Nazis came to power. Unfortunately for him, his name did not sound Aryan, and Karl R. discovered that his application to join the Nazi-dominated Reichskammer der bildenden Künste (Reich Chamber of Fine Arts) was denied. In 1935, at age fifty-six, he vigorously protested the decision to the Regierungspräsident in Düsseldorf, and then all the way to the Reichskulturkammer in Berlin. Unfortunately, his appeal drew unwelcome attention from another quarter. In September 1936, Gestapo authorities in Düsseldorf informed Karl R. that as a nonmember of the Reich Chamber, and a *Mischling* to boot, he was forbidden to engage in the occupation of an architect.

Displaying no little courage, Karl R. continued his protest, reminding the authorities in the Reichskulturkammer in Berlin that he had been a frontline soldier in World War I, had never been involved in politics, and was, furthermore, an accomplished architect whose projects had never encountered any criticism. Simply being a *Mischling* should not deny him his livelihood. A bureaucrat in the Reichskulturkammer, Dr. Gaber, rejected Karl R.'s appeal, quoting his boss to the effect that "the President of the Reichskulturkammer has rejected your claims of hardship. . . . A further appeal is not possible. Any other communications to me will serve no purpose." The Reichskulturkammer then copied its decision on Karl R. to the Gestapo in Düsseldorf once again.

If he was anything, Karl R. was persistent. He sent further statements to various authorities, elaborating on his professional accomplishments and his reliability. Not only had he been a soldier in World War I, he had volunteered at the advanced age of thirty-six to serve on the most exposed forward positions of the western front, where he remained for two years. Yet, in the end his service record made no difference. Karl R. was not permitted to function as an architect in Hitler's Third Reich again. Above and beyond the cruelty of treating a loyal citizen so shabbily, the Nazis had also dispensed with the services of a highly trained and accomplished architect. Karl R.'s fate demonstrated that no vocation and no age group of *Mischlinge* were insulated against persecution.[29]

Like Karl R., Max S. was an older man when the Nazis came for him. His fate illustrates well the growing fanaticism the Nazis were exhibiting toward all age groups of persons of Jewish ancestry as the war lengthened. Born in Berlin in 1899 to Marta S., who was Jewish, and Leopold S., who was a Protestant, Max was in the generational cohort that suffered extremely heavy casualties in World War I. As an eighteen-year-old volunteer in March 1917, he joined a unit that helped stabilize both fronts, be they east or west. Max had volunteered as a grenadier in the trenches and was decorated for bravery. Wounded in August 1918 during the German army's general retreat in France, Max S. became a prisoner of war of the British and was eventually released from captivity on 29 October 1919, a year after the armistice. In 1931 he married Marta D. and settled in Essen. Marta was a Protestant, and Max was nominally a member of the Jewish community — at least he allowed his church tax to be paid to them. However, he was not interested in religion, he claimed, and in a later statement to police authorities announced that he had formally disassociated himself from the Jewish community in October 1938, several years after he had ceased to have any contact with it. His reason was straightforward: "It was totally alien for me to disguise myself as a Jew," he explained to the police. Although his statement could be interpreted as opportunistic and an effort to avoid the harsher treatment meted out to Jews, Max S. was already known to others as a person who never minced his words with anyone. All his friends and acquaintances knew him to be plainspoken, calm, and direct.

Unfortunately, those traits could not shield him from increasing persecution. After 1933, he described himself as a *Mischling* first degree. Yet, in 1941, the state police used his previous affiliation to the Jewish community as a pretext to categorize him as a *Geltungsjude,* and they required him to use the middle name Israel in official documents. After 1 September 1941, new regulations also demanded that, like Jews, *Geltungsjuden* were also supposed to wear the yellow Star of David in public. Unbeknownst to Max S., his wife, Marta, had appealed to the authorities for an exemption for him early in 1942, but her appeal had been rejected. For reasons that are not clear, she chose not to tell her husband of her efforts. For a time it seemed to make no difference. Max held a humble job as a deliveryman and bill collector for a textile firm in Essen, earning only twenty-five Reichsmarks per week. Certainly no one would have envied him his job, and given his modest nature, he had no trouble maintaining the low profile that most *Mischlinge* adopted. However, on 22 February 1943, the state police in Essen, having learned of his wife's efforts in 1942 to secure Max an exemption from wearing the star, arrested him without his armband during deliveries. It was true that he was married to an Aryan woman, Marta, but the marriage was childless and therefore not "privileged." The authorities contemplated sending him to a concentration camp, but then relented. He was released from jail a month later.

Max S. was still in a far from enviable position. By this time he had lost his job with the textile firm and was forced to find casual work wherever he could. One day, a policeman in Essen overheard a conversation among some shoppers during which one party stated that a Jew was selling tobacco products, cigarettes, and cigars from a table in a partially bombed-out apartment building nearby. The patrolman investigated and found Max S., filling in for the tobacconist while the latter hurried to the Essen housing authority to get approval for repairs for the damaged structure. The policeman questioned Max S. closely. Then he demanded to see his identity papers. Having determined that Max was a *Geltungsjude,* he filed a report with the Gestapo. On 29 November 1943, the Gestapo arrested Max S. again and charged him with failure to wear his yellow Star of David, with failure to use Israel as his middle name on official documents, and for selling tobacco products without a license. Despite pleas for his release from Marta, he was confined to a police prison and barracks in Essen.

In late April 1944, Essen endured a heavy bombing attack. Afterward, a police official from the prison described Max's behavior while in custody:

S. had been placed at the barracks for about four months and was assigned janitorial duties. S. carried out all of his various assignments with industry, reliability, and prudence. During the terror bombing on the night of 26–27 April 1944, he provided noteworthy support to the police authorities with his calm and levelheaded comportment. At the height of the bombing raid he personally extinguished several incendiary bombs and thereby helped to save the barracks. Courageously, he opposed an attempted escape by other inmates and was a genuine help to the authorities. His industriousness also helped to make it possible to make repairs to the barracks and to return the prisoners to it within a short time. S. gives the impression of a person who is thoroughly calm, unassuming, and hardworking.

Unmoved by the local police official's glowing endorsement for Max S., the Gestapo ordered his transfer to Auschwitz a few days later. He arrived there on 31 July 1944. The record does not disclose his ultimate fate. However, few survived at Auschwitz for long. Thus, Max S., a decorated combat veteran who had survived his wounds in the trenches of World War I, and who had been a model prisoner under arduous conditions in the Essen police barracks, probably did not survive. One Nazi-contrived snare after another had felled him. After all, a *Geltungsjude* failing to use the name Israel or wear a Star of David, and caught selling tobacco without a license deserved no mercy.[30]

Some *Mischlinge* entered sufficiently important technical occupations early enough that the Nazis hesitated to remove them — at least right away. Dietrich Goldschmidt, son of Hans Goldschmidt, a prominent civil servant, archivist, and historian in the time of the Kaiserreich and of the Weimar Republic, was one such person. The elder Goldschmidt was able to patch together private jobs following his dismissal from public service, but it was obvious that meaningful careers were becoming increasingly impossible. The Goldschmidt family convened after the *Kristallnacht* violence in November 1938 and made several decisions. The elder Goldschmidt, who had an international reputation as a historian, contacted colleagues abroad about refuge. Dietrich and his older brother, who were far along in their secondary education, would look for careers in specialized technical areas or else move abroad. On the eve of World War II, the elder Hans Goldschmidt migrated to Great Britain — where he was immediately interned as an enemy alien — and his oldest son also moved abroad. Younger son Dietrich, who was mathematically and technically gifted, chose to remain in Germany.[31]

At first his decision seemed to pay off. Dietrich completed his degree in engineering in Berlin's respected Technische Hochschule (Institute of Technology) in Charlottenburg in 1939 and found employment with a Berlin automobile manufacturer, Kemperer Motoren, which merged with the giant DEMAG Motorenwerke in 1942. Thus, Dietrich enjoyed full-time employment up to the autumn of 1944. Goldschmidt explained later that he had been able to obtain so prized a higher education because the very system encouraged technical expertise. At first, he worked as an assistant to one of DEMAG's directors. Then, as the dragnet closed, it became obvious that *Mischling* Goldschmidt was a liability. Reluctantly, his employers finally moved him to a less obtrusive post. In his last career move in Nazi Germany, Dietrich Goldschmidt, onetime engineering protégé, transferred to DEMAG's lowly replacement parts division. Even for persons who were technologically skilled, a career in Nazi Germany had become impossible if they were racially "impure" and had no protector. In September 1944, following numerous appeals and delays, Goldschmidt was forced to don the "uniform" of a forced laborer.[32]

Mischlinge who had the misfortune to carry a name that the Nazis could immediately stereotype as sounding "Jewish," often faced severe persecution from an early age. Given Adolf Gersonsohn's family name, it seemed as if persons in authority in Nazi Germany actively looked for signs of his being Jewish. Adolf was not blond and did not look Aryan. Therefore, officials were especially inclined to ascribe Jewish looks, Jewish activities, and Jewish vices to him. Born in 1927 in Düsseldorf to Hermann and Liselotte Gersonsohn, Adolf was age fifteen in 1942 and had not had the option of finishing school. Neither did he have the option of entering the HJ, joining a flak battery, training in the RAD, or performing military service as the other boys in his age group were doing. Given his name and his looks, elementary school had already been a trying experience. Even so, Adolf was lively, quick in conversation and repartee, and, given his experiences with society, he was quick to defend himself verbally.

At age fourteen Adolf had his first run-in with the law. Convicted of petty theft in 1941 while a laborer in a local Düsseldorf construction firm, he had been confined to a juvenile center for two weeks. Worse followed. In 1942, Adolf was assigned to a sheet metal factory in Düsseldorf, but his new supervisor was already acquainted with Adolf's allegedly unsavory past. As earlier, Adolf's name and appearance seemed to arouse animosity from supervisors and coworkers alike. Six months into his new job, the Gestapo arrested Adolf on more serious charges. "Adolf [Gersonsohn] has repeatedly committed acts in recent months which are tantamount to sabotage," his employer wrote. "All of our warnings have been without avail. Yesterday, in the railroad switching yard, he damaged a freight car by climbing aboard and turning on a brake." The supervisor laid other charges too. "Despite warnings, he was found among the French [prisoners of war] who gave him cigarettes." However, a more dire accusation soon followed. "A further reason for the dismissal is that [Gersonsohn] should be separated from another teenager, Wilhelmine D., who is employed here." Both of them had been seen in close proximity, the employer stated. "There is a strong suspicion that . . . they have had relations which might eventually have consequences." The employer fastened on Adolf's ethnicity: "His father is Jewish. It really seems to be the case that Jewish blood is dominant here. The youth is degenerate in every sense of the word, and it would be best that he be delivered to an institution."[33]

Gestapo interrogations ensued. Adolf's answers were typical of a bewildered, terrified youth. His answer to the charge of "sabotage" of the railroad car's brakes was: "I don't know why I did it." When asked about his "fraternization" with French prisoners of war, he stammered: "I may have accepted a cigarette *once* from a Frenchman because he insisted that I smoke it. Otherwise, I have never tried cigarettes ever after." A third incident involved a metalworking machine, which a coworker, Maria L., operated. She had asked him to tend it while she attended to maintenance. Adolf stated that he tried to monitor the unfamiliar machine while under the supervision of foreman Untersfeld, who gave no indication of disapproval or warning whatsoever.

However, the real reason for the intensive interrogations of Adolf Gersonsohn (there were several sessions) soon came to light. The authorities were obsessed by a potential friendship between him and sixteen-year-old Wilhelmine Dotterweich. "I was around Dotte almost every day," Adolf admitted. He also conceded that they had a half-hour lunch break nearly every day, too. Otherwise, he added, he never saw her outside of working hours. Upon further prodding, he admitted that he knew from conversations that she lived in a Düsseldorf suburb. However, he knew nothing more precise than that and had never contacted her after work. The Gestapo was not satisfied and after several weeks of close confinement interrogated him again. Its protocol revealed a change with respect to his "true" feelings toward his sixteen-year-old coworker. "Her looks and her personality pleased me greatly," he admitted to an interrogator. "I carried the thought constantly to become her friend and then to get close to her later. I wanted to invite her to movies, take her on trips along the Rhine, and take her to sporting events." Further prodding finally elicited what the police questioner really wanted to hear: "I also wanted to have sex with Dotte." Not content with even this admission, Adolf's interrogators wanted to know exactly what kind of sexual activities he had in mind. Thereupon, the interrogation report became extremely explicit, recording in pitiless detail what he meant by having sexual relations with "Dotte." In reality, the transcription described the normal desires of a fifteen-year-old boy interested in girls of a similar age. The same transcript also revealed that the authorities were extracting such details under heavy pressure in order to make his fantasies sound as lurid and shameful as possible. Their concluding report reveals a chilling hostility. They noted once again that his father was a full Jew while his mother was "allegedly" *deutschblütig*. Technically, they classified him as a *Mischling* first degree but added a qualifier:

Gestapo Reports

> In Gersonsohn's case it is obvious, given his characteristic traits, that Jewish blood predominates in him. Therefore, he will always be inclined towards criminal activities. He already demonstrates cunning and is a thoroughly bad character. He only admits guilt when he can no longer lie his way out of a charge. During police questionings he constantly tried to talk his way out. . . . Only after repeated warnings did he gradually concede any of the offenses of which he had been accused by his former employer.

Convinced that he was incorrigible, the authorities rendered a decision. "Because of his criminal tendencies, he poses a genuine danger to society if he is not removed from it in timely fashion. Therefore, it is in the interests of the Volk community that he be removed from it entirely so that he will not have the opportunity to perpetrate further criminal activities." For those *Mischlinge* who carried "Jewish-sounding" names and who did not look Aryan, the greatest occupational hazard was to work in proximity to an Aryan member of the opposite sex.[34]

Although many *Mischlinge* were from urban, middle-class homes and led normal, orderly lives until caught up in the Nazi persecution, not everyone so persecuted was innocent and law-abiding. Siegfried G. was born near Fulda in 1906 to a Jewish mother who never married. After finishing elementary school, Siegfried G. was apprenticed to a butcher, but that arrangement did not last long. He drifted from one job to another and achieved the reputation of being lazy, ignorant, and unreliable. Often drunk and disorderly, he railed publicly against whatever party or political system was in control at the moment. Perhaps because he was unaware of his parentage, he actually aided the Nazis in the years before the Seizure of Power, posting National Socialist placards during elections, making donations, and raising money for Hitler's movement. He drifted from job to job, and while serving as a truck driver's assistant in the summer of 1936, he uttered some provocative statements in the presence of several employees. Siegfried announced that there was yet another food shortage in Germany and that it was all the fault of the Party. They had covered up shortages while the Olympic Games were in progress, he fumed, but now there was no reason to do so, and people were starving. Sooner or later, Siegfried growled, someone was going to do away with Hitler. "The bullet has already been made for the Führer," he assured his coworkers.

Siegfried G. soon discovered how times had changed, especially for *Mischlinge*. His buddies informed on him, and within a few days he landed in a Gestapo jail. Word of his arrest spread quickly, and other witnesses came forward. With each denunciation the prosecutors took special pains to point out his status as a *Mischling*. Sometimes the denunciations were lurid. One indignant woman, a former girlfriend — Siegfried's marriage did not interfere with his social life — claimed that he had made love to her in a quarry in broad daylight and then photographed her in the nude. Now that she learned he was half-Jewish, she felt it was her civic duty to report the incident. Other eyewitnesses related additional provocative political statements by the accused. Consequently, Siegfried G. was sentenced to prison, first for weakening the morale of the German people, and then for committing *Rassenschande* (i.e., race pollution) during his tryst in the quarry. The fact that he was married to an Aryan woman and had two children may have saved him from a harsher fate. Released from prison on the eve of the war, he became a lowly laborer in a rural Hessian sawmill and, amazingly, survived the war. Perhaps

his prison sentence had heightened his survival skills in unpleasant surroundings. In any case, his marginal job in a remote location helped him to avoid
further unfriendly notice.[35]

Rudolf H. was a Krefeld *Mischling* born in 1921 to Otto and Maria H. Rolf,
as he was called, was loosely connected to the local Jewish community, a
technicality that the authorities used to designate him as a *Geltungsjude*. He,
too, was supposed to wear the yellow Star of David, sign his middle name
with Israel, and receive meager rations. Banned from any post–elementary
school education, Rolf H. became a driver's assistant with the trucking firm
of Heinrich Pöllen in Cologne. He proved reliable, was mechanically adroit,
and was a good driver of the firm's heavy trucks. However, Nazi laws
began to take their toll. As a *Geltungsjude* he was not permitted to keep his
driver's license (i.e., he was not a *Fahrjude*, a person of Jewish heritage who,
under limited circumstances, might have special permission to drive a
motor vehicle). Even so, Nazi restrictions had at least one advantage for
Rolf H. As a *Geltungsjude* he continued to work in Heinrich Pöllen's trucking firm when other employees were drafted. Owner Pöllen complained that
by late 1943, he had lost eleven of his employees to the armed services.
In addition, one of the firm's owners plus another employee had been
killed in a bombing raid in June 1943. Now, more than ever, they needed
every able-bodied man to maintain shipments to the Luftwaffe and the
war effort.

Such necessities counted little for the Gestapo. On the afternoon of
29 November 1943, Rolf H. and a driver, Fritz Schmitz, were delivering freight
to a local Cologne warehouse. Schmitz was a disabled war veteran who still
suffered from injuries to his right hand and elbow. Aware of his driver's dis-
comfort and of the difficulty Schmitz was having in working the gearshift,
Rolf H. took over. Unfortunately, as they rounded a corner and approached
a bridge, they came upon a police checkpoint. The crew quickly traded seats,
but an alert policeman spotted them and took them into custody. Accordingly, on 12 December 1943, both employees were forced to give accounts to
the Krefeld police. Driver Schmitz stated that it was he who had asked his
assistant to take over the driving. Rolf H. stoutly maintained that it was he
who had suggested the switch even though that put him in a worse light.
Using the conflicting accounts, the Krefeld authorities fined both men fifty
Reichsmarks or ten days in jail in January 1944.

The matter should have ended there, but it did not. The Krefeld Gestapo got wind of the charge and quickly launched its own investigation. On 15 March 1944, agents arrested Rolf H. (not Schmitz). "Rolf [H.]," the arrest report stated, "failed to enter his middle name of 'Israel' in his signature to the police authorities in Krefeld during his deposition on 12 December 1943." Therefore, the local Gestapo strongly recommended that he be placed in a concentration camp. Pleas on Rolf's behalf by driver Schmitz and by the truck firm's owner, Heinrich Pöllen, seemed to have little effect.[36] In fact, the Gestapo files contained an anonymous denunciation report from someone who lived near Rolf H. "I have taken an interest in this Jew," the informer wrote to the Gestapo, "and as a German I can no longer remain silent." He proceeded to give a rambling account of rumors and allegations that Rolf H. had been seen driving a truck on pleasure trips and that he maintained apartments in Krefeld, Cologne, and Bad Godesberg. Such charges were preposterous given his paltry wages as a driver's assistant as well as the keen attention police authorities had already showed toward him. The ultimate fate of Rolf H. is not clear. However, his experiences made it obvious that *Mischlinge*, especially *Geltungsjuden*, were under constant surveillance by police and by self-appointed informers. Jealous Aryans seemed to take special umbrage at the notion that Jews or *Geltungsjuden* might be seen driving motor vehicles.[37]

By dint of location, other half-Jewish citizens were luckier and largely escaped the discrimination that dogged *Mischlinge* in heavy population centers such as Cologne and the Ruhr. Martha Rohr, a Berlin orphan who had been raised with the Knebels, a peasant family in Wintersdorf on the Luxembourg border, had largely escaped discrimination in childhood because she, a *Mischling*, was so exotic and because she had already reached young adulthood by 1933. Then she received a jolt. Wintersdorf's newly installed Ortsgruppenleiter, Hans Dokter, developed an intense dislike for likable Martha because she was half-Jewish. Besides, there were no full Jews to target. Hitherto, the villagers, all of whom had known about her origins as she grew up among them, had shown no hostility. However, their mood shifted in 1933. Periodically, Ortsgruppenleiter Dokter ordered public celebrations of the Nazis' "high holy days" such as Hitler's birthday (20 April), or the failed coup of 1923 (9 November). All villagers were expected to give the Hitler salute and shout a loud *"Heil!"* It was at such ceremonies that Martha felt Hans Dokter's gaze upon her. He seemed always to be examining her minutely to see if she was giving the proper salute. Annoyingly, other villagers began to stare, too.

Mercifully her work on the family farm allowed her to avoid most harassment, but she encountered problems elsewhere. When she passed fellow villagers in the streets, they sometimes shouted insults at her if she failed to return the official Hitler greeting. But it was in her capacity as serving girl in the Knebel family's pub that she faced the greatest perils. It had been her good fortune to be graced with a friendly personality, intelligence, and good looks. Periodically, her birth father sent her fine clothing, making her one of the best-dressed women in Wintersdorf. Alas, the combination made her a standout in that most public of places, the village pub. Because Wintersdorf was so close to the Luxembourg border, the Nazis had chosen it in 1936 as a hub for the construction of their "West Wall" against a possible French invasion. Scores of military, construction workers, and Party officials descended upon the village, and after hours they congregated in Wintersdorf's only inn. Nazi laws notwithstanding, the customers, mostly young men, did not concern themselves with the finer points of Hitler's Nuremberg decrees. They frequently asked her out on dates, much to the annoyance of Ortsgruppenleiter Dokter, but prudently, she turned them down. Thus, Martha Rohr continued to enjoy full employment down to the end of the Third Reich. To be sure, she had to eschew dates, dared not marry, and had to reckon with Ortsgruppenleiter Dokter's constant gaze.[38]

Like Martha Rohr, Gerda Leuchtenberg from Frankfurt am Main had similar luck in finding a secure job. Unlike Martha, Gerda, who was slightly younger, grew up among sophisticated, big-city dwellers. She had just completed her *Abitur* in 1939 and was searching for career possibilities. Her Aryan father was a highly respected financial adviser who kept in order the books of government officials and industry leaders. In return, the latter kept him unusually well informed about developments in the NSDAP. Accordingly, he could forewarn his Jewish wife and his *Mischling* daughter of trends that might affect them. It was at her parents' suggestion that Gerda had prudently ended a budding romance with a young soldier in the summer of 1939, even though that decision had devastated her. Thereupon, Herr Leuchtenberg enrolled her in a private vocational training institute where she obtained a certificate as a chemist's assistant. It was in 1942 that Gerda's well-placed father realized that the persecution of Jews and *Mischlinge* would only worsen. He also learned from his contacts that Allied air attacks would concentrate on Germany's biggest cities. Using the benefits of his influence and calling in old favors, he contacted friends who knew friends. He sent his wife to trusted acquaintances in southern Austria. He also told other contacts that his technically trained daughter needed a job. As a result Gerda Leuchtenberg left Frankfurt to work in a chemical plant that produced industrial coatings in a small city near the Swiss border. She stayed there working in anonymity as a chemist's assistant for the rest of the war. Part of the reason for her success was that she made no complaints in her work and assiduously avoided any social relationships. She successfully resisted her attractive supervisor's advances and was relieved when he accepted her rebuff without rancor. Nevertheless, Gerda was a deeply unhappy young woman when she returned home at the end of the war. Scarred by her forced rejection of her true love, and fearing for her family and her own personal safety, she had withdrawn from any personal relationships. In so doing, she had erected invisible walls against almost everyone.[39]

At the other end of the age spectrum from Gerda Leuchtenberg was Alfred F., a native of Dortmund. In 1942 Alfred was forty-five years of age and at the peak of his professional abilities. He was the director of a middle-sized construction firm employing over sixty workers in Leichlingen near Cologne. Alfred F. was also a German patriot, a decorated combat veteran of World War I, and since 1933 a member of the DAF, the German Labor Front. In early February 1943, a labor dispute erupted at the firm and W. Zons, a disgruntled employee whom Alfred F. had recently dismissed, sent a letter of denunciation to the police authorities in Leichlingen. Herr Zons claimed that Alfred F.'s construction firm was squandering hundreds of tons of iron and timber on projects that were not essential to the war effort. Furthermore, wrote Zons, the director was also wasting the productive energies of sixty *deutschblütig* workers. "It is not my style to make accusations," the informant added. "However as a German and a Party Member, I see it as my duty to the Fatherland to point out these evil doings, which the public would describe with the word 'sabotage' and which has already caused bad blood." Herr Zons had been careful to point out at the beginning of his letter that Alfred F. was a *Mischling*. For someone claiming to be nonaccusatory, Zons had prepared a remarkable document.

Predictably, the Gestapo entered the picture. Their investigation conceded that Alfred F. had indeed been a decorated soldier in the 1914–18 war and later a DAF member, and that it was a disgruntled former worker who had denounced him as a *Mischling*. However, they also noted his high income of one hundred thousand Reichsmarks per year. Further, they noted that there were allegations (not proofs) that Alfred F. had withheld certain worker benefits. However, they were particularly outraged that he held a supervisory position over sixty *deutschblütig* employees. Worse, in his capacity as director of a firm dealing in strategic materials, he had frequent contact with other war-related industries. "There is a distinct possibility," a Gestapo official concluded, "that [Alfred F.] might have access to decisions that should be kept confidential." Alfred F. was promptly dismissed. Proven competence by persons in senior executive roles counted for little in the eyes of Nazi officials if the subject was found to be a *Mischling*.[40]

Helmut Langer had been born and raised in a village near the small Czech-Sudeten town of Gablonz, and his mixed parentage (his mother was Jewish but had died when he and his elder brother were small) had caused him increasing difficulties in society. Be it in school, the Hitler Youth, or his social life, Helmut felt hounded. He could not date girls and could not even enter a movie theater. School officials ejected him in 1944, and jobs were out of the question for *Mischlinge* in the Sudetenland, a region notorious for its anti-Semitism. Meanwhile, his father and second Aryan wife had produced three young children. His father's pay as a sergeant in the Wehrmacht was modest at best, and the older boys' stepmother had her hands full (i.e., the nest was full). It was imperative that Eckard and Helmut leave home as quickly as possible. Fortunately, the eldest son, Eckard, had finished school in 1942 before the Nazis could eject him, and had moved several hundred kilometers north to a small industrial town on the Czech border with Poland. It was there that the brothers' aunt had moved with her husband who was a Party member and a veteran of the SA Brownshirts. Using his Party connections, the couple had created a thriving enterprise, manufacturing military decorations, such as the Iron Cross, for the Wehrmacht. Initially, Helmut found work in a nearby town, but after a few familial visits, he was able to transfer to his uncle's firm. The teenager moved into a nearby dormitory maintained by his aunt for company workers. Keeping a low profile, Eckard and Helmut found steady work producing military decorations alongside eastern laborers. Anonymity provided a far pleasanter life than anything they had known at home. They had succeeded in finding jobs and staying alive in Hitler's Greater

German Reich. Even so, their situation was tenuous. They were German *Mischlinge*, working in a German-owned factory, producing quasi-military items for the Wehrmacht. On 8 May 1945, that job came to an end, and the two boys faced an uncertain future.[41]

Hans B. was born in Frankfurt am Main in 1919 to a Jewish mother and a Catholic father. He was baptized a Catholic and led a normal childhood, attending the local Volksschule. Then, upon completing his schooling, Hans B. was apprenticed to a butcher. In the normal scheme of things, he would probably have led an uneventful life, making a modest living. However, he belonged to an age group where his unwelcome status as a *Mischling* had particularly unfortunate consequences. Aged twenty and physically fit when World War II began, Hans B. was immediately conscripted into the armed forces in 1939 as Hitler's legions advanced into Poland.[42]

Hans served in a Luftwaffe regiment and performed arduous duties in the field, providing perimeter defense for aerial units in front lines and executing myriad other ground support duties. In short, he served basically as a Luftwaffe infantryman. Needless to say, his status as a *Mischling* precluded any higher training for the role of a pilot or an officer. He served in various campaigns, the worst of which occurred in the terribly cold winter of 1941–42 when three million German soldiers were caught unprepared on the eastern front. Like thousands of other German ground troops, Hans B., lacking proper clothing, suffered severe frostbite. Evacuated to a military hospital in Nassau, he recovered and was assigned to a special company of convalescing Luftwaffe soldiers. For three months he and his comrades performed light duties with the expectation of returning to normal military service. Then the bureaucracy discovered that Hans B. was a *Mischling* first degree. Dishonorably discharged, he returned to Frankfurt in disgrace.

Although Hans B. was initially able to resume work as a butcher, local Nazi officials in Frankfurt caught up with him again in May 1943 and made him a mechanic's assistant at the Reichs-Adlerwerke, a heavy machinery plant in Frankfurt. Trained as a butcher, conscripted as a soldier, relegated to being a butcher again, and then reassigned as a worker's assistant, Hans B. had, by the spring of 1943, been transformed into an embittered man. This had unfortunate consequences. A prosecuting attorney's report of June 1944 stated the following about Hans B.'s work in heavy industry during the preceding year: "His accomplishments at work have left a great deal to be desired! He conducted every assignment with the greatest reluctance. He was insubordinate, brutal, and always furious and unruly with his superiors." The same authorities noted that he had already been warned about his attitude. "He showed special consideration for foreign workers," they noted, "and because he consorted with Ostarbeiter [eastern workers], he had to be warned by the foreman yet again."[43]

Two weeks before Christmas 1943, Hans B. was ordered to service a heavy motor along with a French engineer in the presence of two female employees. Apparently, Hans B. became confrontational during the servicing of the heavy equipment and asked one of the woman coworkers how old she was. When the coworker remained silent, he burst into a condemnation of the entire war effort: "You German women are so stupid! You are producing goods for two and yet you get nothing to eat! You should be relegated to the piles of debris and the flames! I would rather deal with French women!"[44]

On 29 February 1944, the Gestapo arrested Hans B. and charged him with "weakening the will of the German People." On 22 September 1944, Hans B. was found guilty as charged and sentenced to eighteen months in prison. He was freed only on 18 May 1945, ten days after liberation, when the Americans opened the dungeon. Finding a job had proved hazardous for Hans B. from Frankfurt am Main. He had refused to accept that *Mischlinge* were expected to keep a low profile and to be obsequious and outwardly friendly to all others despite any and every provocation.[45]

Although generalizations are inaccurate, it is fair to describe full Jews and their *Mischling* sons and daughters as having been consistently hardworking and law-abiding citizens in a Germany convulsed by war, inflation, depression, and extreme social tension from 1914 onward. Many, if not all, were well educated and middle-class in their outlook. Faced with continuous social trauma, Germany's full Jews had begun to abandon Germany in increasing numbers after 1933, chased out by Nazi persecution. True, some *Mischlinge* also concluded that it was prudent to seek foreign climes, but those far-off places were often anything but hospitable to Jews. They were also inhospitable to many half-Jews, as the case of Friedl Goldschmidt demonstrates. Friedl's odyssey covered two continents and ultimately spanned three decades of exile. Before the Nazi Seizure of Power, Friedl had built a career as a successful businessman, specializing in textile sales with a major Hamburg firm. In 1933, stigmatized by his very name, Goldschmidt lost his job and fell down the economic ladder quickly. He also drew unwelcome attention from the Gestapo in Kassel and faced terrifying interrogations in 1936 and 1937, having been accused of *Rassenschande.*

Finally, on 1 May 1937, during Labor Day celebrations, friends helped him to flee into the Netherlands. Alas, Goldschmidt rapidly discovered that German refugees in the Lowlands were plentiful, whereas visas, work permits, and financial support were in short supply. It was there that he first entered a beggar's existence, living from hand to mouth, ill and utterly dependent upon curbside handouts, plus charities, for food and temporary shelter. At one point he even visited a recruiting station for the French foreign legion. However, shortly before desperation forced him to enlist, he finally received a temporary *Flüchtlingspass,* or refugee's passport. In December 1938, with borrowed money and in the company of another German refugee, Friedl boarded a freighter bound from Rotterdam to Rio de Janeiro. Ostensibly the two men were tourists, but their down-at-heel appearance fooled no one. After several run-ins with customs officials in Rio, they found temporary shelter in Uruguay where they learned how to bribe properly. Then the two Germans entered Brazil "properly" two months after the onset of their journey.

Reaching South America proved to be the easy part. Completely alone, Friedl Goldschmidt discovered that while his family name had ceased to plague him, his status as a doubtful tourist caused endless trouble. Informed that he could remain in Brazil for 180 days at most, he learned unofficially that if he were to travel into the interior and work on a hacienda (ranch), he could, after four years, seek legalization as an immigrant. Following that advice, Friedl became a farmhand. For two months in the midst of a Brazilian summer, he worked hard in Brazil's interior with other laborers. Then, like many another European, he found that he was vulnerable to tropical diseases. Goldschmidt fell desperately ill, and for the second time in his adult life became totally dependent upon charitable help. Coworkers alerted Benedictine monks in a nearby monastery, and they slowly nursed Friedl back to some semblance of health. He worked on several haciendas throughout the years of World War II and in the postwar period. Meanwhile, Goldschmidt gained greater knowledge and experience of farming in tropical regions. Securing loans from friends, banks, and credit institutions, he finally succeeded in buying his own modest farm in the Brazilian state of Parana, only to face serious crop failures due to rare frosts in 1953 and 1955. Inflation and economic turbulence took their toll, too. In desperation, Goldschmidt finally decided to apply for help from the country where his troubles had first begun. He secured help from a Catholic charity for refugees in the Netherlands and sought restitution for lost income and a hard life in exile lasting two decades. The record is not clear as to what compensation he received, if any. What is clear is that his claims were held up in litigation and bureaucratic delays for many, many years. There is no doubt that so-called *Mischlinge* under Hitler faced daunting uncertainties when seeking jobs and careers overseas.[46]

CONCLUSION

Nazi Germany's *Mischlinge*, the majority of whom were children in 1933, were forced to leave school at various intervals and had to find jobs. Almost invariably, those jobs were marginal, and those mostly young German victims were forced into lives of poverty and drudgery. Yet, over time, discrimination against *Mischlinge* only increased in parallel with the regime's discrimination against full Jews. Although the bulk of *Mischlinge*, now approaching adulthood, had come from urban, middle-class families and had received a proper elementary–secondary education — until dismissed — they realized that under Nazism, higher education and professional careers were denied them. Thereafter, especially in the last years of the war, sheer survival became their chief goal. The best survival strategy for *Mischlinge* was to find an unobtrusive niche in a nondescript job. In short, they sought to keep the lowest possible profile. The worst thing they could do was to draw attention upon themselves through high-visibility positions or indulging in public outbursts against their repressive regime. Therefore, most *Mischlinge* learned to keep silent. Those unfortunates who did not do so often paid a terrible price for their all-too-human reactions toward an increasingly hostile society. All *Mischlinge* knew that the twelve years of National Socialism were wasted years for them personally. Yet, those persons who succeeded in leading anonymous existences considered themselves to be lucky when compared with the full Jews — their own mothers or fathers, aunts, uncles, or grandparents — who were facing transportation to the East. Nevertheless, except for the full Jews, the plight of Germany's sons and daughters of mixed German-Jewish heritage was by any standard lamentable. Sheer survival became their goal. Some merged into the commercial–industrial world with scarcely a ripple, and as anonymous persons, they escaped the worst effects of Nazi persecution — at least outwardly.

Improbably, the Langer brothers, who had suffered blatant anti-Semitism in the Czech Sudetenland, avoided further persecution by working in a war-related factory elsewhere, run by a German with Nazi connections. Most *Mischlinge* were less fortunate. Hans Haurwitz, a so-called *Geltungsjude* and slave laborer alongside his Jewish father, comes to mind. Others, whose parents may have held influential positions, were able to find marginally better employment in war-related industries or other positions that shielded them from the Nazis' direct gaze. Others, like Berliner Meta Alexander or Frankfurt citizen Gerda Leuchtenberg, found employment in south Germany but paid a dear price by entering an existence marked by isolation, intense anxiety for their families, and ultimately a lifelong distrust of all human beings.

Ironically, because the Nazis failed to utilize the considerable talents and abilities of *Mischlinge* during World War II, they did themselves significant harm. Those mostly young people, seventy-two thousand half-Jews and forty thousand quarter-Jews, constituted a valuable human resource to the state. Because of Nazi prejudice, most of those same Germans never contributed in any meaningful way to the war effort. To be sure, this silver lining for the Nazis' wartime enemies provided cold comfort for Germany's *Mischlinge*.

3

Drawing the Line

One of the cruelest developments for young *Mischlinge* was the fact that they could not lead normal social lives even though they continued to remain "free," albeit on the fringes of German society, until the last year of the war. The Nuremberg decrees of 1935 had already singled out full Jews as social pariahs who were not permitted to marry or have intimate relations with citizens who were *deutschblütig* (i.e., of German blood). Offenders were deemed to have committed *Rassenschande* (racial defilement) and were subject to heavy jail terms which, in the later years of Hitler's Reich, were tantamount to sentences of death. However, those same laws were less precise with respect to Germany's *Mischlinge*. The gestation of the Nuremberg decrees as well as their terms are instructive about the irregular and arbitrary way in which the Nazis attempted to deal with half-Jews during their twelve-year Reich.

Of central importance in understanding those 1935 decrees, often called the Nuremberg "race laws," is the fact that Hitler hated anyone with Jewish forebears no matter how remote. Therefore, the very thought that persons of Jewish heritage might have sexual relations with *deutschblütig* Germans, especially women, was anathema to him and to the other party fanatics. It was a highly emotional issue and cut to the core of their profoundly racist attitudes. Hitler's numerous railings against Jews in *Mein Kampf* and elsewhere carried a near hysterical note about sexuality. This frequently quoted passage from his book suffices: "For hours the black-haired Jewish boy, diabolic with joy in his face, waits in ambush for the unsuspecting girl whom he defiles with his blood and thus robs her from her people."[1] In the same diatribe he dwelt at length on the evils of "race mixing" and "bastardization."

Hitler returned to the subject frequently in his rambling discourses to the party faithful. Consequently, *Mischlinge,* most notably *Mischlinge* first degree, were as much the object of Nazi anti-Semitic venom as full Jews. According to the Nazis' distasteful biological reckoning, the offspring of *Mischlinge* and *deutschblütig* citizens would "mendel out" progeny in succeeding generations who would also exhibit "Jewish" characteristics. Therefore, *Mischlinge* figured prominently in the Nazis' heated internal discussions surrounding the Nuremberg laws that Hitler promulgated at his Party rally in September 1935 and issued as decrees on 15 November 1935.

There were peak periods of anti-Semitic outbursts in Nazi Germany, followed by fallow times. One of those peaks occurred in the summer of 1935, driven by propaganda blasts from Josef Goebbels and from Gauleiter Julius Streicher in Franconia. The latter was the publisher of the semipornographic and notoriously anti-Semitic illustrated newspaper, *Der Stürmer,* and Hitler was one of its most avid readers. Thus pressure built for Hitler to make a dramatic announcement on citizenship and race at the Nuremberg rallies in September 1935. Once again, "moderates" centered in the Reich Ministry of the Interior with support from the Foreign and Economics ministries urged caution, attempting to limit the effects of the two Nuremberg decrees to full Jews only. The party fanatics, including those who were fanning the public mood, ardently sought to discriminate against *Mischlinge* to the same extent as full Jews. As he had done before and as he would do again, Hitler equivocated, torn between his own ardent anti-Semitic feelings and his political instincts not to alienate too many Aryan relatives of *Mischlinge* only two years into Nazi rule over Germany. The result, after much inner feuding and numerous drafts, was a compromise. With respect to the decree on citizenship, half-Jews, now officially designated *Mischlinge* first degree on the basis of two Jewish grandparents, would be accorded "provisional" Reich citizenship (i.e., it could be revoked at a future date). This was in contrast to Germany's full Jews, who were declared noncitizens immediately. On the much more emotional Decree for the Protection of German Blood and German Honor, the compromise stated that *Mischlinge* first degree could marry other half-Jews or foreigners but not *Deutschblütige* (i.e., Aryan Germans). The decree did not explicitly bar *Mischlinge* first degree from having sexual relations with Aryan Germans the way it did for full Jews. This presented *Mischlinge* a loophole of sorts. However, in practice the effect of the decree was to deter such liaisons. With increasing regularity, the Gestapo took matters into its own hands in interpreting the 1935 decree. By 1941 it was requiring all *Mischlinge* caught in close personal relationships with *Deutschblütige* to sign statements foreswearing those relationships on pain of removal to a concentration camp. Thus, by wartime local Nazi authorities were treating *Mischlinge* first degree in the same way they regarded full Jews despite the language of the Nuremberg decrees. Given Hitler's turgid prose, few Nazis had ever bothered to read *Mein Kampf*. However, the party's true believers held identical views to Hitler's obsession against Jews — and *Mischlinge* — especially when the issue involved sex and marriage.[2]

Consequently, the Nuremberg decrees turned normal social liaisons into criminal offenses that could be and were actively prosecuted throughout the duration of Hitler's Germany. The ghettoization of Germany's full Jews after 1938 (i.e., their forced concentration into overcrowded dwellings and near isolation from the rest of the population) had in some measure made the laws irrelevant, since Jewish citizens were experiencing almost no social interaction with other Germans anyway. This also held true to a large extent for full Jews married to Aryans in the so-called privileged mixed marriages. However, *Mischlinge* continued to obtain education in public schools, find employment in the private economy, and in some cases perform national voluntary labor service or even soldiering. For them the effects of Nazi restrictions were especially pernicious. Since the laws restricted half-Jews from integrating socially into the rest of society and the persecution and "relocation" of full Jews was in full swing by the time the war began, this meant that *Mischlinge* were confined, according to the race laws, to socializing with each other. Yet, since there were only about seventy-two thousand half-Jews and forty thousand quarter-Jews in this artificially created category — this in a population of over seventy-five million — and since most *Mischlinge* scarcely knew of one another's existence, the severity of the problem is obvious. Under the Nazis, *Mischlinge* became lonely persons who were forced to live quasi-integrated in the very society that was persecuting them.

As teenagers or young adults finishing school, entering the workforce, and sometimes facing the dangers of military service in wartime, the *Mischlinge* found the Nazis' restrictions infuriating. Moreover, World War II, like all wars, brought a quickening of the social tempo. Young people, especially, experienced more intense social and personal relationships as wartime dangers and human tragedies provided urgency to their lives. In short, such phenomena as wartime friendships and romance, universal human experiences, played the *Mischlinge* false, and increasingly they felt the sting of the Nuremberg decrees. By 1939 Nazi authorities became increasingly aggressive in interpreting their race laws, and they meted out harsher sentences against so-called *Mischling* transgressions. In short, the Nazis were drawing a line in society, one which *Mischlinge* dared cross at their own peril.

Sadly, many victims discovered too late that in their own society they had to reckon with the fact that some neighbors, acquaintances, coworkers, and erstwhile friends had no qualms about denouncing them to the authorities. There is some historical controversy concerning the extent to which denunciations took place in society. Some historians view it as a universal phenomenon that saturated German society. Individual citizens became, in effect, the eyes and ears of the Gestapo who were essentially reactive. Other historians see this interpretation as exaggerating the extent of denunciation. In their view, a relatively small but nevertheless significant portion of the population engaged in it. In fact, examination of Gestapo records indicates that the secret police tended to pay attention to the results of their own investigations more than to private citizens' denunciations filed at Gestapo offices. Besides, many of the latter involved relatively trivial cases of citizens denouncing neighbors for uttering anti-Hitler jokes or other statements mildly critical of the Nazi regime. Other common categories included denunciations of individuals alleged to have listened to foreign radio broadcasts or to have expressed pessimism about the outcome of the war. Usually, the Gestapo treated such garden-variety denunciations cavalierly, imposing fines, administering warnings, or meting out short jail sentences. However, denunciations of Jews and persons of partial Jewish ancestry such as *Mischlinge* were treated far differently. When denunciations of such persons crossed a Gestapo official's desk, there was a much greater likelihood that rigorous investigations, arrests, and harsh sentences would ensue. This, too, was clear evidence that *Mischlinge* first degree experienced "invisible walls" rising up around them.[3]

CASE HISTORIES

One of those who experienced firsthand the effects of social isolation was Berliner Eva Heilmann. She had postponed her ambitions of getting a university education, had completed training as a secretary instead, and was finally able to find work in Berlin. Bright, personable, and attractive, she was an avid lover of serious music, and for her a logical social outlet in wartime Berlin was attendance at symphonies, operas, and plays. She became a frequent concert attendee. Eva often frequented performances of the Berlin Philharmonie in the Bernburgerstrasse. It was during one of her many visits there that she made the acquaintance of a pleasant young man who had seen her at the concert hall on previous occasions. They struck up a conversation, and each was attracted to the other. Following the next concert, they found each other in the lobby again and decided to take a late evening stroll to a nearby public park. It was a lovely summer evening, and their conversation began pleasantly. They appeared to be an attractive young couple, possibly romantically involved. Unfortunately, their conversation took a disastrous turn when Germany's current political situation replaced music as the main subject. The young man uttered several anti-Semitic remarks that faithfully reflected Goebbels's propaganda. Eva Heilmann was silent at first, hoping that he would find another topic. However, her companion continued to rail on in the same vein. She finally decided that they had to face the issue straight on, and so she told him that she was a *Mischling*. To this point he had been a decent companion and they obviously had enjoyed each other's company. Therefore, she was utterly taken aback when he reacted not with shame but with indignation. The young man sprang up from the bench and screamed at her. She was endangering his career, he shouted, his face mottled with anger. Then he ran off into the dark, leaving her at the secluded bench. Nighttime Berlin in a darkened public park was not exactly the place for a single young woman to find herself, but Eva Heilmann made her way home to safety. The perils and humiliations of interacting with male acquaintances in Nazi Germany were becoming obvious. Even so, Eva Heilmann did not suffer outright legal prosecution for her association, brief and unpleasant though it was. She decided that she would have to be on her guard with *deutschblütig* men thereafter.[4]

Peter Heilmann, Eva's brother, had also learned to be circumspect in society, avoiding contact with *deutschblütig* women. He also experienced a severe compartmentalization in his life. By day he served as a lowly fumigator, shunned by the public because of his rough, ill-smelling working attire. However, in the evening he served as an unofficial social secretary for his high school class. Peter had earned his *Abitur* in 1941. Even during the Third Reich, the *Abiturienten,* graduates of the elite secondary schools, comprised only 2 percent of their age group. One of the traditions of alumni of Germany's Gymnasiums was that the members of each graduating class remained in touch and held frequent reunions. They also recognized the accomplishments of classmates with newsletters, round-robin letters, or other communications that were usually distributed by a particularly conscientious classmate. It fell to Peter Heilmann to serve, in effect, as class scribe for his fellow alumni, even though he was now a lowly fumigator and a despised *Mischling.* Barred from military service, unable to visit places of cultural enrichment or popular entertainment, or to socialize in any normal way, Peter found that he had much free time in the evenings. His classmates began asking for his assistance: "After we were conferred with the Abitur, most of them became soldiers, some officers, the others non-commissioned officers. We met twice yearly when my classmates were on leave. I was permitted to write the invitations and to send out all the official announcements. I was also permitted to organize the entire event. Yet, finally the moment came when, at some opportune moment, I was informed that I should not put in an appearance. After all, that might disturb the gentleman-officers." After several reunions took place without him, Peter Heilmann vowed that he would never meet with his high school classmates again.[5]

Andreas Heintz, an architect in Frankfurt, was older than the Heilmann siblings, born in 1911 to Franz and Käthe Heintz in Frankfurt am Main. His situation was somewhat unusual because a legal case that had caused his imprisonment hinged on whether or not he was designated a "full Jew" as was initially assumed by the authorities or "merely" a half-Jew. This was because his parentage was not clear. The Nuremberg laws of 1935 had contained ambiguities, subjecting half-Jews to some persecution but remaining silent on the issue of intimate relations with *deutschblütig* citizens. Andreas Heintz, the victim, suffered two bouts of persecution, first as a full Jew and then as a half-Jew. His was an involved legal case, but it reveals how the wheels of Nazi justice spun.

In early 1937 the Gestapo arrested architect Heintz, age twenty-six, for *Rassenschande* (i.e., race defilement). He had been living with Karin Ebert, a woman who was *deutschblütig.* After several months in a Gestapo jail, he went on trial, and because the prosecution viewed him as a full Jew, he was convicted and sentenced to a lengthy jail term which he began serving on 12 May 1937.

The case did not end there. His mother, Käthe Heintz, appealed the decision, stating that her husband, Franz, who was Jewish, was not Andreas's real father. Rather, it was one Dr. Härtner, an Aryan and an intimate friend (now deceased). Eyewitnesses testified to the truth of Frau Heintz's claim, and accordingly a detailed medical examination of the Heintz family took place. Two medical experts, who were also anthropologists, minutely examined the physical proportions and characteristics of father, mother, and son. Professor Dr. Otto von Verschuer, the director of the University of Frankfurt's Institute for Inherited Biology and Eugenics, and his youthful assistant, Dr. Josef Mengele, conducted the examination. On 9 July 1937, they delivered their results. Their judgment was based on such factors as the child's and parents' blood groups and types, hair color and texture, color of eyes, shape of eyebrows (which received elaborate attention), fingerprints and palm prints, and head shape (which received especially elaborate scrutiny). They also used photographs of the subjects, including images of the deceased Dr. Härtner. Medical scientists von Verschuer and Mengele issued an unequivocal verdict: Herr Heintz was the true father. Therefore, son Andreas was a full Jew and should remain in jail. He was guilty of "race defilement."[6]

However, at his mother's urging other eyewitnesses testified that the real father was indeed Dr. Härtner. After examining all the testimony, an appeals court in Frankfurt overturned the verdict. Accordingly, Andreas Heintz, now categorized as a *Mischling* first degree as opposed to a full Jew, was released on 14 September 1937. Despite this reprieve, four months in a Nazi jail had opened his eyes to what kind of justice Jews and *Mischlinge* could expect in Hitler's Germany. Keeping a low profile, Andreas slipped over the German border the following winter, bound for South America and destined never to return to Germany. It was just as well. The Nazis' legal system continued to churn, and on 30 March 1938, shortly after his departure, the Gestapo issued another arrest warrant for Andreas Heintz for race pollution with the same Karin Ebert. By their reckoning, *Mischlinge* were race polluters, too. In short, the Gestapo was proving to be a law unto itself. As noted earlier, by 1941, the same Gestapo was systematically forcing any and all *Mischlinge* first degree to sign affidavits foreswearing any liaisons with *deutschblütig* citizens under threat of incarceration in a concentration camp. Fortunately for Andreas Heintz, such harassment was academic, since he had already fled Germany. The Second World War, the Holocaust, and the postwar years followed, at which time Andreas Heintz finally appealed his conviction. On 6 February, 1958, the attorney general for Hesse issued a brief statement. He exonerated Andreas Heintz. The architect had not committed race pollution after all. To be sure, the newly sovereign Federal Republic was no longer carrying Nazi racial laws on its books. Nevertheless, Heintz wanted a clear and unequivocal statement from legal authorities that his "crime" of 1937 was not a crime. The fate of his resourceful parents remains unknown to this author.[7]

The Andreas Heintz case is instructive in a number of ways. First, it demonstrates that the German medical profession was largely in league with the Nazis and had accepted the theories of rogue anthropologists like Otto von Verschuer and his protégé, Josef Mengele. The Reich doctors' leader, Gerhard Wagner, and two other medical leaders, Walter Gross and Friedrich G. C. Barthels, had played a central role in drafting the provisions of the 1935 Law for the Protection of German Blood.[8] As a result, physical examinations became commonplace for *Mischlinge* in situations where parentage was contested or appeals for whatever reason against the individual's racial categorization had been raised. Furthermore, the denunciation of Andreas Heintz and the rapid reaction of the Gestapo to accusations of *Rassenschande* in his situation demonstrated that the Nazis were deadly serious in enforcing their 1935 race decrees against Jews and, de facto, against *Mischlinge* first degree. Legally speaking, half-Jews might have been exempt from *Rassenschande* suits, since the Law for the Protection of German Blood and Honor did not specifically ban intimate relations between *Mischlinge* and *Deutschblütige*. It simply banned marriages.

Most *Mischlinge* who were coming of age under National Socialism were likelier to suffer discrimination in youth organizations rather than in personal liaisons. Given their success in creating the Hitler Youth as their organization of choice, the Nazis took a dim view of any competing group. By the eve of World War II, at least 90 percent of all German youth were officially listed as members of the HJ and the BDM. Only a few holdouts, usually organized among the major churches, lingered on for any length of time. Not surprisingly, the Nazis were suspicious of youth groups that had a foreign or exotic character. They were especially wary if *Mischlinge* were found to be among the participants. Thus, a Frankfurt District Court counselor, Dr. Amrhein, was upset to discover that two private youth clubs had sprung up in the spring of 1939. One was called the Harlemklub, and the other carried the curious title of OK Gang Klub. The members assembled at the Hauptwache in Frankfurt on certain afternoons "in brightly colored coats," where, according to Dr. Amrhein, they made arrangements to go to certain dancing clubs in the evening. "The club members had a special fondness for English dances and records," he noted in an official report. "One specific record with a melody named after the Harlem District of New York, was so loved that they named their club the Harlem Klub." A few months later the OK Gang Klub came into existence among a group of high school–aged youths at the instigation of one boy who from age six to thirteen had lived in the United States and who had returned to Germany with certain "foreign" ideas. The members wore club pins in nightspots for identification purposes. Especially disturbing to the authorities was the fact that teenagers, boys and girls in equal numbers, danced to "swing" tunes. Many also boasted of their sexual experiences. One boy's parents allowed him the use of their ski lodge in the nearby Taunus Mountains, and club couples stayed there overnight without adult supervision. One aspect of this activity particularly shocked Dr. Amrhein: "In that ski lodge several club members are alleged to have consorted with a half Jewish girl who lives in the vicinity." Thereupon, the authorities cracked down, placing twelve girls under state supervision. Many boys avoided trials and imprisonment by joining the armed forces, but an original founder of the Harlem Klub was not so lucky. He was sentenced to eight months in jail.[9]

Club activities continued nonetheless. In February 1942 another district attorney was shocked to find that two more club members were *Mischlinge* first degree. The authorities hastily established charges against the new cohort but went out of their way to charge the two *Mischlinge* with additional crimes. One youth was charged with supplying quantities of scarce leather to members sufficient for resoling eight pairs of shoes. He had done this without a license, they noted. The other *Mischling*, who was an apprentice salesman, was accused of providing textiles for the sewing of garments without a license. Both were accused of gambling. In sum, the authorities leveled multiple charges against the two teenagers. There were eighteen youths identified by representatives of the Gestapo, the Sicherheitsdienst (SD), Kriminalpolizei (Kripo), the Frankfurt City Jugendamt (Youth Office), and the Hitler Youth.

They decided that the other sixteen be sent to a reeducation camp in the Schongau to prepare them for military service. The two *Mischlinge* against whom the more serious charges were raised did not have that dubious honor. They went to jail. Nazi authorities were only too happy to throw the book at *Mischlinge* caught in minor offenses.[10]

Sometimes exclusion from society combined with the stigma of being a *Mischling* was simply too much for an individual. The seventy-two thousand persons categorized as *Mischlinge* were so spread out that the possibility of half-Jews forming social networks did not exist. In general *Mischlinge* had no one to whom they could turn for moral support outside their own immediate families and perhaps a few trusted friends. If even that limited support were missing, then the individual in all likelihood faced a life of near seclusion and extreme loneliness. Unless a *Mischling* possessed maturity and inner resilience, the effects of social isolation could be devastating.

Heinz Ullmann was a seventeen-year-old, listed as a schoolboy and engaged as a film laboratory assistant in Frankfurt during the war. He was from Prague and had German parents, but one of them was of Jewish or half-Jewish ancestry — the record is not entirely clear. Therefore, Heinz Ullmann was a *Mischling* in Nazi eyes, either a *Mischling* first degree or a *Mischling* second degree. Following a hurried departure from school in the autumn of 1941, he had moved to Berlin but encountered difficulties with the authorities there. Consequently, he moved on to Frankfurt am Main. Ullmann had no family or friends in that region, but Frankfurt suited him, since he was unknown to the local authorities. At first his desperate move seemed to work. He found employment in a photo laboratory in a Frankfurt suburb but lived in Frankfurt proper in furnished rooms in the Josef Hayden-Strasse. His landlady, Barbara Preiss, did not know him well but described him to others as *anständig,* or law abiding. He socialized with no one but came and went to work with great regularity. Then on Friday, 13 December 1941, seven weeks after his arrival in Frankfurt, Ullmann received a distinctive piece of mail: his draft notice.

Landlady Preiss delivered his call-up papers personally, stating that she knew she was handing him something that would bring him joy. He was to report for induction on 18 December, the notice said. She claimed later that in a previous conversation she had heard Heinz say that he would serve gladly. However, she could see now that he was anything but happy. Suspicious, Frau

Preiss and her grown daughter, Ingeborg, questioned him more closely that evening. The youth replied that he had weak lungs and would once again be found ineligible for military service. The landlady and her daughter reacted with extreme skepticism, whereupon the boy broke down and admitted tearfully that there was another factor involved. He was a *Mischling*.

Upon hearing this, Ingeborg Preiss arose and announced that under such circumstances, Heinz Ullmann must vacate the premises immediately. After all, she was a member of the Party! "Ullmann was obviously depressed," Frau Preiss admitted afterward and noted that the boy had withdrawn quickly to his room. By this time it was 10:00 P.M. and the house quieted. The next morning Frau Preiss, not hearing her lodger's alarm clock or any movement in his room, knocked but received no reply. She called another male lodger, who found Ullmann's room empty.

That same Saturday morning at 8:00 A.M., a small boy ran into a nearby police station and announced that at the Hohenzollern Anlage near the post office, he had just spotted a man slumped over on a park bench who appeared to be dead. The police quickly found the body of Heinz Ullmann. During the night he had settled himself upon the bench and shot himself through the heart with a revolver with one bullet in it. There were no witnesses. A German teenager from Prague had died alone at his own hand in a strange city without friends or family. Under police questioning, Landlady Preiss opined: "If Ullmann committed suicide, then it must be assumed that his motive is to be found in the fact that he was non-Aryan and therefore felt unhappy."[11] The only real mystery about Heinz Ullmann's suicide was how he had obtained a revolver and ammunition in that tightly controlled society.

Most *Mischlinge* discovered that the isolation process that had begun in schools, youth organizations, and everyday life worsened in young adulthood, although few felt compelled to commit suicide. Not only did they face difficulties in finding jobs or careers, they also had to confront the reality that the National Socialists had criminalized normal social behavior. In that increasingly male-dominated society, far fewer young women had reason to defer courtship and marriage for a higher education and professional careers than did women of later generations. Homemaking was the logical alternative. Many young German women accepted that reality and went on to lead normal social lives. They married in their late teens and early twenties. Yet, the 1935 Nuremberg decree protecting German blood and honor virtually forbade all *Mischlinge* that option. Even the decree's silence on liaisons between unmarried persons counted for little, as Nazi authorities, especially the Gestapo, detained *Mischlinge* caught in intimate relationships. Instead, the agents forced *Mischlinge* to sign statements admitting that *Rassenschande* would be cause for incarceration. However, it was not merely the threat of harsh punishment that deterred many young persons, especially women, from having close relations with Aryan Germans. Premarital or extramarital relationships, although hardly unknown in German society either before the advent of the Nazis or after, were nevertheless frowned upon by large segments of society. In traditionally tight-knit families all across class lines, the notion of a daughter having an affair with a man to whom she was not married was "not the done thing." Therefore, *Mischling* women who, as eligible young adults, were inclined to socialize and in the normal course of events find a suitable mate and marry, found that they could not. Nor were they prepared because of their upbringing to have extramarital affairs. This, too, was a part of the invisible line the Nazis drew in society, and it grew even more pronounced in wartime, when the tempo of life quickened in the face of danger, especially to young people.

Gerda Leuchtenberg from Frankfurt am Main was the only daughter of middle-class, professional parents. Born in 1920, she had just finished high school in the spring of 1939 and was contemplating what she would do with her life when she met a young man. They fell deeply in love in that last peacetime summer. Then, in the last week of August, her suitor, a young Luftwaffe lieutenant, asked if he might pay a formal visit to Gerda's parents. It was the decent thing to do in that society, and it meant that he would be seeking her parents' permission to marry her. Although she loved him, she knew something that he did not. She was a *Mischling* first degree. Given the severity of the Nuremberg laws, such a marriage would have required special consideration by the National Socialist authorities, a lengthy appeal process that would almost surely end in failure. Moreover, it would bring unwanted attention both to Gerda and to the man she loved, and in all likelihood it would ruin his career. She also knew that he, too, held to a high code of personal conduct, and she was convinced that once he had asked for her hand in marriage, he would never renege on his pledge. She wanted desperately to be his wife and for them to have a family. Yet, Gerda had already taken the time that summer to consider the consequences and to discuss them with her parents, whom she loved and respected and from whom she held no secrets. Gerda's parents could only counsel her to hold off any marriage proposal. Thus, when her suitor asked permission to meet her parents, she refused him. His first reaction was one of astonishment, quickly followed by profound grief. Unable to bear it any longer, he ran from her presence. They never met again. He was killed some months later in one of the early campaigns of World War II.

Immeasurably saddened by what she had had to do, Gerda vowed to avoid any further romantic attachments, and she succeeded in this throughout the war years even though a secluded life did not come naturally to her. Furthermore, the experience of rejecting her lover continued to affect her ever after. It was her destiny to marry only in middle age, long after the Nazis were gone, and far too late for her to have children of her own. Thus, Gerda Leuchtenberg never produced the family she had so desperately wanted to start when she fell in love in that summer of 1939. The effects of Nazi racial discrimination on *Mischlinge* continued for generations.[12]

Other *Mischlinge* suffered hardships similar to those endured by Gerda Leuchtenberg, although sometimes the outcome was more benign. Karl Metzger, a Hessian, was already a successful salesman with a company located in Friedberg in 1933 when the Nazis seized power. He had fallen in love with a young woman by then, and in 1935 they wanted to marry. Alas, the timing was wrong. Karl Metzger's mother was Jewish, and he, a *Mischling,* found his marriage application was promptly denied. Furthermore, the vengeful Ortsgruppenleiter for that section of Hesse saw to it that his fiancée was drafted into the women's auxiliaries; she was one of the few women in Friedberg to suffer that fate. Karl was convinced that her betrothal to him, a half-Jew, was the reason why. Toward the end of the war Karl was placed in a forced-labor camp. Conditions were atrocious there, and he lost nearly seventy pounds before the Americans liberated him in April 1945. Yet, both he and his lover, who had been drafted, survived. The happy part of their story was that Karl and his fiancée of ten years were finally married in May 1945. Unlike the unfortunate Gerda Leuchtenberg, the Metzgers promptly started their family.[13]

Although *Rassenschande* became one of the most feared "crimes" under which Jews and *Mischlinge* might run afoul of Nazi laws, it was hardly the only one. As other cases noted earlier indicate, almost any infraction of Nazi laws could produce serious consequences for Jews and partial Jews. For example, many Germans listened to foreign broadcasts even though the Nazis had made it a crime. They did so because even in that tightly controlled society, the police and notably the Gestapo were not omnipresent. Almost always it required an effort on the part of one citizen to report or denounce to authorities the listening habits of another citizen. If it acted at all, the feared Gestapo might issue a reprimand to an "ordinary" German who had been betrayed. However, if the person being denounced was a full Jew (unlikely after 1941, since the Nazis had removed virtually all of them from German society) or else a *Mischling* or some other undesirable category, the consequences could be far more severe, especially in wartime. Denunciations fragmented German society under the Nazis. Yet, denunciations were far more dangerous to those whom the Nazis had already ostracized.[14]

In 1943, housepainter Hermann C., a middle-aged *Mischling* from Wiesbaden, was happily married with a family. As such, he had not been drafted. Hermann C. was quiet and hardworking and had never had any trouble with the law. He was on friendly terms with his neighbors, including several who lived in the same apartment building. In the evening he often invited an elderly widower plus the neighbor's adult son and the family's foster child, a young woman, to join them. They would listen to the evening news on his proudest possession, a solidly constructed Siemens radio. Habitually, Hermann C. and his neighbors discussed the day's events after the news. Alas, his trust in his neighbors was not reciprocated. On 25 September 1943, Hermann C. was arrested. Someone had reported him to the Gestapo for listening to radio broadcasts from London since September 1941. Furthermore, he had discussed those broadcasts with his houseguests. Hermann C. was speedily convicted. His jailer demanded that he prepare a list of persons with whom he had discussed "poisonous Allied propaganda," but Hermann refused, saying he could not remember with whom he had discussed the broadcasts. Alas, his loyalty to friends only angered the Gestapo further, and the authorities sentenced him to four years at hard labor, levied a heavy fine, and removed his citizenship rights for five years. They also confiscated his radio "for service to the Reich" (i.e., it became loot). The authorities' rationale for their draconian sentence is revealing: "As far as the severity of the punishment is concerned, it must be kept in mind that the accused, who as a *Mischling* had a special obligation to comport himself correctly and irreproachably, has through his actions committed a heavy offense." In short, his blameless past was irrelevant. "Even if the accused has led an innocent life beyond reproach until the present," the concluding report announced, "even if he has performed his work well and conscientiously, and even if he committed his crime inadvertently by tuning into enemy broadcasts by chance and admits to doing this, then even so he must reckon with a harsh sentence." Hermann C. remained in prison until liberation in May 1945. A mere reprimand was out of the question for a *Mischling*.[15]

Even imminent defeat did not deter the Nazis from meting out harsh punishment against "undesirables." To the bitter end all citizens had to reckon with informers in their midst, and *Mischlinge* had to be especially wary. Margarethe W. was an unusual person to have ended up in Nazi custody. She was the middle-aged housewife of a superpatriotic German, Heinrich W., who had joined the Party in 1930. Their son had become a Gruppenführer (i.e., a high official) in the Kyffhäuserbund, an ultranationalist organization until the Nazis absorbed it in 1933. They had remained loyal Nazis until 1934, when party officials discovered that Frau W. was a *Mischling*. Reluctantly, Herr W. left the NSDAP to avoid being expelled. Nevertheless, the couple remained doggedly loyal to the Party. Their only son became a soldier and was currently serving at the front.

For whatever reason in the autumn of 1943, Margarethe W. and a neighbor, Else D., decided to sing a silly song that mocked Hitler slightly. Someone among their neighborhood circle informed on them and reminded the authorities that Margarethe W. was a *Mischling*. Local police quickly arrested the couple, and after chastising and releasing Herr W., they threw the book at Frau W. A harmless housewife, Margarethe W., at age fifty-seven, was sentenced to two years of hard labor, her husband's pathetic offer to pay one thousand Reichsmarks to the Party notwithstanding. In early 1945, one year into her prison term, Margarethe W. sought a pardon. Thereupon, on 20 March 1945, a representative of the supreme court of Hesse finally replied. He informed Margarethe W. that there were no grounds to reduce sentence. Yet, he was reasonable. He added that he might be willing to review her sentence in three months' time. One week following his decision, on 28 March 1945, the American Third Army entered Frankfurt. The record does not disclose how former Nazi Heinrich W. and former *Mischling* Margarethe W. reacted to Allied victory and to her immediate release from jail. Their experience reinforced one point: the longer Nazis held sway, the more that denunciation poisoned the lives of Germans. Furthermore, its virulence, already bad in peacetime, worsened for *Mischlinge* in wartime.[16]

However, it was *Rassenschande*, not mocking songs, that was the emotional benchmark for the Nazis, and it was allegations of *Rassenschande* that worked so heavily against Anna H., a native of Krefeld. Born to poor working-class parents, Anna was nineteen years of age in 1939 when she met a young man and had her first affair. In the normal scheme of things, such a relationship would have aroused little comment. However the Nazis held two strikes against her. Anna's mother was Jewish (her father was Aryan), and Anna H. had attended a Jewish school in the 1930s. Consequently, she was placed in the special category of *Mischlinge* known as *Geltungsjuden* (i.e., equivalent to full Jews). That may have been another reason why she had been called to account by the Gestapo so promptly. Then, for reasons that were not entirely clear, the authorities dropped the charges. Perhaps the evidence was not entirely ironclad, or else her Aryan friend had found a way to mollify the authorities.

Relieved to have escaped the indictment, Anna H. apparently assumed that she could resume a normal life. Unfortunately, she was unaware of a sinister fact. Once identified to the authorities in 1939, she no longer enjoyed anonymity. The local Gestapo had marked her for further scrutiny. She was a *Hilfsarbeiterin*, or unskilled laborer, earning a paltry eighty-eight Reichsmarks per month, and of necessity lived with her parents. Anna H. and her parents did not know that a fifteen-year-old girl, living right next door, had become a Gestapo informant. The officials told the girl to look for any infractions of National Socialist laws such as failure by mother and daughter to wear the required *Judenstern*, or Star of David, in public. Finally, in March 1942, they felt they had what they were looking for and arrested Anna H. After several days in confinement she was released with a stern warning to comply with the law. Chastened, Anna H. returned to the family apartment.

Her teenage neighbor, emboldened by success, continued to spy. In August 1942, she decided that she had enough evidence of further failure by Anna and her mother to wear the Star of David and filed another denunciation report. On 17 September 1942 mother and daughter were placed under arrest. It was the third time for Anna, the first for her mother. After two and a half weeks, the Gestapo released the mother even though she was a full Jew (she belonged to a "privileged mixed marriage"). Anna was not so lucky. Convinced that she was incorrigible, they kept her in jail, then shipped her to Auschwitz on 15 January 1943. The following spring a telegram arrived from camp commandant Rudolf Höss to Gestapo authorities in Düsseldorf, who forwarded it to Gestapo authorities in Krefeld, who, in turn, notified Anna's father (not her mother) that Anna H. had died on 5 May 1943 of "diarrhea" at the age of twenty-three. Allegations of *Rassenschande* at age nineteen had started her on her fateful journey to a death camp.[17]

It is widely accepted that the Nazis expected women to confine themselves to traditional sex roles such as the devoted housewife and mother. The historical record shows that under National Socialism, all women faced severe restrictions in higher education, the professions, and senior positions in business and commerce. The National Socialist credo of the three Ks, *Kinder, Küche, Kirche* (children, the kitchen, and religion), for women was not an exaggeration. While this held true for all women, the notion of capable Jewish women and *Mischling* women serving as professionals or achieving social prominence was abhorrent to National Socialists. Therefore, few female *Mischlinge* sought to break into such circles. However, there were exceptions to this rule, as the case of Magdalene G. demonstrates.

Magdalene G., born in 1908, was the daughter of Sophia and Bernhard G. He was a prosperous confectioner who owned a factory complex in Krefeld, producing waffles, cookies, and zwieback. Bernhard was Aryan and a Catholic, and Sophia was of Jewish ancestry but had converted to Catholicism. Magdalene was in Nazi eyes a *Mischling* first degree, although she, too, like her parents was a Christian, hardly surprising in the heavily Catholic Rhineland. In 1938, Magdalene G. was a vivacious and cultured thirty-year-old who had much leisure time on her hands. Until 1933 she had moved easily in the upper social circles of the Lower Rhine. Nevertheless, under the Nazis she had become a social pariah who, despite her family's wealth, lived in isolation. That same summer of 1938 saw diplomatic negotiations brewing over the Czech Sudetenland, and various diplomatic contingents were arriving in Germany to try to avert a crisis. Over a busy weekend when international dignitaries congregated in Bad Godesberg, a bored Magdalene G. made a bold decision. She checked into Godesberg's luxury Hotel Dreesen, which was soon to attract world notice when Hitler met Chamberlain there. It was true that female *Mischlinge,* no matter how attractive, were not supposed to socialize with *deutschblütig* German males, and the shadows of the 1935 Nuremberg race laws were lengthening year by year. But who had said anything about *Mischlinge* dating foreigners? Admirers of Magdalene G. were not long in materializing. Afterward, the irate mayor of her hometown, Krefeld, explained to local Gestapo authorities what happened in Bad Godesberg:

> Fräulein G., whose profession is well known [his insinuation that she was a prostitute was patently false], knew how to attract the attention of the Italian Mission and its German accompaniment. She was able to inveigle them into offering her an invitation to the ball last Friday in Düsseldorf, hosted by the Gauleiter at Schloss Benrath. At that ball she danced with an entire string of prominent personalities, including His Excellency, M. Russo.

The mayor was furious: "Naturally, these gentlemen were not aware that Fräulein G. is a half-Jew, or that her mother is a full Jew." Especially maddening for the mayor and local Nazi bigwigs was the fact that her Italian social partners exhibited not the least concern about Magdalene G.'s bloodlines. Nevertheless, her appearance at the Gauleiter's ball had raised eyebrows among German officials from the Foreign Ministry in Berlin as well as from local Party leaders. Stung by his fellow Nazis' remarks, the mayor stated to local Gestapo headquarters: "I am presenting information of this incident to you because various gentlemen in the Party have complained to me. Among them are Oberführer Pahlings and Schlutkothen. Moreover, the Führer of Standarte 40, Thiel, knows about this." In short, the local Nazi hierarchy was not amused at Magdalene G.'s entrée into the international social scene or her success in crashing their Gauleiter's ball. Yet, in the end nothing could be done. The accursed Italians were not *deutschblütig.*[18]

Although Magdalene G.'s courage was admirable, her bold social profile was not prudent. *Mischlinge* were supposed to remain anonymous. Furthermore, time was not working in favor of Magdalene G. or her parents, now that the Party fanatics increasingly were dictating their own harsh interpretations of Nazi racial policy. Then, with the onset of the war, Magdalene's family suffered a severe blow. Bernhard G. died suddenly in 1940 at age fifty-six. He, the Aryan partner in the marriage, could shield his wife and daughter no longer.

Following her father's death, former socialite Magdalene G. had to assume heavy responsibilities, since the family business was not small. It was forbidden for Magdalene's Jewish mother, Sophia G., to run the firm, so her daughter took up the reins, and against all expectations, she performed splendidly. A local Gestapo report in May 1942 admitted as much: "After G. . . . died two years ago, his daughter directed the firm, to universal approval, especially the DAF [Deutsche Arbeitsfront or German Labor Service]." In short, even the factory workers were happy with her performance. However, the authorities were anything but pleased. The report revealed new developments: "About two months ago the factory was leased to a Krefeld waffle concern with the option to purchase." In short, the Nazis had squeezed Magdalene G. and her mother out of a once prosperous and by all accounts (including labor) well-run family business.

Even worse, the reports from local Gestapo authorities revealed that they were taking an extremely jaundiced look at Sophia and her daughter Magdalene. "It has been recorded here at least once that the Jew, Sophia Sara G. . . . was treating her household personnel badly. She behaves repulsively and in a truly Jewish manner." The authorities were equally vitriolic about the *Mischling* heiress: "The daughter Magdalene is strongly suspected of having same-sex affairs with other women. The exact details are not available. However, certain well-informed circles are fully convinced of the abnormal tendencies of the half-Jew G." This was a remarkable revelation concerning the same woman whom the mayor of Krefeld had been denouncing as a favorite of the Italian diplomatic delegation a few years earlier.[19]

The same local Gestapo official also reported another "egregious" incident, a social happening in September 1941 between Magdalene G. and a prominent radio singer, Wilhelm S., who was employed by the Westdeutscher Rundfunk (West German Radio). Impressario Wilhelm S. had sung with great success at a KdF (Kraft durch Freude, a Nazi recreation organization) gathering at Krefeld's Convention Center. A local Gestapo official reported:

After the conclusion of the performance, he [Wilhelm S.] was invited to dinner by the half-Jew, Magdalene G. . . . and he accepted. By mere chance, the Director of the City Convention Center, Herr Kreische, was present during this conversation, and he made it known to K. . . . that he was being invited to a Jewish family for dinner. The latter then turned to him with a smile and replied that if the Chief of the SA [Viktor] Lutze could present an autographed picture of himself to the Family G. . . . then he could just as well go there for dinner.[20]

In short, she had charmed yet another celebrity.

Alas, Magdalene's social successes served only to further enrage the Gestapo, and they monitored her activities intensively. Agents read all of her mail, noting that she was corresponding with certain persons in Wiesbaden and Chemnitz. Most sinister of all in their estimation was the fact that she was still corresponding with her mother. This was hardly surprising considering that the luckless Sophia G., a full Jew, had in the meantime been "evacuated" to Theresienstadt. The Gestapo man wondered why the daughter was so brazen as to continue communicating with her mother with the help of the Reichsvereinigung der Juden (Reich Organization for Jews). Why indeed.[21]

In early November 1942, an agent intercepted a deeply personal letter from a young Luftwaffe pilot, Hubertus L., who had just flown back to Wiesbaden from a dangerous long-distance mission to Casablanca. The aviator explained to Magdalene G. that he had just lost a large number of his squadron mates, had barely escaped death himself, and realized now for the first time how precious life was. Further, he referred to the fantastic night they had enjoyed together and hoped they would be able to remain in contact. The Gestapo copied down the letter verbatim, leaving out no detail. By this time their file on Magdalene G. was starting to bulge.[22]

Meanwhile Magdalene G. had to confront other problems. In late September 1942, the local SS Führer in Düsseldorf needed an alternate command central. He reported that confectioner Bernhard G. and his wife were now both deceased (actually Sophia G. was in Theresienstadt). The factory was closed due to a lack of critical food ingredients. Thus, waffle heiress Magdalene G., a *Mischling* first degree without any visible means of income, could now be stripped of both her German citizenship and her factory. The latter would serve nicely as an SS reserve command center.[23]

The final Gestapo report of 1943 on the heiress indicated success of another kind: "Presently, she has retreated into the background. Every now and then she visits a theater or a concert in Düsseldorf. The house she had been occupying in Krefeld . . . has in the meantime been assigned to bombed-out persons, so that she is now living in one of its attic rooms." While she was still unruly enough to correspond with acquaintances in Chemnitz and Wiesbaden and with her mother in Theresienstadt, the Gestapo authorities admitted that her communications contained nothing subversive. Neither was Magdalene G. in touch anymore with celebrities such as impressario Wilhelm S. or war heroes like pilot Hubertus L. The Gestapo decided that she had gotten their message, and they could now dispense with intensive monitoring of Magdalene G. Her isolation was complete.[24]

To be sure, young men relegated to the category of *Mischling* also suffered evil consequences from the Nazis' Nuremberg race laws. As noted earlier, nothing aroused their visceral hatred of Jews more than the notion of a Jewish man having sexual relations with an Aryan woman. Repeatedly, Hitler railed against the idea in *Mein Kampf*, and it was one of the favorite themes in Julius Streicher's pornography-riddled publication, *Der Stürmer*. Since full Jews had begun disappearing from German society, starting with the pogrom of 9 November 1938, a process that was virtually complete with the removal of all Jews to the East by 1941, the offense of *Rassenschande* came to be leveled by default against half-Jews in wartime Germany.

Born in 1920 to a Jewish mother and a Christian father in Elberfeld, Rolf B. was raised as a Christian. In fact, through most of his childhood he was unaware of his mother's religious persuasion. His working-class parents separated when he was young, and Rolf struggled to complete his elementary education while living with his mother. However, if family life and school were not exactly ideal, he found other outlets. In 1932, at age twelve, Rolf B. entered the Hitler Youth, before the Nazis seized power. As an early HJ member he was exhilarated at entering in timely fashion into what became Germany's mainstream youth movement. Then, in 1935, the bottom fell out of his life. With the Nuremberg laws in effect, his mother admitted to Rolf that she was Jewish. Devastated, he resigned from the youth organization, avoiding a painful scene whereby youth leaders and other boys could have stripped him, a *Mischling*, of his prized badges and uniform. Never a keen pupil, Rolf nevertheless finished elementary school and found employment as a clerk. In 1939, his Jewish mother, now divorced and without the protection of a "privileged mixed marriage," was sent to the East, ultimately to Theresienstadt. Somehow, Rolf carried on despite his mother's uncertain fate.

Then in the autumn of 1940 he got his big chance. Aged twenty, Rolf joined the Luftwaffe and became a member of a signals company in Augsburg. At last he experienced success, and the Luftwaffe seemed to be none the wiser about his *Mischling* status. Applying himself, he completed basic and airman specialist training. Best of all, he fit in well with his mates. Training complete, Lance Corporal Rolf B. departed with his comrades to an aerodrome in Bavaria. At last he was experiencing that sense of comradeship that he had felt earlier in the HJ. Then, on 3 June 1942, Rolf's world fell apart — again. Ordered to report to his company commander that morning, he came to attention and saluted smartly. Without any preliminaries, the officer informed Rolf that as of that moment, he was dismissed from military service. He was *wehrdienstunwürdig* — in short, dishonorably discharged. The authorities had finally discovered that he was a *Mischling* first degree. Devastated, Rolf returned to his hometown of Elberfeld. Hounded by his dismissal plus the stigma of being a *Mischling*, he had to accept work as an unskilled laborer, earning thirty-five marks per month. Still, somehow he got by, enduring long days of heavy labor and loneliness. Then, in July 1942, he met a young woman who would forever change his life.

Hilde S. was also from Elberfeld, and in the summer of 1942 she was an unhappy woman. At age twenty she had married the man with whom she had had her first affair. Even so, she made that decision only after learning that she was pregnant. From the first their marriage was a disaster. Her new husband was conscripted within a few months, and she heard almost nothing from him while he was away. He never called and seldom wrote. In fact, in one of his letters he even admitted that he was seeing other women. Moreover, when he returned on leave, he brazenly dated other women, too. Finally, in April 1942, during yet another home leave, he was sitting in a local pub with one of his dates when by chance Hilde S. entered the establishment. Infuriated by his wife's chance encounter, he became abusive and created an ugly scene, whereupon she ran out of the bar. Soon after, her husband/soldier/philanderer returned to his unit. It was just at this time that their only child became gravely ill, and Hilde S. hospitalized the boy. Dutifully, she sent word to her husband but received no answer. That was the last straw for Hilde S. She filed for divorce.

A few months later and by sheer chance, she met Rolf B. in the local market when the two fell into conversation. Hilda S. was solicitous and obviously lonely. She was impressed by Rolf B. and was not put off by his shyness. Understandably, Rolf was flattered by the attentions of an interested young woman, and they began to see each other more regularly. In the autumn of 1942, they fell in love. Initially, Rolf visited Hilde briefly on weekend evenings. Then, he began staying with her overnight. True, Rolf departed early each morning in order to avoid contact with neighbors in the apartment complex. Unbeknownst to Hilda and Rolf, a woman who lived next door had observed the budding romance and quickly informed one of her friends, Aurelie S., who, in turn, informed other neighbors. Soon, the entire apartment building was abuzz. One of the neighbors was aware that Rolf B. was half-Jewish, and armed with this knowledge, the neighbor then informed the police. On 2 December 1942, the police arrested Rolf B. and charged him with having "sexual relations with a soldier's wife." They remanded him to the custody of the Gestapo. The latter noted that he was a former HJ member, Luftwaffe veteran, and had no criminal record. Furthermore, he was single, employed, and not a burden upon the state. And yet, this counted for little. From the very beginning the Gestapo officials took an intense dislike to Rolf B. They underlined the fact (literally) that currently his income amounted to a measly thirty-five marks per month. "He gives the impression of being soft and unmanly," one official added. "He seems to be slow and is terribly anxiety-ridden." Meanwhile, Rolf B., emotionally crushed for the third time in his life, crouched alone in a Gestapo cell.

To her credit, Hilda S. came forward immediately on Rolf's behalf (although he could hardly have known that). On the day following his arrest, she produced a frank testimony to the Gestapo, recounting in excruciating detail her loveless marriage and virtual abandonment by her faithless husband. She tried to dispel vicious rumors by her neighbors (who unbeknownst to her were making depositions on the same day). For example, Hilda confirmed that she was not pregnant, contrary to neighborhood gossip. She stated emphatically that Rolf B. had had absolutely nothing to do with her decision to obtain a divorce. She admitted to only one fact. Initially, she said, she had not known that Rolf was a *Mischling*. A neighbor had told her, and when queried, Rolf had immediately admitted to her that he was indeed a *Mischling* first degree. Hilda S. assured the authorities that she had continued her relationship with open eyes.

Hilda's defiant testimony did her lover little good. After a few weeks in Gestapo custody and following a new empowerment of 17 December 1942 granted to the Gestapo's powerful Abteilung II in Berlin, the secret police sent Rolf B. directly to a camp on 1 February 1943. Then, in early May, an anonymous official typed in a simple footnote under Rolf's prisoner photograph: "Died at Concentration Camp Auschwitz on 17 April 1943." The chronicler did not feel it necessary to note cause of death. Rolf B. had not yet attained his twenty-third birthday.[25]

Some *Mischlinge* paid a heavy price simply for having the wrong friends. While it was true that the Nazis always considered Jews as enemies, they initially saw Communists and hard-core Social Democrats as their more immediate threat. That was why they incarcerated large numbers of them in 1933 and intensively monitored the activities of exile groups. Jews or others thought to belong to either of those political groups were especially suspicious and could expect no mercy from the Nazis. The case of Erna M. is instructive. Erna M., a native of Düsseldorf, was a *Mischling* first degree who had married an older man, Karl H., of Aryan background. By the time war had broken out, the couple was residing in Cologne with their two young children. Erna and Karl had both been Social Democrats before 1933, and they still had contact with former Socialist friends, including an émigré couple who had settled in Brussels after 1933. Erna M. had visited them several times in the late 1930s, and her exile friends asked her about general conditions of life in wartime Germany. Then, at one point, the émigré couple began to ask more probing details about conditions in the Third Reich. The war came, but the two couples remained in touch.

Then, sometime late in 1942, their friends in Belgium made an unusual request. They asked Erna M. to provide hospitality for one of their Dutch friends who was traveling through Cologne. She did so, unaware of the man's true identity. In May 1943, the Gestapo, who had been following the stranger's movements, pounced. They arrested both Erna and Karl for aiding a member of the Dutch Resistance. He was also a Communist by Gestapo standards. It was not at all clear that Erna and Karl had known of the status of the person they had aided. In sentencing Karl H., the Gestapo gave him, an Aryan, the benefit of the doubt. He received one year of imprisonment. The Gestapo's judgment upon Erna was vastly different. She was a *Mischling* first degree.

Various protocols from forced interrogations, each harsher than the one before, revealed that she, by now a terrified woman, had been eager to help the alleged Communist Dutch agent. They sentenced her, a half-Jew, to twelve years of imprisonment. The chances of any prisoner surviving twelve years of incarceration in a Gestapo-run prison were remote. Unfortunately, the records do not indicate the ultimate fate of Erna M. and her husband, Karl M. Clearly, Erna M., mother of two children, received no mercy at all. After all, she was a *Mischling*.[26]

By European standards, Germany was a sizable nation in terms of territory, and, even under the Nazis, economic and social conditions varied from region to region. Moreover, the National Socialist party apparatus often reflected those regional variations. Some areas were more ardently National Socialist than others. Protestant Franconia in northern Bavaria (mostly Bavaria was Catholic), an economically depressed area, had been an early hotbed of National Socialist fervor, and its local Nazi leadership seemed to be especially virulent in its anti-Semitism. After all, the Gauleiter in that region was Julius Streicher, editor of *Der Stürmer*. The Sudetenland in the former Czechoslovakia was another center of anti-Semitism, and the Gauleiter of Rhineland-Pfalz (Palatinate) was especially ardent in trying to make his Gau *judenfrei* (free of Jews) earlier than anyone else. Thus, in the end, it came down to local officials and the varying intensity of local prejudices in the population making the difference as to whether Jews or *Mischlinge* would suffer milder or more extreme effects from persecution. There were some areas of Germany where traditionally there had been few Jews, and as a consequence, the notion of anti-Semitism seemed remote. This is not to say that anti-Semitism was absent in such areas. It was simply less obvious. The case of Martha Rohr bears this out.

Martha Rohr, a *Mischling* orphan born in Berlin in 1918 but raised by the Knebels, a peasant family in remote Wintersdorf near the Luxembourg border, had suffered no discrimination in childhood. She finished elementary school at age fourteen like all the other village children and divided her time between working in the fields by day and working evenings as a waitress in the family pub, the Gasthof zum Bahnof. It was the only pub in town and a busy place in the late 1930s, since so many construction workers, military personnel, and Party officials were laboring on Hitler's West Wall (Siegfried

Line). They gathered at the inn after work. Thus, Martha, blessed with good looks and a pleasing personality, served hordes of appreciative young men every evening.

Her status as a social standout carried its attendant dangers. It was widely known in the village that Martha was an adopted daughter and half-Jewish. Wintersdorf's Ortsgruppenleiter, Hans Dokter, had taken an immediate dislike toward the girl when he arrived in 1933. Lacking full Jews as targets of discrimination, he fastened on her even when she was a schoolgirl, monitoring her public conduct during Nazi ceremonial occasions to see if she had rendered the proper Hitler salute. However, as she blossomed into adulthood, he became obsessed with the fact that she was now in daily contact with numerous engineers, construction men, military personnel, and Party members. Martha was cautious and dated none of the pub's patrons and hardly any village youths. Even so, her social life bothered Ortsgruppenleiter Dokter. Finally, in mid-1940, he acted. Hans Dokter demanded that Martha be subjected to an intensive physical examination by a team of three public health officials in the district capital, Trier. Accordingly, she set off for the Öffentliches Gesundheitsamt, Trier's public health bureau.

The three National Socialist medical examiners told her outright that they were there to determine from her physiognomy whether or not she was more Jewish than Aryan. Under humiliating circumstances, Martha Rohr was forced to disrobe before three strange men and was subjected to a minute examination of every part of her body. Thus, Martha Rohr suffered the same humiliations that other young Germans like Eva Heilmann in Berlin, Alexander Heintz in Frankfurt, or Anna H. in Krefeld had had to endure. Like Krefelder Anna H., Martha was age twenty-three when this decisive moment of her life arrived. In contrast to Anna H., Rohr had never attended a Jewish school; neither had she attracted the attention of the Gestapo. It was Ortsgruppenleiter Dokter who had initiated the examination. The three medical officials set about measuring the shape of her head. They noted the color of her hair and eyes. They paid special attention to the shape of her earlobes. They examined her body mass, gauged the shape of her breasts (not so pendulous as to arouse suspicions of her carrying too much "Jewish blood," the judgment that had befallen Eva Heilmann). They also took evidence about her personality and looked through official records to see if she had committed any crimes or had been found to be antisocial. Finally, the Nazi examiners reached their conclusion: Martha Rohr was more Aryan than Jewish in appearance. She could return to Wintersdorf. Unlike so many other hapless *Mischlinge* in Germany, Martha retained her job in the private sector, albeit as daytime field hand on the family farm and as serving girl in the family pub.

However, Martha Rohr was still very much a *Mischling*, and there were sharp limits to her socializing. Aware of Ortsgruppenleiter Dokter's continuing malevolence, Martha exercised extreme caution in dealing with others. Long attuned to local customs, she noticed that not only the Ortsgruppenleiter was monitoring her relationships with everyone. Other villagers who had known her from infancy were doing the same. Then it occurred to her that she had never been asked to join the BDM, the girls' youth group, in her teenage years, the only village girl so excluded. During the war, especially when the tide turned against Germany, she noticed that fellow villagers grew ever cooler toward her. Thus, it was of questionable advantage when one of the young men of her village, Nicholas Rohr, fell in love with Martha. They went out on innocent dates, and she was impressed with his sincerity. However, marriage remained out of the question for her, the only *Mischling* for miles around. The crime of *Rassenschande* had become widely discussed in the war years, and it had reached even remote Wintersdorf. Besides, she did not want to endanger Nicholas either. Consequently, the would-be lovers kept their distance even though such isolation ran against their desires, especially in wartime.

It was a moot point anyway. Drafted in 1943, Nicholas went off to war, and he and Martha lost touch. The village gave him up for dead, but in 1947, an ill and emaciated Nicholas Rohr limped home from captivity in Lorraine. Martha helped nurse him back to health, but by then the ravages of his ordeal had stolen all his teeth and his youthful good looks. Nevertheless, they married, stayed in Wintersdorf, and started a family. Although her social life and courtship had not been ideal, compared with the experiences of most other *Mischlinge*, Martha had survived comparatively intact.[27]

German citizens who were simultaneously homosexuals and *Mischlinge* were at least as rare as rustic *Mischling* orphans like Martha Rohr. Ever since the late nineteenth century, homosexuality in Germany had been defined as illegal under Paragraph 175 of the Kaiserreich's criminal code, and it remained illegal under National Socialism. Although as many as fifty thousand men (almost no women were prosecuted) were punished for homosexuality between 1933 and 1945, even Heinrich Himmler estimated that as many as two million German men were homosexuals. Of those punished, between five thousand and fifteen thousand men (estimates vary) were sent to concentration camps. It was then that real horror ensued. Once incarcerated, homosexuals suffered especially harsh treatment. Over 60 percent of them died in those camps, a higher mortality rate than was the case for other non-Jewish groups such as Jehovah's Witnesses or political prisoners. Nevertheless, the Nazi leadership, including Hitler, displayed some ambivalence toward (i.e., tacit tolerance of) homosexuality, as the prominent career of SA leader Ernst Röhm demonstrated — at least until his murder out of political expediency during the purge of 30 June 1934. Thus, the Nazis never attempted systematically to comb out all homosexuals from society with the intention of killing them the way they did with full Jews. Most homosexuals were either never caught or else were reprimanded and warned, "reeducated," or "cured." This was the experience, at least, of "ordinary" Germans.[28] Those who were not ordinary (i.e., *Mischlinge* still living within society) had to reckon with an utterly different attitude toward homosexuality by authorities. In short, *Mischlinge* faced severe consequences for having the wrong kind of friendship. Not surprisingly, they experienced severe inequality of treatment under the National Socialist legal system even by comparison to so-called Aryan homosexuals. The following episode bears out this aspect of Nazi discrimination.

Heinz K., the eldest son of Georg and Elfriede K., was born in Upper Silesia in 1919. Heinz's mother died when he was two. His father remarried and moved eventually to Dortmund. The boy finished school there and was apprenticed to an iron and steel works in Dortmund. Heinz K. was an idealistic youth and at age twenty volunteered for military service. He had already been an eager Hitler Youth participant, admitted first to the elite Naval HJ and then to the equally selective Motorized HJ. He performed his RAD (National Labor Service) enthusiastically in 1938–39, and in late August 1939, only a few days before the outbreak of war, Heinz K. volunteered for the Wehrmacht. He was "as fleet as a greyhound, tough as leather, and as hard as Krupp steel," to use Hitler's favorite phrase about National Socialist youth. Nor did Heinz disappoint his leaders. He served in a highly respected battalion of combat engineers and distinguished himself as a first-rate soldier at the front.

Günther O., born in Essen in 1922, also turned into a fine young soldier. At age eighteen, he volunteered and was soon serving in active combat on various fronts from 1940 onward. In fact, he was rated as one of the best soldiers in his company. It also transpired that in 1940, while on home leave back in Germany, Günther O. met Heinz K. The two young men found that they had much in common, being enthusiastic former HJ members and now highly regarded soldiers. What set them apart from most other German youth was the fact that Heinz and Günther proceeded to have an affair with each other.

Given the stigma attached to homosexual relationships in Nazi Germany, it was surprising that the two young men were able to continue their relationship undetected for several years. In fact, their relationship only came under official scrutiny after Günther O. was discovered to be a *Mischling* first degree. Despite his exemplary record as a combat engineer, the authorities dismissed Günther from the Wehrmacht on 21 December 1942. Stripped of his uniform (and decorations), Günther O. returned in disgrace to his native Essen and became an electrician's assistant. However, he continued his affair with Heinz K., who by this time was back in Germany, serving in a medical unit. Apparently neither of the young men was aware that civilian Günther O. and in Nazi eyes a *Mischling*, might come under special scrutiny. In the spring of 1943, the police suddenly took Günther O. into custody (Heinz K. still enjoyed the protection of the Wehrmacht and was not arrested). Günther O. posed thorny problems for the chief prosecuting attorney in Essen. Whereas normally, the National Socialist legal system would have come down with great severity on a *Mischling* who was simultaneously a homosexual, it balked when confronted with Günther O. He had compiled an unblemished civilian record and a glowing military record. "It has to be recognized," admitted the chief prosecuting attorney for Essen, "that the accused has comported himself extremely well at the front. It must also be emphasized that he was regarded as one of the best soldiers in his company." Nevertheless, the official noted, Günther O. had continued his long-term affair with Heinz K. and was undeniably guilty of having committed "unnatural acts." Therefore, on 4 May 1943 the authorities sentenced him to three months of imprisonment in a civilian jail plus a hefty fine. As sentences went in National Socialist Germany — at least for a *Mischling* — the verdict was mild. Then again, Günther O.'s Aryan partner, Heinz K., had not suffered the indignity of being dishonorably discharged from military service the way that decorated soldier Günther O. had been dismissed. Nor was he prosecuted or imprisoned and fined by civilian authorities as his *Mischling* friend was (in the meantime a military court-martial had examined Heinz K.'s offense and issued a mild rebuke). It comes as no surprise that there was a double standard in the Nazis' legal system for Aryans and *Mischlinge,* even with regard to homosexuality.[29]

To an overwhelming extent, the Nazis treated homosexuality as a male abnormality and seldom applied its criminal code against women. For example, approximately a thousand men in Germany were convicted of homosexual acts in 1934, with the figure rising to over five thousand in 1936. By contrast only four women received convictions in 1934, and only six were found guilty two years later.[30] Such lopsided statistics notwithstanding, women who were *Mischlinge* were far likelier to suffer unwanted attention from the authorities if claims arose that they were conducting lesbian affairs with Aryan women, especially if the woman was married to a soldier in wartime. The case of Friedl and Hans E. as well as "the other woman," Edna S., demonstrates this point.

Disintegration of marriages in wartime was common. Essen natives, Aryans Friedl E. and Hans E. had married in 1933 while in their twenties. It was in March 1943 that Hans, by now a lance corporal in the Luftwaffe, came home on leave to a less-than-joyous reunion with Friedl. Friedl had undergone an operation in January 1943, and during her convalescence, a young woman of her acquaintance, Edna S., had moved into the apartment. Friedl needed care during her lengthy recovery. Edna had recently been bombed out of her dwelling and needed shelter. For both women the arrangement made good sense.

Unfortunately, Hans E. did not see it that way. Despite the fact that their marriage had shown severe strains for years, Hans E. convinced himself that Friedl and Edna were conducting an affair. He immediately denounced his wife and the unfortunate Edna S. to the state police, alleging a lesbian relationship. "My wife's attitude towards me reveals that she no longer has any use for me," he stated to the authorities. "I discovered that at the beginning of January of this year a woman who had been bombed out had now been relocated in our apartment. This woman is, according to my inquiries, a half-

Jew. Because of the relationship that exists between my wife and this half-Jew, I must conclude that they have established a lesbian relationship." Hans E. demanded an investigation, and if, as he expected, the authorities confirmed his accusations, he would sue for divorce.

Divorce for Friedl E. was one thing. Charges of homosexuality against Edna S. were another. Fortunately, after their arrest both women filed depositions that corroborated each other's claims. "Our marriage has been broken for years," Friedl E. told the state police. "My husband is so furious and so jealous — without reason — that he has turned my life into a living hell. His low character has become obvious now that he has accused me shamelessly of having a lesbian relationship with [Edna S.]." Friedl E. maintained with great vehemence that the presence of Edna S. had nothing to do with the repulsion she had developed toward her husband. Meanwhile, Edna S., who knew full well the Nazi attitudes toward *Mischlinge*, stated emphatically that Hans E.'s accusations were ludicrous: "I have normal desires," she explained to her interrogators, "and I have no need for such relationships. Therefore, I never noticed if Frau E. had any such desires. In my opinion Frau E. in the aftermath of her operation and as a consequence of her disappointments in her marriage no longer had any interest in her husband. However, as a result of our conversations, I could tell that with respect to sexual orientation she was perfectly normal."

That statement was not precise enough for her questioners. Edna S. added, or was forced to add: "Upon questioning, I declare to you explicitly that I have never exchanged any intimacies with Frau E. We have never kissed each other or exchanged any intimacies of any kind. Also, we never slept together in a bed." Evidently, at this point her questioners finally gave up their attempts at eliciting any admission of a lesbian affair from the hapless Edna S. Even so there was one more item on their agenda. Under pressure from her interrogators, Edna S. was compelled to add a corollary to her statement concerning any future relationship she might have with men: "I am fully informed that I, as a *Mischling* first degree, am not allowed to have any relationships with *deutschblütig* men. I am especially not permitted to have sexual relations with them. I have been warned once again explicitly against such relationships by possible measures by the authorities of the State Police."[31] It was well that Edna S. had warded off such accusations. By 1943, the Nazi authorities, had they acquired any confirming evidence, would gladly have charged her with destroying the marriage of a German soldier, thereby weakening the morale of the German nation. As several of the cases described in this study demonstrate, *Mischlinge* convicted on such charges would have ended up in a concentration camp, and by 1943 that fate was nearly always fatal.

To be sure, heterosexual women placed in the status of *Mischlinge* were far likelier to attract the unwelcome attention of nosy private citizens, the police, and the Gestapo than were Aryan lesbians. As noted, denunciations by private citizens had become a plague on German society, and while these "eyes and ears" of the police were often ignored if they targeted Aryan Germans, that was not the case when denunciations targeted *Mischlinge*. Moreover, in wartime the tempo of denunciations increased perceptibly. With it, a peculiar danger arose for female *Mischlinge* perceived by snooping individuals as being too friendly to soldiers. Allegations of *Rassenschande* in wartime could have nasty consequences, as the case of Johanna B. reveals.

Johanna B. was young and attractive in 1941, and she lived in the center of Düsseldorf, close to its well-known nightlife. Given her friendly personality and good looks, it was inevitable that young men in her age group would find her attractive. In wartime Germany, such suitors were mostly men in uniform. Unbeknownst to Hanni — she preferred her nickname — another apartment dweller in the same building, Parteigenosse (Party Comrade or simply PG) Heinrich Johannes, was monitoring her social activities carefully. Finally, in the spring of 1941, Johannes denounced Hanni B. to the Ortsgruppenleiter in Düsseldorf. She was immediately detained and interrogated. Courtesy of PG Johannes, Hanni's questioners even knew the names of her Wehrmacht friends. The interrogators got to the point quickly. Had she had sex with Lieutenant Richard S. or with Sergeant Alfred P. or with Lance Corporal Edward S., they asked?

Showing considerable poise, Hanni B. answered with equal frankness: "With respect to the explicit question as to which Wehrmacht personnel with whom I have had sexual relations, I must reply that I have had no such relations with any soldier!" She did admit that three years earlier on New Year's Eve 1938, she had gone to bed with Edward S., but that was long before he became a soldier. The same interrogation also revealed to her why she was currently being interrogated by the authorities. Someone in close proximity to her apartment had informed on her. The police demanded to know why she had had Heinz W. in her apartment the previous night! Unflustered,

Hanni B. stated that Heinz W. was a musician whom she knew casually from a performance at a popular nightclub nearby. After the evening performance, he had accompanied her home, since it was dark and she was alone. Just as they reached her apartment, the air-raid sirens sounded. They had taken cover in her building, specifically at the apartment she shared with her parents. Suddenly, after taking shelter, there was a sharp knock at the door. It was a policeman who demanded Heinz W.'s identity papers. After Hanni B. asked why he had happened to appear, he explained that he had just received a telephone complaint. The caller claimed that an Aryan was staying overnight with a Jew and had given the apartment building and Hanni's apartment number. Obviously, PG Johannes had spent a busy night, spying on Hanni B. She reiterated her statement that she was not having affairs with anyone in uniform.

However, frankness and courage could carry a *Mischling* like Hanni B. only so far with the Gestapo. Under pressure, she signed the following statement: "I am aware that marriage to a man of German blood requires official approval." However, she could not resist adding a slight qualifier. "To be sure, I was not aware that I am not supposed to have any interaction with men of German blood at all." Nevertheless, recognizing that too much defiance could be dangerous, she gave the minimum necessary obeisance: "It has now been explained to me that in interacting socially with men, I am to show the greatest restraint. The Staatspolizei [State Police] will not tolerate my having sexual relations with men of German blood. Should it transpire that I have violated this lesson and this warning, I can reckon with the most severe consequences from the State Police." Hanni B. then signed the document with a defiant flourish, unusual for prisoners who had just been subjected to interrogation. It was countersigned by Assistant Criminal Inspector Putz, who, following Hanni's lead, tried signing with a flourish, too. In his case the result looked swollen and artificial.[32]

For Hanni B. it was just as well that PG Johannes's denunciation had occurred early in the war. A similar denunciation and subsequent Gestapo interrogation in 1943, 1944, or 1945 might have ended differently. Her case also revealed that the Gestapo was in many ways becoming a law unto itself. The 1935 Nuremberg decree that banned marriages between *Mischlinge* and *deutschblütig* Germans had been silent about unofficial liaisons. Yet, by 1941, the Gestapo, as several cases mentioned earlier demonstrate, was systematically requiring signed statements of *Mischlinge* in cases of suspected

Rassenschande. The threat was not idle. Repeat offenders could reckon with the concentration camp, and *Mischlinge* convicted of destroying a soldier's marriage could expect no mercy whatsoever. Even so, Hanni B.'s experience showed another dimension. Without being openly defiant, she had nevertheless demonstrated composure and self-control during her tense interrogation. That was just as well. Not known for their sensitivity, Gestapo officials tended to show less mercy to victims who quailed, pled for mercy, or in other ways demonstrated fear.

For *Mischlinge* who, for whatever reason, found themselves caught up in the legal system, there was the danger that, once noticed, their situation became precarious. Marital status was critical. If the *Mischlinge* were unmarried or divorced, then they were often subject to special scrutiny by neighbors, coworkers, and busybodies who seemed to take pleasure in spying on non-Aryan "strays." Denunciations could have a devastating effect because, as noted earlier, once a *Mischling* was enmeshed in the legal system, its authorities often found ways to conjure up additional charges. Then the authorities could isolate the victim from society in the most drastic way: permanent incarceration. In the Nazi experience, that often meant transfer to a concentration camp. That was the authorities' ultimate demonstration of drawing the line between *Mischlinge* and the rest of a society in which full Jews had, for all practical purposes, already disappeared. The fate of Karl M., a native of Elberfeld living in Wuppertal, bears out this generalization. His fate also demonstrates how the coincidence of birth, growth, and coming of age in combination with evolving Nazi persecution could affect people's lives profoundly.

Karl M. was born in 1912 and therefore was age twenty-one when Hitler came to power. He was already engaged in January 1933, and subsequently married Alwine S. a few months later. The timing was important, given the fact that Karl M. was soon to become, by Nazi standards, a *Mischling* first degree and Alwine S. an Aryan. Had they deferred their marriage longer, the Nuremberg decrees of 1935 would have forbidden such a union. The marriage of Karl M. and Alwine S. was not happy, and it remained childless. The two divorced in the autumn of 1941.

In the meantime, Karl M. had reported for military service in November 1939. Had he done so even a few weeks earlier, he would have probably been one of thousands of young men who entered the armed services despite his status as a *Mischling*. However, the hardened attitudes within the NSDAP were such that the authorities, instead of inducting him immediately (as they would have done in September 1939), placed his file on hold pending further investigation. Then they ordered Karl M. to appear before a Reichssippenamt (Reich Office for Genealogical Affairs) in Berlin. He filed a formal statement to the Berlin office in late 1939 and enclosed all genealogical records available on his family. He also laid out his family's background and his religious affiliations from childhood to the present. For unknown reasons, the bureaucratic wheels ground especially slowly in his case. Two years passed. Finally, on 4 April 1942, Karl M. was informed that according to the Nuremberg decree of 1935 on citizenship, he was, by current definition, a Jew. It transpired that because he had formally left the local Jewish community of Wuppertal only on 8 May 1939, he was, according to their definition, worse than a *Mischling* first degree. He was a *Geltungsjude*. Furthermore, he no longer had an Aryan wife to shield him.

In the meantime following his divorce, Karl M. had become a common laborer in Remscheidt, earning forty Reichsmarks per month. To be sure, by 1942 such work and meager earnings had become commonplace among *Mischlinge* like Karl M. His situation had also grown precarious in other ways. All Germans had to carry identification cards, but Karl M. had not been able to provide final information for that card during the two years his files were pending in Berlin. Finally in June 1942, after the Reichssippenamt had made its decision, a local police official sought him out and demanded three identification photos that would be affixed to his *Judenkennkarte* (i.e., his identification card as a Jew). Since the autumn of 1941 his reduced circumstances had meant that he had to live in a room provided by his aunt who was Jewish. They lived on a small residential street in Wuppertal-Elberfeld.

It transpired that a young woman, Erna B., also lived on the same street in a small apartment. Her husband had been on active duty as a soldier since the spring of 1940. They were childless, and she worked full-time for the city's public transportation service. Karl's aunt, an elderly woman, lived across the street, and her daughter helped Erna B. by cleaning the entranceway to her apartment periodically while she was at work. Then, in October 1941, nephew Karl began residing with his aunt and her daughter. The two families on opposite sides of the street were on friendly terms, and Karl M., while helping maintain his aunt's and cousin's apartment, also helped neighbor Erna B.

with her apartment. For example, he made sure that the emergency kerosene lamps were functioning and that the heavy air-raid curtains met city standards now that Allied bombing raids were common. These acts of neighborliness had fateful consequences.

At the end of July 1942, a nearby housewife informed on Erna B. to the Gestapo in Wuppertal. It transpired that Hedwig Birkenstock did not like Erna B., and she claimed that she had seen Karl M. and Erna B. in intimate contact with each other. By this she meant that she had sat down at her apartment window and had stared across the street into her neighbor's window. Erna B., aware of this unwanted attention, stared back, and the two women exchanged words. Shortly after, Hedwig Birkenstock filed her denunciation with the Gestapo. As was often the case, the wheels of Nazi justice moved quickly, since a *Mischling* was involved. Within days, the Gestapo took depositions from three neighborhood women, all of whom stated that they had seen Karl M. in Erna B.'s apartment. Thereupon, the Gestapo arrested Karl M. and interrogated both him and Erna B. Each stated unequivocally that they had not engaged in *Rassenschande*. However, Karl M.'s status as a *Mischling* and worse, his status as a *Geltungsjude*, aroused intense interest. As they had done with other *Mischlinge*, the Gestapo threw the book at Karl M. The authorities forced him to confess that, as a *Geltungsjude*, he was supposed to have worn the yellow Star of David in public. Furthermore, he had to confess that he should have signed all documents with the obligatory middle name of Israel. Karl M.'s counterarguments that he had only had a final decision of his status by the Rassen-und Sippenamt in Berlin and the subsequent allocation of a *Judenkennkarte* just the previous month counted for nothing with the Gestapo. They kept him under arrest.

In early October 1942, the Wuppertal Gestapo reviewed his status, noting particularly that he was not only a *Mischling* first degree but also a *Geltungsjude*. They repeated the previous charges of failing to wear the Star of David and of signing his name improperly. Then the Gestapo rendered its judgment. One official observed that "M. . . . gives an impression of inscrutability. He appears anxious and he promises everything but then does not hold to it as his previous existence demonstrates. Therefore, continued protective custody and delivery to a concentration camp appear justified. M. . . . is divorced. His marriage was childless. His wife was an Aryan . . . and is now remarried for the second time." Other officials agreed. Since Karl M. had no dependents and was, in effect, unprotected, and since he could not perform military service, the local Gestapo had no qualms about their decision. At the end of October 1942, they transported Karl M. to Buchenwald. Subsequently, he was "relocated" to the East. On 1 March 1943, Camp Commandant Rudolf Höss at Auschwitz forwarded another of his terse telegrams to Gestapo headquarters in Düsseldorf, announcing that on 22 February 1943 at 1:45 P.M., Karl M. had "died in the Camp Infirmary of KL [Concentration Camp] Auschwitz from an infection of his heart muscle." Höss informed the Gestapo authorities that Karl M.'s ashes had already been interred and that the same authorities could inform the father of his son's death. National Socialist Germany had no use for *Mischlinge* and especially no use for divorced *Geltungsjuden* with a penchant for neighborly kindness to Aryan war wives.[33]

CONCLUSION

Because of the increasing fanaticism with which the Nazis interpreted their race laws, such as the Nuremberg decrees of 1935, those German citizens relegated to the category of *Mischlinge* suffered increasingly harsh restrictions. Like Germany's full Jews, they, too, discovered invisible walls rising up around them, the main difference being timing. Intensified restrictions and increasingly hostile interpretations of those restrictions by officials meant that the *Mischlinge* had become the targets of choice in the next wave of anti-Semitic fury (now that Germany's Jews were already socially isolated and destined for the camps) propagated by the Nazis in the war years. Those Germans of partial Jewish descent who experienced National Socialist persecution as they advanced from childhood through adolescence to young adulthood were particularly vulnerable to this isolation. Not confined to ghettos or sent to camps — yet — they were forced to function within society. The normal human desire to interact, to work, to socialize, to form romantic attachments, and to marry posed great hazards for them. Faced with the real prospect of incarceration by the Gestapo or by other authorities for such so-called crimes as *Rassenschande*, they found themselves sealed off from the very society in which they still lived. Furthermore, it became obvious that infractions that other citizens might have committed, but which were often overlooked by the authorities, were infractions for which the *Mischlinge* paid dearly. Equally disheartening for them, the *Mischlinge* began to realize that informers were in their midst and that almost no one could be trusted. As a result of these dangers, which only worsened over time, almost all *Mischlinge* withdrew inwardly from society. Consciously or unconsciously, they adopted a low profile. In their desire for anonymity, they took fewer and fewer friends into their confidence and in self-defense built walls between themselves and others. It was a survival strategy that helped most — but not all — to survive until May 1945. However, it was a survival technique that took a heavy emotional toll. German citizens cast in the role of *Mischlinge* in Hitler's Germany were destined to suffer the effects of social ostracism for the rest of their lives.

4

The Penultimate Step: Forced Labor

Raul Hilberg in his study of the Holocaust and Jeremy Noakes in his essay on *Mischlinge* pioneered in tracing the bureaucratic and legalistic steps the Nazis took to isolate racial undesirables: first Jews, then other categories, including Roma and Sinti, Jehovah's Witnesses, homosexuals, half-Jews, Jews married to Christians, and quarter-Jews (to a more limited extent). In the larger context of the Holocaust, the escalating persecution of *Mischlinge* provides striking proof of accelerating fanaticism and racial intolerance within the National Socialist movement. The longer the Nazis exercised power, the more aggressively they interpreted and applied their discriminatory laws. Starting with the Nuremberg decrees of 1935, Hitler and his true believers increasingly relegated Germany's half-Jews to the status of full Jews — with all the consequences that such discrimination entailed. To be sure, the process evolved in stages because of ongoing internal disagreements between the "moderate" bureaucrats who were mostly concentrated in the Ministry of the Interior and the fanatics in the Nazi machinery such as Hitler's deputy, Martin Bormann, members of the Party Chancellery, and SS leaders Heinrich Himmler and Reinhard Heydrich. True, Hitler often equivocated for tactical and political reasons, but the fanatics found his ear more and more, and, emboldened by signs of their Führer's growing fanaticism, the Nazi hard-liners pressed their case at every opportunity.[1]

Thus, it was predictable that the Nazi faithful would promote extensive discussions of *Mischlinge* at the notorious Wannsee Conference, held in a Berlin suburb in January 1942. Traditionally, those interested in the Holocaust have seen that secret meeting as a kind of crossroads where the move to murder European Jewry became irrevocable. However, historians who have concentrated upon the Holocaust have also engaged in a lively debate on two issues, namely the degree to which Hitler was personally involved in the decision making, and when exactly a Führer order (if any) was issued for the mass murder of Europe's Jews. British historian Ian Kershaw has summarized this debate in exemplary fashion in a recently revised chapter in the fourth edition of his book *The Nazi Dictatorship*.[2] Although debate continues, it is likely that Hitler had already made that crucial decision weeks or even months earlier, possibly in the late spring or summer when Operation Barbarossa was executed, certainly by early December 1941. He conveyed his wishes by means of personal discussions and closed meetings with party, government, and military leaders. No Führer order has ever been found, probably because one does not exist. Given his passion for secrecy, Hitler spoke only in euphemisms and innuendoes on the subject, even within his innermost circle. Nevertheless, his hatred of Jews was unequivocal, and like many other violent anti-Semites of his time, he had spoken out publicly for the destruction or the removal — sometimes he and the other extreme Nazi anti-Semites used the terms interchangeably — of Jews from Germany and preferably from all of Europe. Almost two years before, in January 1939, Hitler had threatened in a public address that if Europe were enveloped in a world war again, it would be the Jews' fault, and it would result in their death. In his eyes, World War II became truly a "world" war when the Soviet Union launched its counteroffensive in front of Moscow on 5 December 1941, followed by the Japanese attack on Pearl Harbor two days later. Additionally, Hitler's declaration of war on the United States on 11 December meant Germany was centrally placed in that world war. A flurry of meetings with Himmler, Heydrich, Göring, and others in those crucial December days, plus accounts by other eyewitnesses, most notably Josef Goebbels in his diaries, suggest strongly that Hitler had made the fateful decision or else caused to make the decision to murder *all* of Europe's Jews in December 1941 at the latest. He referred constantly to his "prophecy" of January 1939 (in his faulty memory he persistently dated it — wrongly — to September 1939, i.e., the outbreak of the war) in addressing the upper echelons of his party. The Wannsee Conference, originally planned for 9 December 1941 but postponed until 20 January 1942, was convened primarily to settle the bureaucratic muddle that had developed on the fate of the Jews, including the fate of the *Mischlinge*.

The stages by which full Jews were isolated from German society and then ultimately murdered are instructive when considering the Nazis' decision to round up all *Mischlinge* for forced labor by 1944. The Nazis began discriminating against Jews by stages, starting in 1933 with "spontaneous" boycotts and their first discriminatory Law for the Restoration of a Professional Civil Service with its Aryan paragraph. The two 1935 Nuremberg race decrees isolated them further but did so in such a way as to initiate a difference in the degree of discrimination between Jews and *Mischlinge*. Following the 1938 pogrom, Hitler began to ghettoize and relocate the Jews but not *Mischlinge*. Finally, in wartime when "removal" of Jews outside of Europe to a place like Madagascar ceased to be feasible, the Nazis began mass murders of European Jews in the East starting in the summer of 1941. It was a telling lesson to the half-Jews who tracked as best they could the fate of their own relatives. To be sure, the pace of persecution was uneven, and the *Mischlinge* escaped the worst effects at several crucial turning points. For example, when Nazi officials ghettoized Germany's full Jews in 1939, they allowed Jews in "privileged mixed marriages" and their *Mischling* children to remain in society at large, a crucial distinction, one caused by the Nazis' ongoing fears of alienating too many Aryan relatives of Jews and of the children of Jewish-Christian marriages.[3] In September 1941, Hitler approved a program proposed for some time by Himmler, Heydrich, and several of the more fanatical Gauleiters to "resettle" (i.e., deport) German Jews to newly conquered eastern territories. It was announced at virtually the same time that French Jews were to be resettled in the East, too. German *Mischlinge* were not included in those resettlements initially. Already in that same summer Himmler's Einsatzgruppen had begun their "special operations" against non–German Jews in large swaths of territory recently conquered during the Wehrmacht's advances into the Balkans and the Soviet Union. It was in such geographically diverse areas as Ukraine, White Russia, the Wartheland (formerly western Poland), Serbia, and Greece that the Einsatzgruppen first began their campaign of mass murder. The gruesome shooting of nearly thirty-four thousand Jewish men, women, and children in open pits at Babi Yar outside Kiev in September 1941 was among the first mass atrocities to take place in the Holocaust, the inhuman path upon which the Nazis were now embarking.

Actions against German Jews soon followed. The first large transports of Jews from Germany, including Austria and the Protectorate of Bohemia and

Moravia, began departing for places like Minsk, Lodz, Kaunas, and Riga in October 1941. The inflicting of death on a large scale by Nazi-controlled forces upon unarmed civilians in war zones in the East had by this time become commonplace. Even so it is significant that some German midlevel bureaucrats did not view the "relocating" of German Jews to the East as a prelude to murder. True, centrally placed Nazi organizers, led foremost by Himmler, Heydrich, and Eichmann, had from the first calculated such relocations as the initial stage in the wholesale slaughter of all European Jews including German Jews. Thus, in a certain sense, there was, among midlevel groups of German officialdom in the East, bureaucratic confusion as to the ultimate fate of Germany's Jews once the regime began sending them into conquered Poland and the Baltic littoral to so-called resettlement camps. In short, the Nazis' unbelievable cruelty in combination with bureaucratic incompetence was creating chaos such that indigenous Jewish populations and waves of Jews from Western Europe were being sluiced into confinement facilities that could not possibly accommodate them.

Thus, upon their arrival in Lodz in Poland in October and November 1941, German Jews were crowded into primitive camps or ghettos, only recently vacated when local Nazis hurriedly removed or murdered the resident Jews. The conditions for the new arrivals were terrible, but no outright executions took place even though the local German administration and the SS, trying to stem the increased overcrowding, began transporting the Polish Jews (as distinct from the recently arrived German Jews) of Lodz in January 1942 to Chelmo, one of the first extermination camps. In Minsk the same Security Police and SD executed thousands of White Russian Jews in November 1941, just in time for the newly depopulated ghettos to receive trainloads of German Jews. As had been the case in Lodz, these new arrivals were not murdered — yet. In fact, many survived on into 1942 before being transported to the death camps. It was in places like Kaunas and Riga in late November 1941 that German Jews were murdered wholesale for the first time, many of the Riga-bound Jews being shot immediately upon arrival by order of Friedrich Jeckeln, the higher SS and police leader of the Ostland. It is noteworthy that Jeckeln's SS units were operating under orders from Himmler rather than under the direction of local occupation authorities or the Wehrmacht. It was those murders in the Baltic, especially at Riga, that bore repercussions.

Unprepared for such outright public violence against Germans, even if they were German Jews, some party officials such as Hinrich Lohse, the Reich commissar for the eastern region (Ostland), and Wilhem Kube, Hitler's general commissar for Belorussia, contacted their superiors in Berlin to seek clarification on policy and to protest or at least express reservations about the killing of those same German Jews, many of whom, even by Nazi standards, should not have been executed. For example, the local officials spoke out against the killing of World War I veterans, some of whom died wearing their military decorations. The officials also noted that the victims included Jews married to Aryans as part of "privileged mixed marriages," also *Mischlinge* and other categories of persons who should have retained some measure of protection from outright murder.[4] Word spread. Even Allied broadcasts made mention of massacres in the East. Therefore, Hitler and his followers had to react to the unwelcome airing of their sordid crimes. Their reaction was typical. Far from retreating from their intended course, under Hitler's over-all guidance they set about finding ways to hide their crimes more effectively from public view. As noted, the Nazis had created their own nightmare by herding eastern Jews into ghettos in the East, confident that the Soviet Union would disintegrate (it did not). Therefore, incoming waves of Jews from Germany and elsewhere in Western Europe had led to the inhuman condi-tions that the Nazis "solved" by mass executions conducted in public, and which they could not fully hide. It was in this context that the Wannsee Con-ference of 20 January 1942 (originally scheduled for 9 December 1941 but postponed by the Soviet counteroffensive, Pearl Harbor, and Hitler's decla-ration of war on the United States) became a conference seeking to regulate the mass killings that had already begun. What is pertinent to this study is that a significant portion of the Wannsee meeting was devoted to defining who was a Jew, that is, which victims were to be murdered. It was in this milieu that the fate of Germany's seventy-two thousand *Mischlinge* first degree hung by a thread.[5]

One personality dominated the Wannsee Conference: SS Obergruppen-führer Reinhard Heydrich (Hitler did not attend, in keeping with his policy of distancing himself from specific persecution agendas and their horrifying details). As is well known, the Wannsee Conference sealed the fate of Europe's Jews by settling details on the creation of the machinery of mass killing. That is why conference leader Heydrich wanted to make a clean sweep to include all *Mischlinge* first degree, all Jewish spouses married to Germans, and even some of the *Mischlinge* second degree in the categories destined to be killed. Already, the SS considered half-Jews among non–German Jews in the eastern territories to be the same as Jews, and they did not hesitate to include them in the mass murders that had started in 1941. During that same period, Adolf Eichmann at the Reichssicherheitshauptamt (RSHA) had tried to define Dutch half-Jews as Jews too in hopes of "surrounding" the Reich with territories that adhered to more stringent definitions. In this way the party hardliners sought to force the same harsher policies upon Germany. That effort ended when Göring and Hitler failed to agree to a new definition of who was a Jew.[6] However, Heydrich at Wannsee refused to abandon the matter, and he had considerable support at the conference. Five of the participants were from the Security Police and SD, two from the Party, one from the Party Chancellery, and one from the Race and Resettlement Office of the SS. All of them except possibly the last were hard-liners. There were also eight politicians and representatives from the civil administration. However, of these only one official, Wilhelm Stuckart from the Reich Ministry of the Interior, spoke out for a differentiation. Stuckart, the "moderate," was undoubtedly briefed beforehand by his chief assistant on Jewish affairs, Bernhard Lösener. Hoping to deflect Heydrich's unyielding approach at Wannsee, Stuckart immediately proposed involuntary sterilization of all German *Mischlinge* as an alternative to transporting them to extermination camps. As it turned out, later investigation showed that mass sterilizations would have imposed impossible demands on already overtaxed medical facilities, and the policy was never adopted. Stuckart proceeded to raise other technical objections at Wannsee as well. Germany's *Mischlinge* were, he claimed, "biologically insignificant," since their numbers were limited and they bore so few children. Besides, current laws forbade the marriage of eligible *Mischlinge* to *deutschblütig* citizens anyway. Attempts to sort out already married *Mischlinge,* some of whom were parents, from as yet unattached *Mischlinge* would see situations arise whereby older brothers and sisters might witness unmarried younger siblings being transported to camps while the family's protected *Mischlinge* remained behind. Finally, Stuckart reminded the assembled officials that hitherto *Mischlinge* had shown that they were "loyal" to German culture. Because of their high intelligence, good education, and German *Erbmasse* or appearance, they were likely to be natural leaders. Thus, it was better to exclude them from extermination, especially since they had many Aryan relatives who would be embittered by their demise.[7] His last point was telling. Once again, Stuckart had raised the warning flag about public morale, a factor that perennially concerned Hitler and Goebbels, who had to juggle their anti-Semitic desires against their political instincts and their flawed memories of the collapse of civilian morale as the cause of Imperial Germany's defeat in 1918. These arguments by Stuckart, plus several others, derailed Heydrich's all-encompassing approach. Because of Stuckart and especially because of the arguments prepared by his low-profile assistant, Lösener, the *Mischlinge* were excluded from Heydrich's extermination plans at Wannsee. On 29 January 1942, the Party Chancellery released a report stating that the decision was still undecided. In effect, the fate of the *Mischlinge* was to be deferred until the end of the war.[8] True, in the overall context of the Holocaust this development was only a small setback for Heydrich and for the other Party fanatics. After Wannsee they proceeded at an ever-accelerated pace with their Final Solution for full Jews, confident that their all-encompassing approach would ultimately prevail anyway. In their estimation, the fate of Germany's *Mischlinge* first degree and *Mischlinge* second degree was not forgotten; it was merely postponed.

To be sure, the *Mischlinge* were, like virtually all Germans outside the inner circle, unaware that the Wannsee Conference had ever taken place, and they could not have known what consequences it bore for them. What information they were able to obtain as the war continued — and that was spotty — suggested that Germany's Jews, indeed all of Europe's Jews, were disappearing to the East. Furthermore, within their informal family networks, rumors of death grew ever more prevalent as the war ground on.

Subsequent meetings of senior civil servants and party officials from circles involving the SS, RSHA, SD, the Party Chancellery, and the Reich Chancellery renewed the debate periodically. For example, in March 1942, they considered Stuckart's involuntary sterilization scheme again but concluded that it would overburden medical facilities and was impractical. Heydrich apparently argued that Hitler had given approval for redefining *Mischlinge* as Jews, but the latter had not, in fact, made any such commitment. Fortunately for the *Mischlinge*, Heydrich's assassination in late May 1942 in Prague by Allied agents probably delayed yet again the ongoing debate. Later that summer, after hearing rumors that Himmler wanted to round up all *Mischlinge* for execution anyway, Lösener and Stuckart in the Interior Ministry conferred again. Then, in September 1942, Stuckart sent a personal letter, drafted by Lösener, to Himmler to delay a "final solution" for *Mischlinge*. Stuckart used familiar arguments: public morale would be adversely affected because so many Aryan relatives of *Mischlinge* were involved; the numbers of individuals involved was limited; mass sterilization remained an option. Stuckart concluded by proposing that Hitler alone should decide the issue. Stuckart deliberately mentioned Hitler, knowing that the latter and others like Propaganda Minister Goebbels continued to worry about public morale, a fact of which Himmler was keenly aware. Himmler's reaction to the letter remained veiled. However, subsequent inaction on the part of his SS–RSHA–SD circle indicates that their plans to deport the *Mischlinge* were in abeyance, at least for the time being. Meanwhile, new "scientific" information circulated, indicating that experiments in concentration camps with X rays had made mass sterilization feasible after all, a development that seemed to take some of the urgency out of the debate. Himmler made reference to sterilization to Martin Bormann in May 1943, musing that the method should be applied to both categories, namely *Mischlinge* first degree and *Mischlinge* second degree. However, subsequent experiments showed that this new "scientific" X-ray method was also proving to be ineffective. Inaccurate predictions of its success had had at least one salutary effect: they had delayed once more the transporting of Germany's *Mischlinge* into the Nazi killing machine.

Despite Stuckart's limited success at the Wannsee Conference and at later junctures described herein, evidence surfaced that Hitler was starting to make common cause more frequently with the Party's fanatical elements from 1942 onward. A series of ominous government directives circulated periodically after Wannsee about *Mischlinge* that, despite objections from the Interior Ministry, set them on the same downward spiral that had led to the isolation, incarceration, and murder of full Jews. Already in July 1942, Martin Bormann ordered Party officials to take a much tougher line with their political assessments of *Mischlinge* when the latter applied for exemptions such as marriage, military service, or public employment. Other Party officials such as Hans Heinrich Lammers at the Reich Chancellery and Wilhelm Frick, who headed the Interior Ministry, immediately followed suit, issuing orders to government offices to enforce all regulations against *Mischlinge* strictly. For example, any applications by *Mischlinge* seeking exemptions from the Reich

Citizenship Law were to be terminated immediately. It was at this time that the Party banned *Mischlinge* from attending Gymnasiums and other elite secondary schools. Then, in February 1943, a seemingly trivial Party directive forbade *Mischlinge* to employ German female domestic servants. This was not in itself a severe hardship for *Mischlinge,* since virtually none were in a position to hire such help. Even so, the measure portended evil precisely because it paralleled identical measures that had been instituted only a few years earlier against full Jews. Further evidence of the hard-liners' unceasing pressure soon surfaced in another way. Toward the end of February 1943, the Gestapo had suddenly arrested ten thousand of Berlin's last remaining Jews. Many were immediately shipped to Auschwitz for execution. As many as two thousand Jewish spouses (mostly men) married to Aryans were caught in that roundup. The Gestapo held them in Berlin's Rosenstrasse assembly point, awaiting transport. In so doing, the Gestapo was ignoring the Nazis' own law of sparing persons living in "privileged mixed marriages" (i.e., it was taking the law into its own hands once again). This latest roundup showed that Hitler's inner circle of fanatics continued to vie among themselves as to who was most faithful in anticipating their Führer's desires and in finding ways to act upon them. Unexpected repercussions ensued from the Berlin roundup. In a demonstration of true courage, the captives' Aryan spouses, mostly women, gathered by the hundreds in the Rosenstrasse and launched a weeklong public protest. Police and uniformed SS repeatedly threatened to shoot, but the women kept demanding their husbands' return. Finally, in a rare move, the Nazi leadership backed down and released the Jewish spouses. Hitler's sensitivity to negative political consequences continued to work against the hard-liners' ambitions if those ambitions provoked public protests by significant numbers of Aryans.[9] Nevertheless, the fanatics continued to tighten the screws wherever possible. In April 1944, another measure excluded *Mischlinge* from the DAF, the German Labor Front. This, too, was an ominous development, since membership in the DAF was a necessary precondition for most forms of employment, especially blue-collar work, exactly the kind of employment the *Mischlinge* had, for the most part, been forced to take. In effect, the Party was now banning *Mischlinge* from the entire labor market, private as well as public.

Meanwhile, in the summer of 1943, bureaucrats in the Kanzlei des Führers der NSDAP (the Party Chancellery or KdF and not to be confused with the recreational organization, Kraft durch Freude) had been complaining bitterly about so-called *Mischlinge* "escaping" military service. That was a remarkable charge against persons whom the Nazis had been expelling from the armed forces ever since 1940! Yet, among the Party inner circle, the notion of *Mischlinge* dodging the draft rapidly gained credence. The idea had first surfaced on 3 June 1943 with a proposal from a Sergeant Dr. Vogtherr at the Oberkommando der Wehrmacht (OKW) to Hitler's KdF to round up all *Mischlinge* first degree as well as their spouses and even *deutschblütig* Germans married to Jews for forced labor related to the war effort. The idea immediately caught on. Another KdF official seconded the idea, provided that the draftees could not claim afterward to be equated with real Germans, and he suggested the creation of labor battalions for deployment "in particularly unhealthy swamps, etc." Stymied in their attempts to murder Germany's *Mischlinge,* the party's anti-Semites quickly rallied around this new approach. On 27 July 1943, the Reich Propaganda Directorate "disclosed" that there was widespread public dissatisfaction that *Mischlinge* and persons married to Jews were escaping military service. Therefore, they should be conscripted immediately into forced-labor units and sent to work in cities devastated by Allied bombing attacks. For a public dismayed by the news only days earlier of the firestorm that had just destroyed Hamburg, the idea made good sense. This technique of insinuating an idea into the mind of the general public and then "reacting" to a groundswell of that same opinion was not an isolated event. The Nazis had used similar tactics in rousing the public to boycott Jewish businesses in 1933 and in engaging in the fearful pogrom or *Kristallnacht* of 1938. Now, in the summer of 1943, Goebbels's Propaganda Ministry did the same with respect to Allied aircrews after the Hamburg raid, announcing that it was not certain how long the authorities could protect those *Terrorflieger* or terrorist airmen from a wrathful public. Taking the hint, mobs began to attack and lynch downed flyers from that point until the end of the war. Their tool of insinuation fully honed, the Nazis now floated before the public the idea of incarcerating *Mischlinge* in labor camps.

In October 1943, Hermann Göring, speaking on behalf of Hitler, announced that half-Jewish men and Aryan men still married to Jewish women were to be conscripted into labor battalions of the Organisation Todt (OT). The OT was originally a quasi-military corps of engineers that built war-related structures. Thereupon, in March 1944, Fritz Sauckel, Hitler's plenipotentiary for labor mobilization, ordered the conscription of both categories into the OT immediately, although some individuals were still able to escape the dragnet if they were working in war-related industries. However, Himmler closed all remaining loopholes in the autumn of 1944. Furthermore, all women designated as *Mischlinge* were forced to work as members of heavy-labor gangs in their localities.

Thus, starting in the spring of 1944, the Gestapo began to issue summonses to male *Mischlinge* all across Germany to report to assembly points where they would be transported to forced-labor sites. Many *Mischlinge* in the first wave of roundups were sent to occupied France to repair railroads and to help build defenses against the Anglo-American buildup. The conditions in the OT camps and sites varied greatly, depending on the whim of the local commanders, the OT professionals, and the guards. The OT old-timers labeled the forced-labor battalions as OT Hundertschaften or units of one hundred men. The hapless *Mischlinge* who were pressed into those units carried separate OT identification documents indicating that they were half-Jewish. However, not every one in the OT Hundertschaften was a *Mischling*. While the majority of prisoners were composed of men who were of Jewish heritage or who were married to Jewish women, other components included homosexuals, Ostarbeiter (workers from the East), Gypsies (Roma and Sinti), common criminals, drifters, and other "undesirable" elements. Thus, the Nazis transformed the OT into a two-tiered organization. It became a forced-labor system led by a few Nazi overlords and armed guards supervising a much larger workforce of de facto slave laborers, although the word "slave" was not actually employed. Whether those camps were simply bad or utterly deplorable, they were an unmistakable indication of the steep descent of Germany's *Mischlinge* into the category of outcasts being readied for slaughter just like Germany's hapless Jewish citizens. With that precedent freshly in mind, the Nazis were isolating the *Mischlinge* from society the same way they had isolated full Jews from 1933 onward. Once removed to a heavily guarded forced-labor camp, the victims were subject to a simple bureaucratic decision to move them even farther from an OT site to a concentration camp, and thence from there to extermination camps, although the difference between the last two had blurred considerably by 1944. Moreover, anti-Semitic hard-liners like Himmler were plugging any remaining loopholes in the 1944 dragnet intended to snare any *Mischlinge* who remained at large in society, hence the Gestapo roundups that increased in tempo between approximately November 1944 and March 1945. Like the Jewish members of their families, Germany's *Mischlinge* were destined to die if Hitler and his Party fanatics had their way. After all, this was the same route that Germany's Jewish citizens had already been forced to take: social exclusion, physical confinement, forced labor, and then mass murder.[10] Furthermore, by the last winter of the war, any remaining inhibitions Hitler and his minions might have had in sparing the lives of Jews married to Aryans or sparing the *Mischling* progeny of so-called privileged mixed marriages out of fear of alienating Aryans related to them had vanished. After all, on 19 March 1945 Hitler issued his last Führer directive: "Destructive Measures on Reich Territory." In reality, it was a blueprint for scorched earth in Germany itself no matter what consequences that policy bore for the German people.[11] Given this outright nihilistic mind-set in their leader, no German could expect legal protection or protection of any kind, least of all the despised remnants of Germany's Jewish population.

AN EARLY EXAMPLE OF FORCED LABOR: THE ODYSSEY OF RUDOLF KLEIN

The rounding up of *Mischlinge* had actually begun much earlier in the war, even if such actions were not yet part of a coherent, consistent policy as happened in 1944–45. As the following epic tale of survival shows, there were *Mischlinge* who learned much earlier what it meant to be sent to a "labor camp." Some of those who were born and raised in Austria, and who therefore avoided Nazi discrimination until 1938, were among the first to experience incarceration as forced laborers. It was especially true of persons who fled Vienna to adjoining European nations after the Anschluss of March 1938. The four-year travail of Rudolf Klein, a Viennese citizen and soon-to-be *Mischling*, is a case in point.

Rudolf Klein was born in Vienna in 1920 to Bruno and Elisabeth Klein. His parents, both medical professionals, provided him with a happy childhood despite Vienna's general impoverishment. Rudolf was an able pupil and was musically gifted. He yearned to study musicology and organ at the University of Vienna, having already taken private lessons from a widely recognized teacher, Siegfried Oehlgiesser. At age eighteen he earned his *Matura*,

Austria's equivalent of the *Abitur,* but following the Anschluss, Rudolf quickly discovered how times had changed. First, he donned the uniform of the Reichsarbeitsdienst (RAD) and performed national labor service in a quasi-military setting. Although admitted to the University of Vienna for music studies, Rudolf soon discovered that Jews and *Mischlinge* were facing sharp discrimination. At his father's urging, he left Vienna for Brussels in 1939, en-rolling in the Conservatoire Royale. In the meantime, a beloved relative, Rudolf's uncle Danny Brüll, a Hamburg businessman whom he had recently visited, also arrived in Brussels to escape persecution.

Rudolf's departure from the newly expanded Third Reich was a prudent move. The only problem was that he did not go far enough. German armies conquered the Low Countries and France in May 1940. As a result, he became one of the first *Mischlinge* to learn that the Nazis were not imposing halfway measures upon half-Jews caught outside Germany. From the spring of 1940 to early 1943, he led a precarious existence in Vichy France, enduring imprisonment, forced-labor camps, and then life on the run.[12]

Ironically, incarceration began for Rudolf Klein at the hands of non-German authorities. Following the campaign in the West, Belgian authorities, complying with their German occupiers, rounded up all foreign nationals and placed them in a school outside the Belgian capital. Men were separated from women and children, and then they were herded into cattle cars where they began a tortuous three-week journey through France. Rudolf and his uncle Danny, along with hundreds of other cramped prisoners, finally reached the little town of St. Cyprien close to Perpignan where the Pyrenees meet the Mediterranean Sea. Klein described their journey: "Finally, we detrained but under the most trying circumstances, I must add, because the cattle cars were labeled as if we were German prisoners of war. The [French] people pelted us with stones. We were very poorly provided for, and there were far too many people in the railroad cars. It was pretty awful."[13]

There the hapless group stayed for several months, guarded by French gendarmes and not permitted outside of their seaside compound. Compared with later experiences, it was not so bad. They had enough to eat, and for a time the internees even went swimming in the sea until the authorities erected a fence. To ward off boredom, the inmates organized evening entertainment. They held cabaret performances and located a piano so that Rudolf could accompany the performers. However, Uncle Danny became ever more concerned about their fate, and he gave timely advice to his nephew. Despite the relatively benign conditions in the camp at the moment, Danny stated, matters could suddenly take a bad turn. Presently, there were both Jews and non-Jews in the camp, but at some point, the authorities would begin to isolate those of Jewish background. Rudolf, a baptized Catholic, would be well advised to get out of the loosely guarded camp before ethnic distinctions hardened. Rudolf learned in the meantime that his cousin, Paul Krummholz, a Polish national, was living in nearby Perpignan. Encouraged by Uncle Danny, he contacted him and explained his predicament. Paul gave Rudolf money for a train ticket to Marseilles. Perhaps he could go underground there or, better yet, find passage out of Europe. Rudolf wriggled under the loosely guarded fence the next morning, walked into Perpignan, and took the next train to Marseilles. However, escape in Nazi-dominated Europe was hardly that simple. Upon reaching the port city, he was immediately apprehended by French police and placed in a *centre d'accueil,* a detention camp for foreign nationals. Then, following the closing of that camp a short time later, he was sent back to Perpignan. This time he was interned in a separate camp from the one from which he had so recently escaped. The new site was called Argélès sur Mer. After the war it became an attractive tourist resort. "However, at that time the camp, which was right on the edge of the sea . . . was a dreadful place," Rudolf recalled. "We had nothing to eat or practically nothing. We lived on thin turnip soup. I stayed there through the entire winter. There were no barracks as such, only primitive metal huts. We made fires inside in order to get a little warmth now and then. That was a most terrible time for me, that winter of 1940–41."[14] The only silver lining was the fact that it was a different camp than the one holding Jews. Uncle Danny's prediction had come true. He and other Jewish internees were now closely guarded in what had become the "Jewish" camp. Rudolf's fellow inmates in the new setting were an odd mixture. They were mostly Gypsies (Roma and Sinti) plus Spanish Loyalist soldiers who, having fled Franco in 1939, were now interned at Argélès. Then, in the spring of 1941, a Spanish warship took the Loyalists on board at gunpoint. Rudolf never learned their subsequent fate. Klein and the Gypsies remained at Argélès.

In the meantime, Rudolf had met a French priest with whom he held casual conversations. In retrospect he concluded that it was that priest who intervened on his behalf, because one day he was suddenly transferred to a labor exchange at Beaucaire in Provence. Delighted to have escaped slow starvation at Argélès, Rudolf languished for a few days in Beaucaire awaiting a work assignment. It proved to be an aluminum foundry in Salindre, located near the modest town of Alès. Outwardly, the new assignment seemed favorable. It was remote and unlikely to suffer close scrutiny by state authorities. However, conditions in the foundry proved horrendous, and Rudolf soon realized that he had merely exchanged one atrocious form of detainment for another. The foundry workers, mostly illiterate Vietnamese, were called *préstataires* and all were treated badly. Their pitiful wages sufficed only to reimburse the canteen, which provided dreadfully substandard food. Prisoners had to process the bauxite without protective clothing or masks through all stages from ore to finished aluminum, and they were constantly immersed in dust and chemicals. Sooner or later, all of the *préstataires* fell ill. Even so, the foundry worked at full capacity, three shifts a day, seven days a week, producing aluminum for the Germans. As Rudolf's health worsened, he received periodic injections of calcium, he recalled, to stave off complete collapse. After several months of the heaviest manual labor, Rudolf, because he was literate, was reassigned to monitor a high-temperature oven. However, this task continued to expose him to the poisoned environment. Then another minor miracle occurred. The foundry's assistant director had noticed Rudolf's declining health, and it may have been this official — Klein was never sure — who ordered him north to a sanatorium in Chambon sur Lignon in the Haute Loire district.[15]

Life in the convalescence center was vastly better. Many of the patients were students, some of whom were Jewish, and they shared experiences and information. Alas, this idyllic existence lasted only a few weeks. In that same summer of 1942, Vichy's premier, Pierre Laval, struck a deal with the Nazis whereby the latter would return French prisoners of war if France sent equal numbers of laborers to Germany to replace them. Naturally, no Frenchman volunteered, and as a result Vichy authorities rounded up foreign nationals, including those of Jewish origin, in order to fulfill Laval's unseemly bargain. Suddenly, Rudolf's convalescence home became the object of police searches. Fortunately, several patients had established contact with the French Resistance, which gave timely warning of impending raids. Although a *Mischling,*

Rudolf, as a baptized Catholic, was not yet on the authorities' lists, and he remained at the sanatorium. Nevertheless, he could feel the circle tightening. The center soon closed, and Rudolf received an official telegram ordering him back to the foundry. What should he do? He contacted the Resistance, which promptly conducted him to an underground network in the town of St. Etienne. There, he endured a nerve-wracking existence, moving every night from one address to another while wandering the city streets during daytime. He kept a weather eye out for police roundups, trying to look purposeful as he moved aimlessly from street to street. Although grateful to the Resistance, Rudolf realized that he was playing a losing game and vowed to leave France. Besides, sobering news had reached him at St. Etienne. His beloved uncle Danny Brüll was one of those poor souls delivered up to the Germans under the Laval agreement. However, Danny's contingent of prisoners never reached Germany. They were transported directly to Auschwitz instead.[16]

Spurred on by his uncle's death, Rudolf decided that Switzerland was his only hope. In the course of the winter of 1942–43, Klein crossed over the Swiss frontier five times. First, he took a boat across Lake Geneva, only to be detained and sent back. Then he hiked at night over the mountains at Chamonix, was caught again, and ejected. Trying harder, he hiked over Mont Blanc into the Canton of Valais, but was spotted and thrown out. Desperate, he tried Lake Geneva once more, only to be caught again! Each time following his forced returns, he had barely escaped imprisonment. Explanations to the Swiss about his Jewish ethnicity and the dangers he faced from the Vichyites had no effect, and now conditions worsened. By December 1942, the Nazis had occupied all of France following the Allied invasion of North Africa. With help from the Resistance, he hiked up to the remote Cloister of Saint Tamié in the mountainous Haute Savoie district, high above Albertville, one of seven refugees quartered there that harsh winter. They had pitifully little to eat, and the escape party grew weaker by the day. Finally, Rudolf got word from the Resistance that his name was now on a Swiss list of asylum seekers. With his last remaining strength, he trekked over the mountains again, this time in truly dangerous, wintry conditions, dodging German patrols. On reaching the Swiss frontier town of Annemasse, he finally met a friendly face, a priest who recognized his name on the all-important asylum list. His Catholic mother had convinced the archbishop of Vienna to forward his name to

Vatican authorities who, in turn, alerted the Swiss. Elisabeth Klein's intercession saved Rudolf's life.[17]

Even then his troubles were not over. The Swiss sent him to the Prison Saint Antoine in Geneva, where they closely interrogated him for a month. Their background checks plus meticulous examination of his correspondence with his parents finally convinced his jailers that he was an authentic refugee and not a German deserter (he had mentioned his RAD labor service under the Nazis in 1938). Then the Swiss put him in — of all things — a labor camp. Seemingly, incarceration had become his way of life. However, as Klein later admitted, conditions in Swiss work camps were paradise compared to anything he had experienced before. His health returned at the same time the war turned against Nazi Germany. What he could not know was that even as his time of peril was coming to an end, hard times were beginning for the other seventy-two thousand *Mischlinge* struggling to survive across the border in Hitler's Greater German Reich.[18]

MISCHLINGE AS FORCED LABORERS IN OCCUPIED FRANCE

Rudolf Klein's harrowing experiences notwithstanding, most *Mischlinge* began to feel the invisible noose tighten around them later in the war after most Jewish relatives had already been transported to the East. Sometimes families received terse announcements that this or that relation had died in 1942, 1943, or 1944 of such conditions as pneumonia, acute inflammations, bronchitis, failures of heart muscles, diarrhea, and the like. Understandably, bereaved family members quickly surmised that a hitherto robust relative could scarcely have died of natural causes so quickly. Malnutrition, severe mistreatment, unsanitary conditions, and outright execution were far likelier causes. Other evidence of persecution lay closer to home. There was an increased shrillness in Nazi propaganda and a palpable increase of fanaticism among the Party ranks as the war turned against Germany. This was especially evident after the Soviet victory at Stalingrad in early 1943. Devastating aerial attacks upon German cities brought the war home, too. The Nazis wanted revenge, and so they looked inward upon their own population for further scapegoats. It was in this context that members of Hitler's Party Chancellery broached the idea of placing Germany's male *Mischlinge* in forced-labor camps, and sending them off to arduous assignments. After all, to the fanatics they were "shirkers" evading military service.[19]

Werner Jentsch, who had served as an infantryman in France and the Balkans in 1940–41, was one of those *Mischling* soldiers who experienced this new form of Nazi wrath. They had sent him, a combat veteran, back to Germany in disgrace, so that for three years Werner subsisted in his hometown of Halle an der Saale as a casual laborer. Then, in June 1944, the Gestapo ordered him into the Nazi construction corps, the Organisation Todt (OT).[20] The OT wore its own distinctive brown uniform, and until the time when Jentsch and other *Mischlinge* were dragooned into it as OT "Bastarde," it had been viewed as an organization catering to Party blue-collar regulars. The vast increase of war-related construction projects in Nazi-occupied Europe had enhanced its importance by 1944, by which time Germany was experiencing acute labor shortages. Partly for this reason, the Party fanatics convinced Hitler that the time had come to stop "coddling" the *Mischlinge*. Like the foreign workers caught up in the OT, they received meager rations and endured dangerously substandard working conditions. While it was true that OT regulars supervised them, it was armed guards, many of them SS, who watched over them. Work assignments for the OT Hundertschaften (hundred-man units) varied greatly depending upon the region in which they worked and upon the phase of the war. Nevertheless, they all shared one characteristic: OT internees were despised involuntary laborers who could be transferred overnight to other camps.

Werner Jentsch's Hundertschaft was one of the first units of its type to be called up in 1944. Given the intense Allied bombing of French railways during the buildup to the Normandy invasion, his unit was dispatched to northern France. The new arrivals discovered that repairing rail lines and yards entailed heavy digging. The work was inherently dangerous, but since the SS guards refused to allow OT workers (mostly *Mischlinge*) to take shelter during air raids, it became doubly hazardous. Jentsch's group suffered scores of needless casualties as they were forced to continue work in the open while callous SS guards took cover in nearby shelters. Jentsch was lucky. He survived the strafing and bombing unscathed. Many of his companions did not.

Following the Anglo-American breakout from Normandy in August 1944, Jentsch and his workmates observed subtle changes in the way they were being guarded. His gang of *Mischlinge* noticed, first with amusement and then with interest, that their SS minders kept distancing themselves farther from the construction sites as air raids increased. Attempted escapes were still out of the question — the SS would only shoot them down from concealment. However, Jentsch and his mates decided to wait and watch. If the battle lines should advance close enough, the OT prisoners conjectured, they might find themselves in a favorable tactical position. Then, possibly they could find cover and wait for the liberation to roll over them — literally. The plan was risky, but remaining in SS thrall seemed riskier. Finally, one afternoon in late August, Werner's friends heard the distant rumble of Allied artillery. Air strikes continued to unnerve the SS. Their current OT work site comprised a rail line paralleling a hard-surfaced road on their left. The prisoners also took note of a huge bomb crater nearby. Given its size, it was unlikely that any of the other OT labor gangs could fill it by nightfall. That evening, in guarded conversations, Jentsch's comrades weighed the pros and cons over their thin rations. Then they turned in, contemplating what might happen the following day.

With the arrival of dawn, Jentsch's group hefted tools and under the usual guard marched back to the repair site. The men had been at work for less than an hour when, from the western horizon, sudden flashes erupted, followed seconds later by the sound of incoming artillery fire. The SS guards pulled back some distance from the prisoners, and Jentsch, after surveying the situation, concluded that his work gang was at the most exposed position of the entire Hundertschaft. The guards, he noted, remained crouched below the tracks in bushes to the right. With the road and the enormous bomb crater located on the left, the prisoners could, if they summoned up their nerve, race left across the elevated tracks and make for the crater. Jentsch, the group's veteran soldier, gave the prearranged signal, and, as one, the work gang bounded down the grading and raced to the rear. Seconds later, the dozen men, clad in dark OT fatigues, pitched themselves over the edge of the crater. They had made an irrevocable decision. Caught in no-man's-land, they would have to wait for whatever happened next. If the next soldiers they encountered wore black uniforms, then they were dead men. If they were Allied troops, then the laborers had a better chance, although ex-soldier Jentsch knew that the mind-set of troops engaged in assault produced itchy trigger fingers. The risks were high either way.[21]

After a time, the artillery shelling ceased and was replaced by the rumble of engines. Trembling earth falling from the crater walls hinted that heavy vehicles were rolling by. The traffic continued unabated for over half an hour, and logic told the escapees that their SS guards must have fled. Fearfully, the *Mischlinge* peeked over the lip of their crater. Immediately, American soldiers within an enormous armored column wheeled and trained rifles upon them. Holding their hands high, the Germans stumbled out onto the road, trembling before a tense young second lieutenant. Wearing the OT's distinctive brown uniforms (the earliest contingents of forced laborers had been issued them), the surrendering laborers tried animatedly to convey in German their plight as *Mischlinge*. The uncomprehending lieutenant decided that the highly agitated group must be part of a rearguard unit. The result was that Jentsch and his fellow *Mischling* comrades spent the rest of the war in a special camp in eastern France amid thousands of SS prisoners, some of whom had recently been guarding *Mischlinge* just like them.[22]

Like Werner Jentsch, Klaus Muehlfelder from Reinickendorf, a working-class district in Berlin, was caught up in the battles of northern France in 1944 as an OT laborer. The son of a physician, he had been a good pupil, but new school regulations issued in 1942 and again in 1943 barred *Mischlinge* from secondary schools. Also excluded from military service, fifteen-year-old Klaus had watched his ex-classmates go off to serve as *Flakhelfer* (i.e., antiaircraft battery personnel). Klaus became an apprentice *Fernnmeldemonteur*, a workman installing business telephones for a firm called TN. Despite high priority for that work, he too, received a Gestapo notice ordering him into the OT in June 1944. Dressed in hand-me-down work clothes, he, along with several hundred other men, were placed in crude railroad cars and shipped to Paris. They detrained at a former French army barracks, the grim Caserne Mortier where Klaus celebrated — or rather experienced — his seventeenth birthday. He was the youngest member of the OT's Thirty-third Hundertschaft.[23]

Klaus found that his unit was made up of a curious hodgepodge of individuals. Over half were *Mischlinge* like him. Other internees included husbands who had refused to divorce their Jewish wives, homosexuals, and even outright criminals including several violent individuals. From the first moment he was mustered in Berlin, Klaus was thrown together with people from all walks of life with whom he would never have associated otherwise. Fortunately, on his first day of servitude during the muster, he met another youth who, coming from an intact family like him, was equally bewildered by such rough company. The two boys became friends and helped each other survive.[24]

From all across central Germany during the first large OT roundup, hundreds of so-called *Mischlinge* were being herded into Caserne Mortier. To be sure, the prisoners did not call it a *caserne* (barracks), which implied a regular military installation. Rather they called it a *Lager* (camp). The German word implied a place of confinement, which was exactly what Mortier had become. Horst R. from Danzig, and fellow *Mischling* Horst P. from Dresden, were middle-aged members of the same group of *Mischling* arrivals as ex-soldier Jentsch and teenager Muehlfelder. Most of them came from across central Germany, but also from Berlin and Hamburg. The two Horsts had been rounded up by the Gestapo at the end of April 1944 and were now consigned to the same OT Hundertschaft, repairing French railroads. Horst R. related later that his group had been positioned first in St. Cloud, a suburb of Paris. Later that summer, after their removal from Lager Mortier, they were herded north and east along with German armed forces retreating into Belgium. By late August hundreds of *Mischlinge* were strung out along French railroads, all of them engaged in repairs during the general retreat.[25]

Klaus Muehlfelder's Hundertschaft initially cleared debris on rail lines at Beauvais and Soissons. As was the case with all OT prisoners, his group worked long hours with little rest or nourishment under the gaze of SS guards. Like hundreds of other prisoners, they experienced their share of strafing by fighter-bombers, too. By late August, they had joined the general retreat northward, at which time they heard the distant sound of heavy guns. Finally, one morning, they awakened from their crude sleeping quarters to an odd silence. The SS guards had decamped, as had the regular OT supervisors. The prisoners were now on their own! At this point confusion broke out. Some prisoners chose to remain in place and await the Allies. Others, like Klaus, were torn. The desire to rejoin their families was strong, and rumors of an early end to the war were rife. Therefore, unlike Werner Jentsch and his friends, Klaus and several other OT laborers embarked on an unlikely trek back into Germany.[26]

Clad in rough work garments and bearing their few possessions in crude satchels, Klaus's tiny band bore the look of army stragglers. They carried no movement orders, and while each of them possessed an *Arbeitsbuch* (labor permit) and a *Wehrpass* (a kind of internal military passport), those documents hardly guaranteed safe passage. Besides, each *Wehrpass* was stamped with a bold qualifier: "Not to be used for military assignments." The inconsistency between the document and its qualifying statement says much about Nazi terminology! However, the quality of their papers was not so critical. It was the sheer chaos of retreat that facilitated their return to Germany.[27]

At first they made their way on foot, mostly mingling with military stragglers. Fortunately, while marching alone on an isolated stretch of road in northernmost France, a Luftwaffe lorry driver took pity upon them — some of the OT workers were limping visibly in crude wooden clogs. The amiable driver deposited them at a Belgian railway station where they caught an eastbound train to Bastogne. From there the group walked to Luxembourg City, unhindered by roadblocks or security checks of any kind.

Up to this point in their unlikely journey, the *Mischlinge* from Klaus Muehlfelder's OT Hundertschaft had had better luck than some of the other *Mischlinge* who had started out from Lager Mortier the previous June. Horst R. and Horst P.'s Hundertschaft had had to endure especially sadistic security guards, including foreign volunteer (i.e., French) SS members and SD (Sicherheitsdienst) officials. In one of their OT Lagers they came under the supervision of a notorious SD leader, known to them as the "Henker von Prag" (the Prague Executioner). Rumor had it that the latter had organized the liquidation of Jews in Czech territories. Horst R. noted that all of the OT Lagers in which they were imprisoned bore the appearance of concentration camps with quantities of barbed wire and plentiful guards. At Amersfoort in Belgium, one of their last stops before reentering Germany, the camp guards seemed especially eager to assault *Mischlinge*. To be sure, harsh treatment had become the norm at OT camps in France. Horst R. remembered that at St. Cloud, one of the favorite forms of discipline consisted of forcing a prisoner to heft a load of stones and run at high speed in circles within a tightly fenced enclosure. Vicious guard dogs were set upon the hapless prisoner if he did not run quickly enough. The guards commanded the dogs to bite the struggling prisoner's legs and heels. Unlike prisoners from other units that dissolved in that chaotic summer of 1944, the two Horsts and their fellow *Mischlinge* found no opportunity to escape. Their retreat continued all the way through Belgium, and it was only in January 1945 that their Hundertschaft crossed under heavy guard back into Germany. Fortunately, the late-arriving

Mischlinge experienced increased chaos in a Germany facing imminent defeat, and so they survived.[28]

Meanwhile, Klaus Muehlfelder and his companions continued to enjoy better luck. In Luxembourg City, they concocted a new identity. Looking like heavy construction workers (which in a sense they had been), they introduced themselves to local Nazi authorities as such and discovered that the Ortsgruppenleiter and his staff were about to decamp for Germany. Klaus's group helped the panicky Nazis move their possessions onto trucks, meanwhile informing the responsible official that they had been ordered to report to their own construction company in Saarbrücken. Could he help? Courtesy of the grateful Ortsgruppenleiter, they lodged overnight at Party headquarters (!), then boarded a heavy truck. En route they concocted another story for their driver, who drove them all the way to Koblenz on the Rhine. By this time they had outrun the chaos of the collapsed front, so that more orthodox travel arrangements were necessary. To make themselves less conspicuous, they boarded different trains in ones and twos. Klaus and his fellow Berliner obtained tickets to Berlin's Anhalter Bahnhof, and rode a D-Zug (express train) the entire way. During one tense moment they were searched by military police and Gestapo officials. However, their labor permits got them through (wisely, they did not show their compromised *Wehrpasses*). On the outskirts of the capital, Klaus and his traveling companion made another prudent decision. They knew that passengers entering Anhalter Bahnhof were subject to stringent security checks. As knowledgeable Berliners, they detrained at Potsdam instead, then transferred to the outermost station of the Schnellbahn or S-bahn, Berlin's rapid transit system. Within half an hour they had arrived back in the capital. Klaus caught another train to the suburb of Waidmannslust and made his way toward the station exit. What he saw next nearly bowled him over. Just ahead, a familiar figure was walking toward the same exit. At that moment Klaus's father turned around — and was speechless. The Muehlfelders, father and son, embraced, then walked home for a joyous family reunion with Frau Muehlfelder.[29]

Despite his good fortune, Klaus, along with so many others, had made one flawed judgment. World War II did not end upon his return to Berlin in September 1944. The fronts stabilized, and the terrible war ground on. Klaus considered going into hiding. However, his parents vetoed that idea. The family chose a simpler strategy. Klaus should simply return to his old firm, TN, and act as if nothing had happened. Reluctantly, the boy agreed, and astonishingly, the plan worked — for a month. Then, in October 1944, Himmler issued his hard-nosed proclamation, closing all loopholes for *Mischlinge*, and the Gestapo resumed its dragnet. Klaus received another call-up notice for induction into the OT. On the day before his physical, the teenager smoked strong tobacco incessantly, which made him ill. The examiners found him to be in wretched health and gave him an attestation that he was physically unfit for any kind of service.[30]

Matters hardly ended there. The Gestapo interrogated him sharply, trying to trick him into admitting that his illness was feigned. However, Klaus, who had hardened since the previous June, stuck by his alibi. The Gestapo authorities allowed him to return home, but a few days later they summoned him to yet a third physical examination. Although by now he found tobacco abhorrent, Klaus subjected himself to another bout of smoking, and this time the ruse finally worked. The OT examiners marked him as medically unfit. He was placed in a firm producing greenhouse materials and survived the war at home. Few *Mischlinge* earmarked for OT forced labor achieved that feat.[31]

FORCED-LABOR CAMPS FOR *MISCHLINGE* WITHIN HITLER'S GERMANY

The experiences of *Mischlinge* like Werner Jentsch, Klaus Muehlfelder, Horst R., and Horst P. were atypical in one sense. They had been dragooned into the OT several months earlier than the bulk of *Mischlinge*. The major call-up did not occur until the autumn of 1944, with smaller drafts taking place during the winter of 1944–45. Although the forced detention of *Mischlinge* was a watershed in anti-Semitic actions against *Mischlinge*, the general population of Germany scarcely noticed it. The OT drafts coincided with the call-up of all remaining reserves of manpower into hastily trained Volksgrenadier divisions, or into the largely untrained Volkssturm. The latter were holding mass demonstrations and inductions all over Germany in October and November 1944.[32] Besides, many other quasi-military units were in the process of formation late in the war. The continuing presence of millions of foreign laborers and prisoners of war in a nation denuded of manpower meant that legions of badly clothed, poorly fed men were tramping the width and breadth of Germany in 1944 and 1945. Under full public gaze, those formations performed all manner of heavy labor, often under armed guard. The roundup of *Mischlinge* was hardly as obvious as it would have been in quieter times.

Many *Mischlinge* who had the slightly better fortune of being placed in forced-labor units later in 1944 were usually assigned to locales closer to home. For example, Berliner Otto Hess, who like Werner Jentsch had served as a Wehrmacht soldier in 1939–40 and who had been dishonorably discharged after the campaign in France, had quietly resumed his prewar job. He worked in Telefunken-Platten in Berlin in advertising. Hess excelled at what he did, and his superior, a nominal Party member, placed Hess in the back room. Then, in September 1944, Hess, like hundreds of other Berlin *Mischlinge* combed out in the late-war dragnet, had to report to the suburb of Eichkamp for induction into the OT.[33]

All over Berlin the same thing was happening. Horst Hartwich, who had found low-end employment since his dismissal from school in 1943 (and who had twice survived being buried alive in bombing attacks), was another unfortunate *Mischling*. He joined Hess and others at Eichkamp, where a medical examiner glanced briefly at the stripped *Mischlinge* and then stared lingeringly at a pretty nurse. Any humor in their situation ceased when he turned back and announced that all those present were *frontarbeitsfähig* (i.e., fit for assignment to the front). Hartwich, Hess, and the others were photographed — at their own expense — and issued *Dienstbücher* or service records. However, the latter were marked not only with an "OT" but also displayed a prominent "B." The *B* stood for "bastard," meaning, in Nazi bureaucratic jargon, that they were of mixed race. None of the inductees knew what was happening, and wild rumors circulated within the bewildered group. Some thought that the term "fit for assignment to the front" meant that they would be issued rifles and marched off to battle. Others were convinced that the *B* stood for Buchenwald and that they were now on a one-way trip to a gas chamber. The authorities confounded them all by sending them home.[34]

However, their home stays proved short. On 7 November 1944, a ragtag assemblage of hundreds of men, clad in whatever civilian clothes they could find, returned to Eichkamp, were issued rations, and then marched to Berlin-Grunewald, where another surprise awaited them. There, waiting at a station platform, was a passenger train whose long line of cars presented an unexpected luxury in wartime. After a lengthy pause, the train finally steamed out of Grunewald, heading westward although no one knew where. One of Horst's traveling companions was Hans Hempel, recently returned from years of exile in Turkey. Although a *Mischling,* Hans was not accustomed to Nazi intimidation, and so he struck up a well-known tune from wartime England: "We're going to hang out our washing on the Siegfried Line! Have you any extra washing, Mother dear?" Amazed at his boldness, the other occupants stood up and cheered. Then they joined in. Soon the whole train was chorusing the lines. Ultimately, word came down from the front car that it might be best if they stopped provoking the guards. Reluctantly, the singers acknowledged the warning, and silence returned. Hitherto, Germany's *Mischlinge* had endured Nazi persecution in isolation. If there was any silver lining in what was happening to them now, it was the knowledge that at last they were not alone. This time they had each other's company.

Finally at three the next morning, the train pulled into a station labeled "Zerbst." It was a small city east of Magdeburg near the Elbe River. *"Aussteigen!"* the guards screamed. "Climb down!" The OT forced laborers filed into heavy trucks. After a half-hour journey, they halted at a large aerodrome where they wearily trundled through the cold into a large hangarlike building and waited. Finally at dawn, Horst's small group was sent to a squat barracks, only to find it already full. It was a depressing place, one made grimmer when one of the arrivals committed suicide. Unable to find a place to deposit their bundles, they were eventually resettled in another hut, ten men to a stall.

Later that morning after a sleepless night and without breakfast, they stood before their captors, who revealed their purpose. Now that Germany was denied airfields in the West, the Organisation Todt was expanding other airfields for the Luftwaffe. Immediately, the authorities enumerated camp restrictions. Forced laborers were not to communicate with regular OT personnel or guards. They were not to communicate with Aryan women (none were there anyway). Postal communications were strictly censored. And so forth. Without further ado, they began work, shivering in their inadequate garments. Nighttime brought no relief. The men shuddered in their unheated stalls.[35]

It was in Zerbst that many Berlin *Mischlinge* first made each other's acquaintance. Otto Hess met future friends such as Horst Hartwich, and Hanns-Peter Herz. The Heilmann boys, Peter and Ernst-Ludwig, were there, too, as were Thekla Brandt's brothers. Hanns-Peter remembered clearly that the hapless inmates had to make do with any and all clothing including bits of old Italian army uniforms. Leather footwear had become a luxury. Many wore wooden shoes.[36] As elsewhere, the OT "Bastarde" at Zerbst came under the supervision of OT regulars. The latter carried the title of Bauleiter (i.e., construction foremen). There was even a reserve SS Oberführer at Zerbst, Luftwaffenbaurat Erfurt. He was especially proud of his SS reserve status. Then there was Herr Meindelschmidt, a corrupt OT procurement officer, and Herr Rein, the camp commandant. Fortunately for the *Mischlinge*, their guards were Luftwaffe rather than SS. The inmates soon concluded that the young airmen were behaving relatively decently toward the OT Hundertschaften — in distinct contrast to the callousness of the OT regulars. Even so, their situation was hardly envious. Food was scarce. Hanns-Peter Herz recalled that they ate a thin gruel made of grains and occasionally sweetened by carrots or turnips, or, rarely, a dollop of tough horsemeat. Potatoes were a luxury. Hanns-Peter resented being ordered once by an SS man to peel a bag of potatoes for the latter's horse. Prisoners ate the peelings.[37]

Despite the grim atmosphere, Horst Hartwich recalled occasional diversions. Two cousins, Rainer and Heiner L., were Luftwaffe enlisted men, the first of whom had arrived from a punishment battalion, the other from convalescence leave after a crash landing. The *Mischlinge* thought Heiner was slightly addled. He proved it one day by removing the white strip from the camp's red-white wind indicator and driving on his errands with what amounted to a Communist flag. The OT laborers cheered him on. Yet, such light moments were rare. Dark rumors abounded that OT leaders Erfurt, Rein, and Meindelschmidt had supervised airfield construction in the East, then ordered the execution of all Jewish slave workers at an air base in Hungary — after robbing them. While no outright executions took place at Zerbst, conditions were grim. Rations remained meager, and prisoners continued their heavy, outdoor labor in thin rags throughout the harsh winter of 1944–45. Their drafty hangars and crude wooden huts remained unheated. Despite warnings of reprisals for all, several inmates attempted an escape in January 1945, but most were rounded up and assigned to punishment details. Their acts revealed that prisoner solidarity within the OT camp was shaky. *Mischlinge* at Zerbst were aware that two groups of internees were assembled there: (1) decent people who looked out for each other, and (2) morally suspect characters who looked only after themselves. The latter were often the common criminals who had been rounded up with the *Mischlinge*, although there were a few in their own group who belonged among the opportunists. Not surprisingly, the latter soon established liaisons with OT regulars and avoided tasks involving heavy labor or danger.[38]

The camp's main task was to build a long, heavy-duty concrete runway for the new jets. Given Zerbst's location athwart the air corridors to Berlin, the authorities placed the highest priority upon the aerodrome's completion, and work continued in all weather. Throughout the winter and spring, Hess, Hartwich, and Herz worked alongside hundreds of others, hauling stone and pouring concrete. Besides the OT regulars and OT "Bastarde," Russian prisoners and Ukrainians joined the effort. The *Mischlinge* saw tensions rise between the two ethnic groups after Procurement Officer Meindelschmidt gave preferential treatment to the Ukrainians. Everyone took to calling him *Gemeindelschmidt*, meaning that he was a vulgar, repulsive man. Later, inmates from a nearby civilian prison were added to the labor pool as the work tempo increased.

Even so, the *Mischlinge* soon realized that their labors were pointless. With temperatures well below freezing that winter, the concrete, without proper chemical additives, could not set properly. The cynical OT regulars ordered prisoners to heat water for the cement mixers while other teams hacked holes in the deep-frozen soil for the pour. Such measures were hopelessly inadequate, but pressure to complete the runway remained intense. Large gangs of men labored round the clock with the night shift working under searchlights, Allied aerial attacks notwithstanding. Laborers and guards alike suffered in the intense cold, but no one complained. As long as the OT officials could demonstrate that the runway was making progress, the project would continue. The soldiers knew that the only reward for whistle-blowers would be a transfer to the eastern front. Therefore, an atmosphere of live-and-let-live developed. Guards looked the other way when OT technicians made errands to Berlin with mail from the very prisoners they were supposed to keep at arm's length. The same guards allowed prisoners to trade fuel to local farmers in exchange for produce. A lively trade developed for prisoners holding currency for the purchase of black market bread. The two camp medics also did their bit, providing brief sick leaves to seriously ill inmates. Everyone kept going somehow.

A sobering reminder of what was happening elsewhere appeared in February 1945 when new prisoners from the East arrived in Zerbst. Although cold and hungry, the OT inmates stared with foreboding as seven hundred men from the Warthegau straggled onto the air base. Although forbidden to speak to the new arrivals, the Berlin *Mischlinge* soon learned that the contingent, which originally had numbered thirteen hundred "political prisoners" (mostly former Communists and Socialists), had endured nightmarish conditions. The more observant OT inmates also noticed that those guarding the prisoners were not SS. Rather, they were pink-cheeked, well-fed officials from the Warthegau's now defunct Ministry of Justice. Speculation about military defeat soared. Radio broadcasts reported Soviet offensives in the East and Anglo-American offensives in the West. Nevertheless, work on the runway continued.[39]

As was often the case in such forced-labor operations, the prisoners were not all quartered neatly in one "camp." There were often a series of outlying Lagers contributing to the same effort. Engineer Dietrich Goldschmidt, a *Mischling* who had worked in the automotive industry, had been assigned to an OT unit in Burg bei Magdeburg whose task was to quarry stone for the runway near Zerbst. Conditions in this adjoining site were comparable in most ways to what the *Mischlinge* were encountering at the aerodrome. His camp's Lagerführer was in peacetime a cigar manufacturer from Burg bei Magdeburg who screamed and ranted at the 120 *Mischlinge*. However, he usually left them alone. Like the main contingent at Zerbst, Goldschmidt's group made do with primitive accommodations, living in crude huts that nevertheless kept out the worst effects of the cold weather. Furthermore, their guards usually did not abuse them. He and his Lager mates also traded bits of building materials and small quantities of fuel for farm produce from nearby peasants. They cooked their basic foodstuffs over primitive stoves in the huts. Everyone lost weight, but they survived.[40]

What set Goldschmidt's OT incarceration somewhat apart from the norm was his ability even under confinement to render aid to friends who were full Jews and under SS guard in Berlin. This was possible because his future wife, Berliner Ursula Theune, succeeded several times in reaching him at his work site on her bicycle. Dietrich would insert some of the scarce food (condensed, stewed vegetables) that he had prepared over his hut stove into an aluminum "bicycle pump" (in reality a milk container), which his fiancée brought with her. Despite camp regulations, Theune was able to slip into camp, greet Dietrich, then peddle back to Berlin, outfitted with her "pump." Once home, Ursula visited their Jewish friends, Eugen Schiffer and his daughter Marie, who were imprisoned in Berlin's last remaining "Jewish" hospital at Iranische Strasse 2 under SS arrest. After parking her bicycle in full view of the guards, she prudently entered with her pump in hand, then, when opportunity allowed, quickly unloaded its contents for the famished Schiffers. Dietrich and Ursula's actions were admirable, but their situation remained highly uncertain. The question that remained uppermost in their minds toward the end of that winter, Dietrich recalled, was simple: "*Was wird aus uns?*" (What will become of us?).[41]

It was on 8 April 1945 that the Americans began to provide him answers. First, bombers attacked nearby Halberstadt, and two days later, ground troops took the city. That was enough for the OT Lagerführer and his staff. They commandeered the camp's only vehicle and drove off to the east — directly into the path of the advancing Soviets. Meanwhile, the rest of the guards scattered, and suddenly, the 120 inmates were left to their own devices. Dietrich and Ursula, in anticipation of end-of-the-war chaos, now launched their own plan. He phoned her in Berlin, and she arrived shortly with two bicycles prepositioned for their escape. Aware that Americans were blocking the nearest Elbe crossing, the young couple peddled upstream to an unguarded bridge. Finally, they reached Ursula's parents in Göttingen and were married there on 16 June 1945.[42]

About the same time Goldschmidt made his escape, the OT forced laborers at nearby Zerbst were completing the final grading and surfacing of their runway. On the afternoon of 10 April 1945, Horst Hartwich, who had been written up by the camp orderlies as sick and therefore fit only for light duties, was ostensibly helping a fellow worker scrub out a boiler behind the airfield's main hangar. Momentarily dizzy, he lay down and gazed up at the sky. Suddenly, the air-raid sirens shrilled. This was nothing new. Sirens had been sounding almost hourly in recent days as formations of bombers flew toward Berlin. In fact, Horst was beginning to doze off when suddenly the roar of an aircraft in low-level flight shook him out of his torpor. First he thought it was an audacious Luftwaffe crew, and then it dawned on him. Their aerodrome, object of pointless labor and shabby treatment, and simultaneously guarantor of their lives, was finally under attack! Horst had barely survived two heavy bombings in Berlin and knew they were now in genuine peril. Seconds later, they heard the shriek of falling bombs. Despite his fear, Hartwich also experienced a wave of fury. Why should he, reduced to the status of a draft animal, have to cower in a hole in fear of the Americans? Fortunately for him and most of the other inmates, the bombers concentrated on the runway rather than on personnel. Minutes later, the raid was over. The runway, now in ruins, had never launched a single aircraft nor contributed in any way to the defense of Hitler's Reich. That evening, Horst and other survivors learned that American ground forces were in Magdeburg. On the morning of 12 April, the inmates awakened to a strange silence. The OT regulars, their guards, and the despised "ministry of justice" officials from the Warthegau had all disappeared during the night.

Hartwich and his Berlin friends started off that same morning, heading east. With the sound of distant artillery fire behind them, they reached a main highway near the town of Belzig early the following day. From there they continued their trek, looking into a rising sun as they stumbled in clogs and rags toward Berlin and their families. Finally, on the next morning the ragged group hobbled into Wannsee, the western terminus of Berlin's rapid transit system. Otto Hess, Horst Hartwich, Hanns-Peter Herz, and six hundred other bone-weary fellow *Mischlinge* had finally arrived home. A few days later, Soviet armies forged a giant steel pincer around the capital. For the newly returned *Mischlinge* from Zerbst, that was not such a bad fate. Long faced with the prospect of death at the hands of the Nazis, now they exulted. After all, they had survived Hitler's Germany.[43]

Other *Mischlinge* faced similarly daunting conditions that approached the hardships prisoners encountered in concentration camps — except that these OT victims led a quasi-peripatetic existence. Berlin native Helmut Coper had just turned nineteen in the summer of 1944. His family had suffered harrowing experiences since 1942 when the Gestapo accused his Jewish father of falsifying ration cards for fellow Jews. They had interrogated him repeatedly but could not extract a confession or substantiate their charges. Helmut, too, had been detained and interrogated. The Copers knew they were in peril anyway; close relatives had begun disappearing to the East. The summer of 1944 brought fresh disasters. Tragically, Helmut's mother, the Aryan family member, was killed in an Allied air raid. Frau Coper had been the main support for the family since her husband could not work, and her Aryan status had provided husband and son with a legal shield against deportation. Following her death, the Nazi authorities wasted little time. They promptly arrested Helmut's father and shipped him to Theresienstadt where he soon died. Helmut's turn at Nazi justice came a month later in September 1944.[44]

Unlike many Berlin *Mischlinge,* Coper was not sent to the OT Lager at Zerbst. Instead, he and several hundred other men were put into a separate OT contingent and sent south to the industrial town of Jena in Thuringia to join other groups of forced laborers. Immediately upon arrival, they were ordered to begin digging underground installations for the large firms of Schott and Zeiss. Although the work could have been as "benign" as that experienced by the inmates at Zerbst or at some of the other anonymous OT camps, it proved to be otherwise. The brutal SS guards and the less numerous, equally callous OT regulars created conditions that were tantamount to a concentration camp. Housed in primitive huts outside Jena, and fed even less adequate rations than in other OT camps, all of the forced laborers soon weakened. After each hut-based unit had prepared its own inadequate breakfast, the guards herded them onto a lengthy forced march into the city. They worked eleven hours a day, digging. There was no heavy earth-moving equipment, and only three OT regulars were there to operate drills and place explosives. For weeks the routine never varied. Their diet of poor quality bread and thin soup soon combined with the heavy work regimen to make the prisoners gaunt.

Even under such primitive conditions, Helmut endured. He landed in a hut with some hardened "survivors," and hut life proved important for survival. He was saddened to see that so many *Mischlinge* in his Hundertschaft were uneducated, naïve youths from rural districts who were unable to establish any ties with one another. True, Helmut had begun his ordeal in isolation, too, but it was his good fortune to be quartered with several older Berliners, one of whom had been a skilled criminal, a former member of a *Ringverein* (organized crime ring). "Richard," as the professional criminal was called, was a godsend for inexperienced youths like Helmut. He was an expert scrounger and survivor. Under his tutelage, the members of the hut became a kind of a team. He "organized" coal and foodstuffs and was expert at trading them for other scarce items in order to eke out a better existence. His hut mates soon learned the survival tricks Richard had acquired in prison. He artfully stole turnips, and after bargaining some for a stash of coal plus quantities of sugar, he cooked up an acceptable marmalade, which he shared with his mates. They developed a sense of loyalty to him, and each member began looking out for the others. Psychologically, they benefited from that fundamental fact.

In such harsh conditions, class differences disappeared. Hut mate Paul von Hermann, formerly a banker and a decorated soldier of World War I, was physically weak and perennially clumsy. However, he commanded universal respect from the other prisoners because of his keen intelligence and his determination to struggle on. A third hut mate, Helmut's Stubenführer (hut leader), was a businessman from Chemnitz and a natural leader. When the latter recommended a course of action, the others willingly obeyed. Helmut was lucky to have such companions, and for good reason. Above them was an *Aufseher* or overseer, also known in the context of concentration camps as a *Kapo*. The man was a vicious criminal and a pathological killer. Rumor had it that he had murdered his own mother! It was also rumored that following his conviction, he had escaped from prison. Now, after his recapture, the Nazi authorities had released him to the OT where he was serving as Helmut's foreman. Fortunately, it was widely known that this *Aufseher* was utterly corrupt. Therefore, knowledgeable members of the Lager knew to bribe him periodically with the odd cigarette or some other scarce item.[45]

The SS guards were another matter. They remained aloof, and no prisoner of Coper's cognizance ever established any normal human relationship with them. This was nothing like Zerbst with its indifferent Luftwaffe guards. Helmut's group quickly learned to fear their SS accompaniment after one of their number, an elderly barber from Nuremberg, was publicly beaten to death by those selfsame guards. No one could explain why this happened. Nor was the barber's death an isolated example. Helmut recalled the fate of Hans Neuss, a talented singer from prewar Berlin. The prisoners marveled that such a celebrity was working among them. Thus, one day the entire OT contingent was horrified to learn that Hans Neuss had been shot "while trying to escape." His execution made them fear their SS guards all the more.

Such casual brutality was disheartening, but the strictly enforced rule that OT laborers were never to take cover in public air-raid shelters with Aryans during attacks was especially demeaning. Because Helmut's OT contingent worked in downtown Jena and later in the centers of other cities in central Germany, they came under frequent Allied bombings in the period 1944–45.

During this time their "subhuman" status became crystal clear. Scores of his fellow laborers were injured or killed out in the open, kept there by SS guards who crouched in their shelters just meters away. What made the prisoners' existence even more bizarre was the fact that sometimes following raids, they were called upon to help clear rubble in residential neighborhoods. Often those districts contained the homes of Nazi officials. Suddenly, the OT laborers would find themselves in altogether human situations, salvaging family possessions, helping douse fires, rescuing family pets, and the like. Although hardly a rescue service, they functioned as such, and the grateful *Partei-Bonzen* or Party bigwigs, not understanding at first who was helping them, invited them to join them at mobile Party soup kitchens, the well-known *Gulaschkanonen.* They would stand around canteen wagons, filled with thick pea soup and fatty sausages, and would converse with their newfound Party "friends." Even after it was revealed who the OT Hundertschaften really were, the local inhabitants sometimes gave them food anyway. Helmut remembered that such humanitarian gestures could be risky. The SS arrested one well-meaning citizen and took him away.

As the war wound down the following spring, it became obvious that neither SS guards nor OT regulars wanted any further responsibility for the OT Hundertschaften. By mid-April 1945, rumors of Soviet advances were rife. Then, one evening, Helmut's respected Stubenführer announced that they had no alternative; they had to escape. Chaos was spreading, he said. As many as half of all their camp mates had already died, grown seriously ill, or been injured. Now they, the survivors, had to look after themselves. Following a discussion, the men decided that returning to Berlin was their best bet.[46]

Helmut's Stubenführer secretly called together all the *Mischlinge* in the contingent, many of them Berliners, and repeated his proposal whereupon they all joined in. Pooling their resources, the inmates provided money and valuables for the Stubenführer to bribe the remaining OT officials into producing falsified movement orders for the group. By this time, the risk was low. The hated SS guards had disappeared, and order was breaking down. Thereupon, the OT contingent marched to Jena's main railway station, displayed their movement orders, and commandeered an entire train heading north to Leipzig. Thus, a ragtag group of grimy men steamed in uncharacteristic comfort out of Jena for home. Alas, their jubilation ended at Leipzig where they discovered that no more trains were getting through to Berlin. Soviet troops had just cut off the capital. Now they had to walk.

Tired, hungry, and dejected, the OT group nevertheless embarked upon their final march. Many cringed each time they approached a military checkpoint. However, the Stubenführer's convincing manner and his bogus movement orders worked every time. The OT forced laborers were returning to Berlin, he assured the soldiers, to help build defenses. It was a risky march nonetheless. Even at that late date, some of Helmut's companions were killed in aerial attacks. Still, they trekked on. One time they blundered into a fire fight between Soviet and German forces, but obeying Wehrmacht advice, the group sidestepped the battle. Finally, on 21 April 1945, only hours before Soviet armies completed their encirclement, the group entered Berlin — and promptly disbanded.

It was hardly a glorious homecoming. With his mother and father dead, Helmut had no family to return to. After knocking at many apartments, he was startled when a basement door opened, revealing an acquaintance who had joined the SS. For a moment, the two young men just stared at each other. Helmut explained that he had no identity papers. Assassination squads were hunting down deserters all over the city. Nodding, his SS neighbor glanced around and beckoned Helmut inside. There they called a truce. Soon, another former neighbor, now an infantryman-deserter, joined Helmut Coper and his SS cellar mate. Helmut later dubbed their group a *Kellergemeinschaft* or cellar community. Thus, an impromptu company of former and current unacceptables hid together as awful battles raged above them in Berlin. They survived.[47]

A *MISCHLING*'S TRANSPORT TO A CONCENTRATION CAMP

Bavarian Emil Steiner from Kempten was unlucky in two ways. Kreisleiter Brändle in his hometown was a particularly fanatical Nazi, and, after years of persecution, Emil had developed perforated stomach ulcers. Forced to live apart from his family for long periods in primitive conditions, he grew steadily weaker. Finally, in August 1944, Emil struggled back to his family's apartment in Kempten, bleeding from his mouth. His wife, Eleanor, frantically sought help, but the first surgeon she approached categorically refused to operate on a *Mischling*. After further canvasing, she finally located a kindly retired surgeon who saw immediately that Emil was in a perilous state. He removed part of Emil's stomach, and Emil returned to his family greatly weakened. Even so, only weeks later, in September 1944, Kreisleiter Brändle ordered Emil to be transported to Theresienstadt. Knowing that further communication would be difficult, Emil prepared several postcards with postage and threw them from the cattle car in which he rode. Someone found one of them and posted it to Eleanor. Emil's group of seven Kempten men including Walter R., a former bank director, plus several businessmen, and a few refugees from Berlin, were now known to be in the camp.

Meanwhile wives of the victims stayed in touch as best they could. A week after the deportation, one of the Berlin refugee women in Kempten told Emil's wife that she, too, had received a message from her own husband. The families were relieved, but none knew what camp conditions were really like. Besides, they soon discovered that they, too, were no longer free. Kreisleiter Brändle placed the families of the departed *Mischlinge* in a rundown structure separate from the rest of Kempten. The citizenry promptly dubbed it the *Judenhaus* (Jews' House), a widespread practice in Nazi Germany. Immenstädterstrasse 20 was a modest structure designed to accommodate only three small apartments. Now there were seven families jammed into it, and Kempten's more enthusiastic Nazis strolled by daily, screaming epithets such as *"Judenpack!"* at the dwellers. After a few months of confinement, Eleanor escaped Kempten's miniature ghetto by informing the health authorities that her son, Rolf, had contracted scarlet fever. Worried that the disease could spread, Brändle ordered the Steiners to return to their old apartment. The families still received word occasionally from their men in Theresienstadt including the good news that Emil's condition had stabilized. Thus, the Steiners and the other six families maintained a fragile hope. Nevertheless, Kempten had scored a doubtful first. It was because of Kreisleiter Brändle that they were among the earliest *Mischlinge* in Germany, as a group, to experience what the full Jews had faced several years earlier. Eleanor and her children survived the last winter of the war in their dreary apartment. Rolf and Erika as *Mischlinge* second degree encountered severe harassment in public school, but their resourceful mother transferred them to another school where discrimination was minimal. Some of Kempten's citizens made a special point of being cordial to the three Steiners as peace approached, but hard-liners like Brändle remained ardently anti-Semitic to the last days of the Third Reich. Grimly, Eleanor and her children prayed for Emil's survival.[48]

Amazingly, Emil Steiner did survive. He had met a compassionate medical examiner upon arrival in Theresienstadt who, learning of Emil's stomach surgery (and his status as a World War I veteran), designated him as a medical orderly. In reality, Emil became a patient in the ghetto hospital. The Nazis used Theresienstadt as a kind of showcase where elderly Jews, including World War I veterans, were placed. To be sure, many victims died there, too. The prisoner diet was sparse, but that fact may have saved Emil's life. Subsisting on thin soups, he found to his surprise that his stomach stabilized. Against all odds, Emil Steiner was among the living when Theresienstadt was liberated.[49]

MISCHLING WOMEN AS FORCED LABORERS

As the fronts, east and west, closed in, the Nazis combed out Germany's final labor reserves including the other half of Germany's Mischlinge, the women. Himmler's directive of November 1944, closing all loopholes for male Mischlinge, also decreed that all female Mischlinge and all Aryan wives in mixed marriages were to perform war-related manual labor. They did not place women in camps, but the authorities saw to it that the female Mischlinge were assigned demeaning work. Thus, in the last winter of the war, thousands of mothers, daughters, and sisters in "privileged mixed marriages" were also engaged in forced labor for Hitler's Germany.[50]

Until 1944, Meta Alexander had led a favored existence, at least by Mischling standards. A Berliner, she had secured a job in a pharmaceutical firm in Konstanz on the Swiss border through various connections. She had also kept a low profile, although that was not easy. She had had to ward off eligible men whom she would otherwise gladly have dated. Then, in September 1944, encouraged by Allied radio broadcasts, the local citizens, Meta included, decided that the war was about to end. Fearing for her aging parents, Meta returned to Berlin and reclaimed her old job with the firm that had transferred her to Konstanz in the first place. Alas, illusions of an imminent peace quickly evaporated. Then, one week before Christmas 1944, she received notice from the Gestapo to report to a heavy construction firm in Strehlau, a Berlin suburb. Meta shuddered at what lay in store, but she was hardly alone in getting bad news. Her mother, the Aryan spouse, also received her call-up notice. The labor authorities placed Frau Alexander in a leather goods factory at Alexanderplatz where she assembled heavy work gloves and other leather goods for the Wehrmacht. Mother and daughter rose early each morning for work, and each returned home in the evening exhausted. Meta had to walk great distances when public transportation was disrupted, as it often was. Meta's mother had the worse job and lost a finger in an industrial accident in the unsafe conditions. Yet, no one on the factory floor cared. A lost finger had become small change by this time.[51]

Meta was more fortunate. Her construction firm needed a bookkeeper, and Meta filled the role well. Consequently, her employers winked at Nazi requirements that women *Mischlinge* perform only heavy labor. Many co-workers at her construction company were female *Ostarbeiter* (East European laborers), and they quickly established a modus vivendi. Not wanting to push her luck, Alexander set about making herself useful in many ways, functioning as a *Mädchen für Alles* (Girl Friday). She lit fires and mopped floors, but she also kept the company books. Then, at night, she attended to her parents. Her elderly father, the Jewish family member, had to work out of sight in the basement, stoking the furnace. During air raids, Meta and her parents took refuge in a distant shelter, since some neighbors objected to sharing space with Jews and half-Jews, even at war's end. Finally, in April 1945, the Russian battle lines passed over them. The Alexanders had survived.[52]

Fellow Berliner Thekla Brandt and her family suffered similar dangers. In the latter part of 1944, all four Brandt siblings, two sons and two daughters, became *dienstverpflichtet* (i.e., forced laborers). Thekla's brothers entered the Zerbst contingent. Then, about the time that the Alexander women received their call-up notices, the Brandt women reported to a sweatshop producing uniforms for Blitzmädchen (i.e., female Luftwaffe communications personnel). Thekla and her sister entered an exhausting work routine that taught them the true meaning of sleep deprivation. During the day they helped their father and mother in his medical practice. Then, at night, the two young women labored at the garment factory from 9:00 P.M. until the following morning. Public transportation was sporadic, so they often endured two-hour treks from home to factory. Nightly, they worked amid the din of heavy-duty sewing machines, but despite the noise the sisters sometimes fell asleep, so each looked after the other lest they be caught napping by their brutal overseer. Even so, the Brandt daughters did not complain.[53]

After all, Thekla and her sister were fully aware that their Jewish mother was suffering worse persecution. When Allied air raids struck Berlin, Frau Dr. Brandt, barred from shelters, had to remain in her apartment building while structures all around her collapsed. The humiliation of wearing the yellow Star of David armband in public was awful. When making obligatory appearances for her monthly food ration card, flanked by her daughters, they had to conform to a precise — and galling — protocol. The daughters had to return the Nazi officials' Hitler salute with one of their own while Dr. Brandt, as a Jew, was not "permitted" to do so.[54]

In working-class Neukölln, the Brandts' practice was a godsend. Medical care was scarce for civilians in the late-war period. Moreover, the locals knew that the Brandts, husband, wife (surreptitiously, since she was Jewish), and their daughters, provided good care. Nevertheless unpleasant incidents occurred. A neighboring SA man snooped on them. Thereupon, the police raided the apartment, claiming that they had evidence that the Brandts were cooking with black-market fats. The family proved its innocence, but it became clear that they were under constant hostile surveillance.[55]

Then in February 1945, the Gestapo ordered Frau Brandt to appear at their headquarters the next day. Should she fail to appear, they threatened arrest for the entire family. Knowing that evasion was now impossible, the Brandts finally allowed their mother to go to a Sammellager on Berlin's Grosse Hamburger Strasse, a dreaded place from which thousands of Berlin's Jews had already been transported. The family also knew that Frau Brandt had sewn twenty sleeping tablets into her dress, and that if conditions became bad enough, she would use them. Two days into her captivity, Frau Brandt assembled with the other unfortunates in the Lager's main hall. Then, an official read out the names of ten persons who were now permitted to leave. Frau Brandt's name was one of them. Stunned, she walked home into the arms of her startled family. No one could fathom why she had been spared.[56]

Fortunately, because their parents continued the family medical practice down to the last days of the war, they were able to improvise a kind of medical aid station when Soviet forces entered the capital. In those nightmarish days, the elder Brandts operated nonstop on wounded Soviet soldiers at the same time that Thekla and her sister served as medical orderlies (their brothers had not yet returned from Zerbst). Respected for their deeds by the Soviet officers who occupied the Brandts' apartment building, the Brandt family survived the wild times after the fighting ceased. Then Thekla's brothers returned. Despite harrowing conditions, all of the immediate family members had somehow survived.[57]

As the previous profiles demonstrate, half-Jewish women mostly escaped the outright misery of forced-labor camps or imprisonment, although the threat of incarceration certainly hung over them. Moreover, most female *Mischlinge* had to perform involuntary labor of some kind. Even so, some were simply too young to face such dangers — yet. However, Hamburg school-girl Ursula Kühn demonstrated that there were other forms of discrimination that were as emotionally scarring as outright incarceration. Ursula had led an unsettled life, shunted periodically between her destitute single mother and her Giessen relatives, resented and barely tolerated by several family members there. Even so, return trips to Hamburg were anything but consoling. In July 1943, Ursula and her mother survived Hamburg's terrible firebombing, but their apartment was destroyed, and without a secure job Frau Kühn was constantly seeking living accommodations for herself and for her increasingly distraught daughter. Temporary relief of sorts came in January 1944, when the authorities evacuated Ursula's entire school to Wittstock, a small town in Mecklenburg. One child among many, she achieved some anonymity and was sheltered with a kindly older woman, widow of a former Communist, and no friend of the Nazis. Alas, Ursula's *Mischling* status caught up with her again in June 1944. She was denied further schooling and had to return to her mother. Then, that autumn, an official in the local labor office took pity on Ursula, who was exhibiting obvious signs of emotional stress. He issued travel documents allowing Frau Kühn to return her daughter to relatives in the safer town of Giessen.

Her mother judged that Ursula would find greater physical safety in that small Hessian city where air raids had been infrequent. Besides, Frau Kühn's Aryan sister and her family still had an intact apartment. Yet, upon arrival Ursula found her relatives in deep mourning. Their eldest son had just been killed in action in Russia. Their second son was listed as missing in action in France and was presumed dead. Their daughter, who was only two years older than Ursula, was currently serving as a Blitzmädchen, a Luftwaffe signals specialist, in an active war zone. The Giessen relatives worried constantly for her safety. Thus, comparisons of her status with that of Ursula were unavoidable even though Ursula, a *Mischling*, was banned from military service. Furthermore, as a half-Jew, she could neither hold a job nor obtain further schooling. Giessen was a small city, and because of her previous visits Ursula's *Mischling* status was common knowledge in the neighborhood, so anonymity was out of the question. In effect, she was confined as a prisoner in her relatives' apartment with nothing to do. Privacy was impossible and, while her aunt made some allowances for Ursula, her uncle made none. He exhibited fierce hostility, and she had nowhere to escape.[58]

Several months passed. Although she knew that her mother was leading a marginal existence in Hamburg, Ursula started to write a letter asking permission to return home, but finally admitted to herself that her mother was in no position to take her back. Ursula resigned herself to her miserable existence in Giessen. And it was there that the war caught up with her again. Although one of Germany's smaller cities, Giessen possessed some industries and was a significant rail hub. Therefore, the RAF firebombed it on the night of 6 December 1944. Hundreds of citizens were incinerated, including dozens of Ursula's neighbors. Ursula and her relatives barely survived, and along with thousands of other refugees, they departed on foot, seeking shelter wherever they could find it. Separated in the confusion from her aunt and uncle, Ursula joined a column of civilians heading south, and was quartered with several other girls in a village near Marburg. Conditions were primitive. She walked barefoot much of the time, and her grandfather, aged eighty, expired in the same village from lung damage incurred during the recent firestorm. However, despite the discomforts of refugee life, Ursula derived an odd benefit from her situation. Most of her fellow refugees were unaware of her status as a *Mischling*. For her, chaos was a boon. After all, Nazi authority was disintegrating.

With the advent of spring, signs of Germany's defeat multiplied. Mobs of soldiers passed through Ursula's village. Some were Wehrmacht soldiers trying to survive. Others were SS units bent upon further resistance. In the end it all faded into a confusing blur of soldiers stumbling in one direction or another. By this time a few more relatives had caught up with her, although their reunion brought her little joy. The sound of Allied aircraft overhead became a constant feature. Then, one morning everyone awakened to a new noise. Villagers glanced toward the horizon, Ursula among them. Then suddenly lines of tanks emerged from a nearby forest. Fortunately, the local authorities ordered white flags out, and the village surrendered to the Americans without a shot being fired. Some onlookers cowered, but Ursula Kühn was not among them. She stated with arresting intensity a half-century later: "It was the happiest moment of my life!"[59]

MISCHLINGE IN SMALLER FORCED-LABOR CAMPS

Most male *Mischlinge* finished the war in forced-labor camps. Many were placed in large camps supervised by the Organisation Todt (OT). However, many half-Jews wound up in smaller, sometimes miniature work sites that were often obscure. All the forced-labor camps shared one common feature, however. Their inhabitants subsisted on near-starvation diets, endured miserable shelter, and were barred from interacting with the general population. There were a bewildering number of such camps, and conditions for the incarcerated *Mischlinge* varied markedly from place to place. Some of the larger camps already described held several thousand men and were surrounded by heavy security forces, giving them the appearance of concentration camps, an appearance that sometimes was matched by brutal reality. Other camps were far smaller and less brutally managed. For example, the Gestapo in Wiesbaden rounded up hundreds of *Mischlinge* in late 1944 or early 1945 in the Rhine-Main region for shipment to intermediate-sized camps. Many landed at a multisite complex called Blankenburg/Derenburg. By contrast, a later dragnet by Gestapo personnel in a smaller community such as Kassel netted barely forty unfortunate men for a local project. The Kassel *Mischlinge* were confined to OT Lager Bähr in nearby Bettenhausen where they dug an underground air-raid shelter for a hospital. Yet, there were even smaller forced-labor camps such as one in Witzenhausen, another village near Kassel that incarcerated only fourteen *Mischlinge* in the waning months of the war. *Mischlinge* from all over Germany were interned in these small-to-medium forced-labor camps.

In Hesse's largest city, Frankfurt am Main, which in prewar days had been an urban center for Germany's Jews, the local Gestapo conducted a major roundup of *Mischlinge* in January 1945. It was decided that when enough men were in custody, they would be transported to an OT Lager at a place called Derenburg. Thus it was that approximately sixty of Frankfurt's half-Jewish men found themselves on a remote loading platform of the main railway station in the early hours of 21 January 1945. In fact, departure time was set for 3:00 A.M. (the Gestapo did not want the public to see the *Mischlinge* depart). One of the contingent's better known members was Heinz Karry, formerly a Frankfurt industrialist. Karry was destined after the war to build a prominent political career, but for the moment his challenge was simply to survive. The Gestapo officials jammed the prisoners into frigid railroad cars at the freight station annex. Then the special train rumbled eastward, first to Blankenburg, and then, after an unpleasant transfer amid shouts from ill-tempered guards, to Derenburg where they arrived the next day. There the men sat in squalor and utter tedium for a week. Then Karry's group was marched to a former pub with the benign-sounding name of The White Eagle. This was to be their quarters at the Derenburg Lager.

An OT Hauptführer at Derenburg, Herr Frenke, was on hand to receive them. Wasting no time, he issued a series of announcements and regulations. Aloof and unfriendly, the Hauptführer's chief point was that the inmates were cut off from the rest of the world. In short, they were his! He then announced that it was customary for inmates to choose their own *Lagerältester* (senior prisoner) and a *Stubenältester* (i.e., his deputy). They would be responsible to the OT officials for prisoner conduct. Accordingly, the inmates chose Karry as *Lagerältester* and a lawyer, Dr. Ernst S., as *Stubenältester*. The prisoners' assignment was to dig out a large bombproof cavern for a future oil refinery. Without further ado, Frankfurt's *Mischlinge* were added to a pool of foreign workers and marched immediately to their excavation site. Unfortunately, just as the Derenburg camp began operations, an ugly incident ensued that revealed the brutal atmosphere in the camp to which the Frankfurt *Mischlinge* had just been assigned.[60]

In his opening statement to the prisoners, Hauptführer Frenke had issued an unequivocal warning: anyone attempting to escape would be apprehended and shipped to a concentration camp. Furthermore, guards would hold the other inmates responsible and would transfer them to an even harsher camp, perhaps in the nearby quarries at Blankenburg through which they had recently passed. Most of the men had Jewish relatives who had already been shipped to camps including Auschwitz, and while they were not sure of all their relatives' exact fates, everyone had heard rumors of mass executions. Almost to a man, the hapless inmates agreed among themselves to postpone escape attempts. They might create plans for a mass breakout later, but only when the time was right. Unfortunately, Albert S., a musician, thought otherwise.

Potential trouble with Albert S. had already surfaced during the unpleasant train journey. Willi K., a thirty-five-year-old truck driver from Frankfurt, had sat next to Albert S. during their transport and had not been impressed by his traveling companion. Albert S. had extolled his own accomplishments at length. Willi was disgusted: "He related to us his sizable income, his influential connections, and his abilities as an operator at the very time others were living in misery."[61] Willi and other traveling companions, mostly working-class men, were also unaccustomed to such boasting. Neither were they surprised when Albert S. reported for sick call immediately upon arrival in camp. In fact, Albert S. reported sick every day thereafter despite urgent pleas from the medics to free up space for others — the contingent included many older *Mischlinge* with serious health conditions. Albert S. would hear none of it, claiming he had sciatic nerve inflammations. For about ten days the other inmates covered for him. Then, Karry's deputy, Dr. Ernst S., tried to convince Albert to vacate the sick bay. He commiserated with the musical impresario's outrage over camp conditions. Nevertheless, the lawyer continued, they were all caught up in the same situation and would have to cooperate in order to survive. Despite his pleas, Albert S. escaped the very next evening. During their own *Appell* (evening roll call), his mates discovered his disappearance.

Panic ensued. Rather than passively accept Albert S.'s escape and its consequences, the contingent quickly conferred, whereupon Karry sent two physically fit men to find Albert before the guards were alerted. Besides, the prisoners had an excellent idea of where he had gone. The train station at nearby Halberstadt was the logical destination for anyone fleeing from Derenburg. And so it turned out. The two inmates, at some personal risk, walked into the Halberstadt station, searched the men's and women's waiting rooms, and found Albert S. nestled among women travelers, ticket in hand. They marched him back to the camp, arriving at 3:30 A.M. Livid that Albert S. had risked their lives, the inmates closed in, and one of them suddenly slapped him across his face. Simultaneously, Heinz Karry shouted at him: "You are no *Mischling* first degree. You are a filthy swine!" Another prisoner cursed Albert, took a poke, and walked off. Up stepped the next inmate and did the same. By this time a line had formed, and this became Albert's impromptu punishment. No one, eyewitnesses claimed afterward, ever landed more than one punch on the escapee, and many blows were so soft as to be symbolic gestures. Then, after the last inmate had taken his swing, Albert S. collapsed. Satisfied that he had suffered enough, Karry and others carried him to a quiet corner rather than to a bed. They feared the guards would administer heavy corporal punishment if they found him still abed after wake-up time. By now it was 4:00 A.M. Reveille came at 5:00, and everyone knew that another hard day of labor would soon begin.[62]

In the morning, the prisoners marched back to their construction site and resumed work tunneling out the underground oil refinery. Stubenältester Dr. Ernst S. remained behind to look after Albert. Lagerältester Karry accompanied the men. Spared from a specific work assignment and worried about Albert S., Karry returned to quarters that same morning, wanting to speak to him privately. To his surprise, the prisoner still lay in his corner. Concerned, he and Ernst S. summoned the camp doctor, but discovered that she was unavailable. In reality, the inmates at Derenburg were bereft of medical care. Then they rushed back to Albert S., only to find by this time that he was dead. Aghast, they provided a plausible explanation to the Lager authorities for Albert's death, avoiding any mention of an attempted escape. Then they followed bureaucratic procedures, informing the absentee physician, summoning the coroner, and arranging a hearse to transport Albert's remains for a proper burial. In the meantime, they embellished their story, telling the camp guards that the unfortunate Albert S. had stumbled on an uneven stairway and had died from a head injury. By his own admission, the most painful task Karry had to perform in the affair was to write a letter of bereavement to Albert's widow.

The situation Karry and his fellow inmates found themselves in was awful. However, unlike those unfortunates who had been placed in concentration camps since 1933, or in some of the harsher OT camps since 1944, the inmates of OT Derenburg mostly survived their uncongenial surroundings from January/February 1945 until April when the Americans liberated them. Even so, conditions had been brutal. Karl M., another Blankenburg/Derenburg detainee, had entered camp weighing a healthy 186 pounds. By the time the Americans reached him less than nine weeks later, he had lost over 60 pounds and had developed acute, permanently disabling rheumatism. Executions might have been absent at Blankenburg/Derenburg, but conditions were poor.[63] Albert S.'s death caused additonal woes. After the war, his widow was hardly sympathetic to a court decision exonerating the *Mischlinge* from her husband's death and submitted lengthy legal appeals lasting until 1958. Thus, the sad fate of Albert S. demonstrated that all *Mischlinge* caught up in the appalling Nazi camp system entered an abnormal world where deprivation, violence, and brutalization became the norm. His fate also demonstrated another fundamental fact: *Mischling* prisoners were far better off working together. Adopting an every-man-for-himself attitude was nearly suicidal.

One of the bewildering aspects of life for *Mischlinge* rounded up for forced labor in 1944 and 1945 was the sheer arbitrariness of the process. They could suddenly find themselves placed in ramshackle work sites far smaller than Derenburg and its outlying camps. Instead of Gestapo, SS, or OT, the camp overseers might simply be a hostile village population in tandem with the threat of local police actions. Josef G. from Witzenhausen near Kassel was one of those *Mischlinge* placed in just such a situation. His plight emerged after the war when he applied for restitution. Yet, Josef G. soon discovered that in his case, the very obscurity of his camp worked to his disadvantage. Auschwitz was closely associated with that ultimate form of persecution: mass murder. Obscure locales like Derenburg, Bettenhausen, or Witzenhausen aroused no recognition. In answering one postwar official's disbelief about the very existence of his Lager, Josef H. became bitter: "I regret that you force me to recount for you the evil conditions in my camp because I would have preferred to have erased them from my memory. It is better to expunge the bad and remember the good."[64]

His "camp" on the village's outskirts consisted of an ancient clay-built structure with four crude 20-by-25-foot rooms in the interior with ceilings 6 feet high. Approximately five persons occupied each room. Each prepared his own bed, using stuffed straw or any other fiber he could find. Rations consisted of a thin soup and some bread. When asked about sanitary facilities, Josef H. could only laugh. No, there were no toilets or running water. No, there was no heating, washing facilities, or other amenities. Any further description, Josef stated, better suited a dark, menacing novel. The camp inhabitants consisted of persons found to have had some kind of Jewish connection. Besides *Mischlinge,* there were Aryan men married to Jewish women. The thrown-together inhabitants discovered that their "camp" guards were Gestapo personnel. They were coldly impersonal, and their hatred for the prisoners was obvious. Unsympathetic citizens in Witzenhausen, taking the same cue, labeled the site, as was common by this time, the *Judenlager* (camp of the Jews). The prisoners' work consisted of building tunnels or galleries into the near-mountainous terrain — no one really knew why — and they were subjected to numerous restrictions: no inmate was permitted to leave the miniature camp or communicate with the outside. No one was to frequent public gatherings, the cinema, bistros, or any other kind of public establishment. The prisoners were regarded as the equivalent of "foreigners" and were ordered to have no social interaction with "women or foreigners." Nor were they to enter public air-raid shelters in times of aerial attack. Because Witzenhausen was small, both groups, villagers and detainees alike, knew who belonged where. Thus, even after the Gestapo's departure, the *Mischlinge* and other prisoners dared not interact with the locals whose hostility had become obvious from the first moment of their arrival. If Witzenhausen was any example, incarceration in a small provincial village provided cold comfort for half-Jews. The purpose of its "camp" seemed not so much war related as discriminatory and punitive.[65]

A *MISCHLING* SURVIVOR OF TWO CAMPS

One of Germany's more youthful *Mischlinge* suffered two incarcerations under the Nazis, and his survival was nothing short of miraculous. Wolfgang F. was born in 1926 in Eltville in the Rheingau to an Aryan mother and Jewish father. His parents' marriage failed, and Wolfgang's father was ultimately sent to Auschwitz. In 1940 Rheingau's fanatical local Nazis banned *Mischlinge* from public schools so that at age thirteen, Wolfgang F. decided to become a hair stylist. After all, people would always need hairdressers. However, his applications to a barber college or apprenticeship to a shop got nowhere. Finally, a *Friseurmeister* (master hairdresser) in a nearby town told him the unvarnished truth. *Mischlinge,* she said, were not being accepted for training. Wolfgang F. finally found work in the large construction firm of Jean Müller where he worked for two years as a pick-and-shovel man. What the youthful Wolfgang F. did not know was that following his father's transfer to Auschwitz and his own early dismissal from school, he had come under the scrutiny of the Wiesbaden Gestapo, possibly because he was listed on the welfare rolls (although he was no recipient of welfare). There were two sizable groups of *Mischlinge* who were murdered wholesale under National Socialism. The fate of one group of *Mischlinge* was sealed on 5 November 1942, when Gestapo chief Heinrich Müller issued orders that all Jewish inmates, including *Mischlinge* currently held in German concentration camps, were to be transferred to extermination camps in Poland. The second group comprised *Mischling* children from welfare institutions. In the period 1943–44 the Nazis sent them to a special facility in a place called Hadamar, not far from Wiesbaden.[66]

It was in August 1943 that Gestapo officials came for Wolfgang F. One train ride later, the seventeen-year-old found himself being marched up to a large institutional building in a modest town. The name Hadamar meant nothing to him at first. However, he soon realized that he was being incarcerated in a state sanatorium for the mentally and physically handicapped. Later he learned that Hadamar had acquired notoriety as one of the six sites where the Nazis first carried out their program of euthanasia from 1939 to 1941 against mentally handicapped patients.[67] In fact, it was only adverse publicity and protests in 1941 and 1942 by prominent Catholic Church officials such as Bishop Clemens von Galen that had forced Hitler to shelve the program — or so it seemed. Now, in 1943, Wolfgang learned firsthand that the institution in which he was incarcerated was still engaged in evil acts.[68]

It was only because Wolfgang F. actually survived Hadamar by a fluke that he was able to inform postwar restitution authorities what was happening on the institution's upper floors in the early 1940s. It was hardly a sanatorium. "Rather," he said, "there was a special section in which persons were being confined exclusively for reasons of race. In my section there were eighteen youths, each of whom was half-Jewish. Moreover, there was a similar section for girls with about twenty of them present." The officials called their section on the lower floor of the asylum an "education camp," but that was a euphemism, since no education of any kind took place there. Instead, the teenagers, aged sixteen to eighteen, were put to work, laboring on the grounds and in the gardens, or else performing other menial work in the facility. They did so under the watchful eyes of the staff such as Orderly Willich or Senior

Orderly Rudolf, or else the institution director, Dr. Wahlmann. One other sinister fact emerged. Outwardly a medical sanatorium, Hadamar was in fact operating under the direction of an SS Sturmbannführer, an unlikely choice for a "medical facility." It soon became evident that the staff's interest in their youthful prisoners was anything but benign. Wolfgang F. elaborated:

> During the course of my stay in Hadamar, it began to occur to me that one after another of my fellow sufferers were simply disappearing. After one of us was summoned to go up to see the medical doctor, we began to realize what was going on. Several times we were able to observe how the victim, now dead, was carried back down. During the six weeks I was at Hadamar, starting with my group of eighteen persons, many disappeared like that, and in the end there were only about seven of us left.[69]

Even those inmates who did not make the final climb to the upper floor realized that they were in peril. Their "orderlies" were hard men, capable of violence. Thus, one day Orderly Willich, displeased with Wolfgang F., simply pulled out his truncheon and brained the seventeen-year-old. Dazed, the youth picked himself up somehow and continued working. Later inspection showed that Willich's blow had fractured the boy's skull and caused an abscess that had to be treated for years after the war. In mid-October 1943, shortly after the clubbing incident, Wolfgang F. finally received his summons to go upstairs. Shakily, the youth entered a strange room, but instead of meeting a dreaded physician, he confronted a police official, Inspector Klein. The latter stated briefly that he had an order releasing Wolfgang F. from Hadamar. The boy asked why, but Inspector Klein could offer no explanation. Improbably, Wolfgang F. soon found himself back home, working for the construction firm of Jean Müller.[70]

The fate of Arthur Schmidt's children bears witness to Wolfgang F.'s close brush with death at Hadamar. Schmidt and his wife, Ella, had raised three children, but she had died in 1934, leaving Arthur to care for their two sons and daughter alone. All three children were raised in the Jewish faith and were therefore categorized by the Nazis as *Geltungsjuden*. At some point, their names, or at least those of the two younger siblings, must have been entered into the welfare rolls, too. In 1939, a judge sentenced the eldest, Ludwig, to six years of imprisonment for committing *Rassenschande* with his longtime girlfriend. From prison he disappeared into a camp, never to be seen again. After the war, his father sought official clarification, but restitution officials in Frankfurt could not help. However, in seeking to gain attention for his case, Arthur submitted further proofs of his family's persecution. Unlike the un-certain fate of his eldest son, the fates of his daughter and younger son had never been in doubt. They had been murdered at Hadamar in 1944. Thus, he confirmed Wolfgang F.'s claims that its "sanatorium" had functioned as a killing center for *Mischlinge* up to the end of the Nazi regime.[71]

Although Wolfgang F. survived Hadamar in 1943, the authorities had not forgotten about him. In November 1944, the Gestapo ordered him into an OT forced-labor camp. Thus, at age eighteen, Wolfgang found himself on another prison train. The twenty *Mischlinge* in his group were accompanied by a Gestapo official and by an SS Sicherheitsdienst (SD) officer, high-ranking company for so modest a group. In reality, the presence of those officials not only demonstrated the high priority assigned to incarcerating persons of Jewish ancestry, it also gave Nazi officials a pretext to remain away from the battlefronts. Wolfgang's group first worked in a camp in Mokrena in Saxony repairing roads. Then, in January 1945, they moved to Lager Rochau outside Delitsch where five thousand men were handling heavy munitions under guard for the Luftwaffe.

There were numerous eastern workers and foreigners plus *Mischlinge,* watched over by military personnel and OT regulars. "Our group," Wolfgang F. recalled, "consisting of approximately a hundred men from the Rheingau and from Berlin, was placed in a special barracks, located outside of the main facility and especially heavily guarded." Fortunately, this contingent of one hundred *Mischlinge* discovered that the Gestapo was no longer directly super-vising them. Camp security at Rochau was mostly a Luftwaffe responsibility instead. Even so, living conditions were unpleasant. Shelter was primitive and rations poor, although the *Mischlinge* were relieved to find that their rations were no worse than for the other inmates. The work was hard, and with so many high explosives concentrated at Rochau, the potential for injury or death was high. Some of the Rheingau contingent escaped in late March 1945 and returned home amid late-war chaos. Wolfgang F. and most of the other *Mischlinge* preferred to take their chances in the Lager, unpleasant though it was. Finally, in late April 1945, American troops overran Rochau. With their help the Rheingau *Mischlinge* returned home. Thus, Wolfgang F. at age eigh-teen had survived two incarcerations.[72]

MISCHLINGE AS EVADERS

It was obvious that anyone who sought to escape or avoid the forced-labor camps was courting far worse punishment. Therefore, *Mischlinge* who attempted to evade the Gestapo's late-war dragnet merely exchanged one danger for another. The situation for *Mischlinge* in Kassel in 1944–45 is instructive. Milder though the labor camp conditions for Kassel's *Mischlinge* were (compared with some other forced-labor camps), they were hardly attractive, and in consequence not everyone cooperated. Forty men reported to the work site as ordered, but three of Kassel's half-Jewish citizens refused to do so. Kassel internee Georg B. described their fates: one unfortunate victim committed suicide on the day he was supposed to report for work. A second *Mischling* went underground but was soon uncovered and transported to Buchenwald where he died. A third unfortunate was also ultimately captured and transferred to a Gestapo detention center in Wehlheiden. The Gestapo executed him and his fellow prisoners a day before the arrival of American forces in April 1945.[73] Thus, attempts to avoid roundups by *Mischlinge* carried grave risks. Even so, some individuals tried, and a few succeeded.

The case of Otto E., if it demonstrates anything, is a cautionary tale about the consequences of disobeying Gestapo orders. Otto E. was a young engineer who, like Wolfgang F. described earlier, lived in Eltville in the Rheingau. Otto's mother was Jewish. The Gestapo had arrested her in March 1943 and transported her to Auschwitz where she soon died. Thus, Otto had no illusions as to what fate he might expect from the Nazis. When the Gestapo began rounding up *Mischlinge* from Eltville in late 1944, Otto E. immediately concluded that he must escape. He did so with the help of family members, his fiancée, and the local *Bürgermeister* of Hattenheim, all of whom knew of, and were angered by, his mother's recent fate.[74]

Otto E. had already had an earlier brush with the Gestapo. At the time of his mother's arrest, they had interrogated him, too, including his relationships with neighbors and with a young Aryan woman to whom he was allegedly betrothed. Otto E. denied the allegations, and unable to prove their point, the Gestapo reluctantly released him. Then, on Saturday, 18 November 1944, he appeared before Henrika Z., a young Dutch woman who was in fact his future wife, and who was visiting his family at the moment. He explained to her and to family members about the Gestapo order to appear on Monday in Wiesbaden for transport to a camp in Merseburg. As his fiancée observed later:

"He was in complete despair and stated that he was going to suffer the same fate as his mother and that this order was now the reason for his escape. He did not really know how or where." Henrika Z.'s parents still held Dutch citizenship despite long years in Germany. They resided in Grefrath near Krefeld on the Dutch-German border and might help.[75]

Otto, Henrika, and family members then paid a visit to the city super-intendent for Eltville, Herr Eskelund, who, sympathetic to Otto's plight, produced the necessary travel documents that Otto E. needed for public transportation. On the following Monday he boarded a train, but traveled to Giessen instead of Wiesbaden where by prior arrangement he met his fiancée. From there they traveled by indirect routes until two days later they finally reached Krefeld. However, instead of finding sanctuary, they arrived in the midst of an air raid. Furthermore, Krefeld, as one of Germany's western-most cities, was close to the battlefront by this time with Allied armies poised to break through to the Rhine. The town was crawling with soldiers, and Otto and his fiancée, as civilians, felt terribly conspicuous. Wisely, Otto E. and Henrika Z. waited until nightfall before proceeding westward to her parents' house in Grefrath. Alas, by then it was a doubtful sanctuary. Soldiers were quartered all around them, and Otto E. had to go into deep hiding under-ground. After seeing to her fiancé's immediate needs, Henrika, who knew that her absence from Eltville might raise suspicions, bravely returned there in order to deflect the Nazi authorities' search.[76]

For Otto E. a terrible six months ensued. "During this period I concealed myself in the oddest places in Germany. Because I did not have a ration card, I was utterly dependent upon the goodwill of total strangers. Often, I had to contend with genuine hunger." Otto E.'s travails were not merely physical. "A terrible moral depression fell over me," he continued. Otto knew that he could not resume contact with any members of his family. By this time, it was well known that spouses of Jews were being pressed into labor camps, too, and Otto feared that his father, a widower, might still face such a fate. Despite the temptation to find out, he dared not establish further contact.

Otto's troglodyte existence in Grefrath became untenable. With the Ger-man military presence there so heavy, he and Henrika's parents knew that sooner or later he would be discovered. In a war zone, civilian dwellings were subject to immediate occupation by the Wehrmacht. First, he built a tunnel and hid there for weeks, utterly dependent upon provisions that others brought to him. Each day — and night — brought with it the fear of betrayal, but with the help of Henrika's parents and trusted neighbors, he survived. Nevertheless, by early spring 1945, Allied armies were approaching, and more German troops flooded into the area. Otto E. related what happened next: "In order not to endanger the people who were caring for me clandestinely, I was forced to leave my hideout." Provided with the names of other sympathetic persons, he made his way north to Oldenburg, out of the direct line of Allied advance. Somehow, he continued to avoid arrest but had to lead a primitive, nocturnal existence. Then, in late March 1945, he decided upon a desperate gamble. He would turn south again and place himself directly in the path of the Allies' advance. Walking back from Oldenburg into the Ruhr District by night, Otto H. crossed over the last Rhine bridge at Duisburg hours before it was blown up by departing German troops. Then he made his way back to his fiancée's parents. Americans quickly took Krefeld, and so he survived the war. True, Otto E. had avoided the OT labor camps. However, in so doing he had descended to the status of a hunted animal.[77]

CONCLUSION

Those German citizens categorized as *Mischlinge* discovered by midwar, especially after the Nazi invasion of the Soviet Union in June 1941, that their lives, too, were increasingly in jeopardy. Close relatives who were Jewish had been disappearing to the East. Reports and rumors of the untimely deaths of those relatives increased dramatically as the war ground on. Even though growing evidence of military setbacks on the eastern front, around the Mediterranean rim, and eventually in France gave them secret hope that they might survive the hated regime, the *Mischlinge* saw other trends at home that caused them mounting anxiety. Increasingly, they had to reckon with scrutiny from the Gestapo and also from local police authorities that were anything but benign. As previous chapters have shown, local police officials might find some trivial offense with which to charge a *Mischling* with crimes and infractions. Notification of such charges often provoked Gestapo intervention, almost invariably resulting in harsher punishments and, for some, a one-way trip to a concentration camp. Many *Mischlinge* also became aware that it was not only the police who were watching them. Neighbors and acquaintances were often doing the same. The *Mischlinge* realized that zealous informers who reported even the slightest transgression of Nazi laws could endanger them. Once arrested or otherwise identified by Nazi officialdom, they knew that the legal system could be and was used against them. Thus, the peculiar legal limbo in which the *Mischlinge* lived — namely, superficially integrated into society but not really accepted by it — was not destined to last. It was in the spring of 1944 that their status descended to yet another dangerous plateau when Nazi authorities began rounding up all *Mischlinge,* placing men into forced-labor units of the Organisation Todt and women in menial, often dangerous jobs or work gangs at home where they, too, knew the hostile eyes of the authorities remained fixed upon them. The direct involvement of the Gestapo in rounding up *Mischlinge* in 1944–45 also demonstrated the direction Nazi persecution was taking. By now, the *Mischlinge* knew that forced labor was but a prelude to slave labor. For many, conditions in OT Lagers were tantamount to those of *Ostarbeiter* (eastern workers), or concentration camp inmates. *Mischlinge* caught outside of Germany, such as Rudolf Klein, faced incarceration early on. In exile in Belgium in 1940 when invading German forces placed him in French labor camps, he barely survived the labor camps in occupied France and faced great dangers during his five attempts to reach Switzerland. Domestic *Mischlinge* were hardly so lucky. As noted, the great mass of German *Mischlinge* experienced what Klein had endured several years later when herded into the OT forced-labor camps in 1944–45. Conditions in some sites were merely bad, as was the case for many of the *Mischlinge* of central Germany engaged in railroad repairs in northern France or many of the Berlin *Mischlinge* consigned at work on aerodromes closer to the capital. Conditions in other sites such as those that Helmut Coper experienced came close to the perils experienced by the inmates of concentration camps. Even so, many other *Mischlinge* experienced conditions somewhat in between, confined to small, often obscure sites that most postwar Germans did not even recognize as having been forced-labor camps. While the women *Mischlinge* were condemned to forced labor while still living at home, they soon realized that not only was their work dangerous, but they also had to reckon with hostile overseers and sometimes coworkers who were indifferent to harsh work conditions, accidents, or any other conditions warranting human compassion. Given these experiences, all of those hapless human beings relegated to the status of *Mischlinge* in Nazi Germany came to a common conclusion in the last year of the war: so long as the Nazis remained in power, their fates as part of a despised minority were sealed. The fate of their Jewish relatives informed them unequivocally that they were destined to die, probably somewhere in the East. The Gestapo-led actions in the final winter of the war of rounding up all Jews in "privileged mixed marriages," all so-called *Geltungsjuden,* and all male *Mischlinge* first degree demonstrated that all organizations under the umbrella of the SS were continuing to take the law into their own hands in their irrational and perverted attempts to create a Germany that was *judenfrei.* Desperately, these last intended victims of the Holocaust waited for Allied victory. That and spreading chaos were their only hopes.

5

A Time of Silence

Having narrowly escaped death at the hands of their own government, most *Mischlinge* chose nevertheless to remain in Germany after 1945 for a straightforward reason: they, like the full Jews in their families, had considered themselves Germans like any other citizen until the Nazi Seizure of Power in 1933. Unlike some of their Jewish parents, however, most *Mischlinge* had not been immersed in Judaic traditions and religious instruction. Mostly, they had lived in secular households, and their parents usually had them baptized into either Germany's Protestant or Catholic churches, although the majority entered the former.[1] The exceptions were the approximately eight thousand *Mischlinge* (roughly 10 percent of the group) who chose Jewish religious upbringing and were consigned to the status of *Geltungsjuden* and who suffered severely under the Nazis. Although the "normal" so-called *Mischlinge* suffered significant persecution, too, most of them survived the war, unlike the vast majority of full Jews. Therefore, they desired to resume a normal (for them) life with surviving family members and friends, in familiar surroundings, enjoying cultural life, using their mother tongue, and seeking to rekindle deferred careers. To be sure, there were exceptions. Some *Mischlinge* joined Jewish survivors of the Holocaust in emigrating to Palestine, later Israel. Others emigrated to North America, Latin America, or elsewhere because of their wartime experiences. Especially those persons who had been most severely persecuted developed the greatest distrust of the society that had turned on them. Statistics are lacking, but it appears that many of those *Mischlinge* who chose to leave Central Europe were indeed the former *Geltungsjuden*, the most severely persecuted category of *Mischlinge* because of their hard-earned identity with Judaism. Nevertheless, the great majority of half-Jewish

German citizens chose to stay at home. Part of their motive was their assumption that Nazism had been an irrational aberration in the nation of their birth.

Yet, having already paid a high price for their identity as *Mischlinge* under the Nazis, Germany's half-Jewish survivors continued to pay a heavy, if less obvious, price in the society that emerged after 1945. True, overt anti-Semitism ended with Germany's defeat, and denazification programs initiated by the occupying powers began the process of making racial bias unacceptable to later generations. However, the transition was glacially slow at first. In their daily lives most former *Mischlinge* quickly discovered that friends, neighbors, and bureaucracies in postwar society soon developed a kind of amnesia about the persecution that half-Jews (to say nothing of full Jews) had experienced for twelve years. Whereas until 1945 most Germans had considered Jewish and *Mischling* status to be critically important (in a negative sense), now, suddenly, that same status for the surviving *Mischlinge* became inconsequential. A typical reaction *Mischlinge* heard after the war was the following: "Oh, be quiet. You didn't have it nearly as bad as the full Jews" (which was true — as far as it went). All too frequently, the occupation authorities seemed uninterested in the *Mischlinge*, reserving their own aid and that of private charitable organizations for full Jews who had survived. And if the occupation authorities appeared to be indifferent, emergent postwar German bureaucracies were doubly so. Generally speaking, former *Mischlinge* and their families found the process of seeking compensation for persecution irksome, frustrating, and often futile no matter what postwar agency was involved, be it Allied or German.

Christian Pross, in his study of restitution from the immediate postwar period up to the present, showed that the legal and political system, governmental bureaucracy in general, and specifically the organizations charged with providing restitution to victims of Nazi persecution tended to be highly unsympathetic to applicants. This is hardly surprising, since their society had only recently — and even then only when prodded by the realities of outright military occupation — retreated from overt anti-Semitism and xenophobia. The first standardized state restitution law was not adopted until April 1949. Matters lingered until 1952 when, with the repeal of the occupation statutes, the Federal Republic acquiesced to demands by the former occupying powers to begin setting up the machinery for processing restitution claims on a regular, sustained basis. It was not until 1956 that an initial federal restitution law emerged. However, the finalized law, the Bundesentschädigungsgesetz (BEG), was not passed until 1965. Not surprisingly, the claimants who were at the core of the process were first and foremost surviving full Jews (who were few) and the immediate relatives of those who had perished (who were more numerous). Suffice it to say here, the laws on restitution and the officials who interpreted them came into being slowly and in the presence of a population that was either indifferent or openly hostile to such laws. In fact, many of the bureaucrats, including lawyers and medical doctors, who had to be consulted about levels of compensation, were themselves former Nazis who continued to populate the German legal and medical professions from the postwar years until at least the 1970s. By contrast, the German federal government was not inclined to draw out unduly the time that former Nazi civil servants had to wait in order to be reintegrated back into civil service jobs. On 11 May 1951 the Bundestag passed a law that allowed readmission of former Party members into the federal ranks. On the same day the Bundestag also passed a law granting reparations to civil servants who had been dismissed under Hitler. Those former civil servants would receive restitution under a standardized national law. Compared to restitution (if any) received under later laws established for ordinary citizens, the terms of the civil servant restitution law were extraordinarily generous.[2]

If restitution was fraught with uncertainty and unpleasantness, other evidence of bias surfaced in postwar German society that gave any would-be applicant for restitution pause. As historian Eric Johnson has pointed out in his study of the Gestapo, the secret police, who had sent vast numbers of Germans of Jewish ancestry to their deaths and who had eagerly prosecuted *Mischlinge* for the most trivial offenses, survived the vicissitudes of postwar politics remarkably well. Many dropped out of sight in the immediate postwar period, and even those who were caught in the denazification process (district chiefs or other higher officials) usually were given light sentences by authorities as Category III "minor offenders." During their trials, many of those selfsame officials emphasized their earlier careers in law enforcement as professional police officers in the Weimar years before they had joined the Gestapo. Thereafter, they claimed, they had remained conscientious officials, bent on carrying out the laws of the land along with all the rest of the civil service. Some of those former Gestapo men on trial obtained supportive testimonials from clergy in the Protestant and Catholic churches. It should be noted that such trials and sentences applied primarily to senior Gestapo officials. Almost none of the subordinate officials or staff members of Gestapo district offices were ever charged with any crimes. Even then, those officials who did receive mild sentences, fines, and dismissals from civil service in the late 1940s complained about the harshness of their sentencing after their release a few months or years later. Accordingly, those same officials recovered their full pension rights in the late 1950s, including seniority rights accumulated during their years of service to the Gestapo. After all, it had been part of the German civil service.[3]

Faced with these trends, *Mischlinge,* as potential applicants for restitution for Nazi crimes, gauged the situation warily. Sobered by what they witnessed, many — but not all — simply threw up their hands and refused to enter into the demeaning process of seeking compensation. The game was not worth the candle. Furthermore, half-Jewish survivors decided that out of sheer necessity, they had to adapt to a new set of unwritten rules, the chief one of which seemed to be the following: make no mention of ever having been a *Mischling.* This held true for both Germanys. Accounts of survival by those rare individuals willing to speak out about their experiences reinforce this point.

BREAKING SILENCE, BEARING WITNESS

Werner Jentsch, a native of Halle an der Saale, had served in the Wehrmacht in 1939–40, was dishonorably discharged in 1941, then took menial jobs until placed in a forced-labor Hundertschaft of the Organisation Todt in 1944. He repaired French railroads at SS gunpoint. Then, in August 1944, Jentsch, along with a dozen *Mischling* prisoners, escaped their guards during an American advance, only to be mistaken by their captors for a rearguard detachment. They were interned in a special camp with SS prisoners. Even so, Jentsch and his *Mischling* comrades experienced a marked improvement in their standard of living. Besides receiving adequate food and shelter in their admittedly bizarre POW camp, the captive *Mischlinge* discovered another, unexpected dimension to their new collective existence. Concentrated by the Allies, but without having to perform forced labor under threat of execution, the mostly young *Mischlinge* found time to communicate, to discuss their lives and their futures together. In the process they also found solace in each other's company. Not least, they sat out the last phase of the war together in relative safety.

It was in the late autumn of 1945 that the Americans released Jentsch and his fellow *Mischlinge*. Under the envious gaze of the SS contingent, the once despised half-Jews marched out of camp with a spring in their step. Mostly natives of central Germany, Jentsch and his companions walked eastward (there was no public transportation) toward their homes in states like Saxony and Thuringia. Jentsch set course for Halle an der Saale. However, before he left the American zone, he obtained a few prized books on mathematics — Jentsch had always loved math — and some days later finally reached Halle, the site of a respected university and once the center of German Christian missionary activity overseas. Over the succeeding years, Jentsch advanced from the status of student (he was finally accepted for university studies) to academic assistant. Then he completed a doctorate in mathematics and ultimately advanced to the prized status of a full professor at Halle's Martin-Luther Universität. Decades later in 1978, Jentsch met this author and poured out his life story, since apparently no one in the German Democratic Republic had any interest in his experiences as a *Mischling*. As noted in the preface to this book, Professor Jentsch's revelations convinced this writer that future generations would be well served in learning what Jentsch and other German citizens had once endured as *Mischlinge*.[4]

Repeatedly during his personal account, Jentsch gave assurances that his story was not unique. Rather, he said, the disruptions and tragedies caused by Nazi persecution of its partially Jewish citizens had run far and wide. Moreover, they caused social, professional, and political reverberations that continued long after the victor nations had ended their military occupations. Jentsch also indicated that in his experience, most former *Mischlinge* had had remarkably varied experiences coping in German society since 1945. Therefore, engaging in generalizations about them could be misleading. Sometimes the victims' life stories had been so dramatic that they attained a kind of celebrity status. Much more frequently, the victims — like him — had suffered in anonymity, and they had learned to live quietly with their emotional scars. For most of them, their lives had developed in unremarkable, mundane ways. Even so, he hinted at the possibility that the lingering effects

of persecution, even if subtle, could be and often were painful to those who
had experienced it. This author discovered in subsequent researches that
Werner Jentsch was a master of understatement.[5]

CASE HISTORIES

Ruth W. was one of those *Mischlinge* who was destined to suffer the effects of
persecution in less obvious ways than arrest by the Gestapo or incarceration
in a camp. Racial discrimination stunted her career potential instead. Born
in 1920 as an only child to lower-middle-class parents in Frankfurt, she received a normal primary education, but one of her teachers made a forceful
case that she was a gifted pupil. Thus, with scholarship aid, Ruth transferred
at age ten to the Elisabethenschule in Frankfurt and until 1933 fulfilled all
expectations. Then the Nazis seized power and matters soon went wrong
for her. She had to transfer to the Philantropin, Frankfurt's only Jewish secondary school, and then in 1935 the educational authorities informed *Mischling*
Ruth that her public schooling was at an end. Thereupon, her now impoverished parents made a heart-wrenching decision. They sent their fifteen-year-
old daughter to live with relatives in Philadelphia. Lacking English and utterly
dependent upon her aunt for financial support, Ruth coped as best she could
with life in her new country. Somehow she earned her diploma at one of
Philadelphia's public high schools in 1938. Money was tight, college out of
the question, and so Ruth became a secretary. Stigmatized during the war
years by her German heritage and lingering accent, Ruth nevertheless coped
with her situation in ways that *Mischlinge* in Germany also found familiar.
She remained unobtrusive, deferential, and accommodating to everyone no
matter what her private mood might be. Her status as a gifted German schoolgirl became a remote memory.

Following the war, Ruth W. married and became a housewife and mother.
Alas, the marriage was unsuccessful and as a single parent, she struggled to
make ends meet, working in the only capacity she knew: as a secretary. Years
passed. Then, Ruth S., as she was now known, learned in 1958 that victims of
Nazi persecution could apply for compensation. Having had no connection
with Germany for two decades, but realizing that she had lost priceless edu-

cational opportunities, an embittered Ruth S. decided that she should confront the shabby treatment that Hitler's Germany had dealt her. She filed an affidavit with a Philadelphia attorney. The historical record does not address exactly what compensation she may have received. However, the authorities in her native Hesse had to acknowledge her claims and deal with them. To be sure, no one could truly compensate Ruth S. for lost opportunities. What she, a gifted scholarship recipient, might have achieved employing her own language in her own country would remain forever conjectural. Neither was there an index to measure the mental anguish and bitterness she suffered during her lonely transition from one culture into another in her adolescent years. The record does show that the effects of that persecution had lingered. In her attorney's letter, written twenty years after her hasty departure from Frankfurt, Ruth S. admitted to bouts of depression and bitterness. Memories of her youthful potential served only to plague her now.[6] Ruth W. possessed one slight advantage over *Mischlinge* who continued to reside in Germany after 1945. Persons living abroad and making such claims were twice as likely to receive restitution as persons who remained in Germany.[7]

Many citizens categorized as *Mischlinge* under the Nazis quickly discovered after the war that their deplorable status would go unrecognized among the vast majority of Germans. Having been mistreated, humiliated, and malnourished, be it in OT camps or individually in jail cells, especially in the later war years, many *Mischlinge* had expected postwar compensation. However, *Mischlinge* frequently could not produce incontrovertible proofs of that persecution. Frankfurt citizen Walter S. understood this phenomenon from bitter personal experience. In 1945 he filed a detailed statement of his downward spiraling fortunes from 1938 onward. It was his fate to have gone from gifted schoolboy at an elite Gymnasium to salesman apprentice, meatpacker, casual day laborer, homeless drifter, OT forced laborer, and finally brutalized prisoner in a special punishment camp, all within the space of six years.

In fact, Walter S. had submitted not one but rather a series of increasingly detailed statements about his past to postwar German restitution officials in the U.S. zone. His applications revealed that as a *Mischling* he had been dismissed from one of Frankfurt's finest Gymnasiums and then had to accept entry-level jobs ever after. He moved from city to city during the lean war years, and finally, unemployed and homeless, returned to Frankfurt in 1944 only to be placed in an OT forced-labor camp. Alas, these facts seemed to count for little with the restitution authorities, and stung by their indifference, Walter S. submitted more information. He recounted in graphic detail his OT forced-labor assignments in and around Frankfurt and how, with many other prisoners and because of chaotic conditions, he had undertaken an eight-day unofficial leave at Christmas 1944. Honoring his private pledge to a camp guard, he returned to the OT Lager when he said he would, but new camp officials transferred him and other "deserters" to a disciplinary camp in the heavily bombed Ruhr District. Walter S. then described the horrors of incarceration at Lager Deutsche Eiche (German Oak) in Remscheid from January to May 1945. At war's end the American army transported him, a very sick man, back to Frankfurt for recovery.[8]

The restitution authorities remained unimpressed, dismissing his claims as those of a German civilian who had been placed in a late-war labor battalion. Besides, they noted, he had taken illegal leave at Christmas 1944 and deserved his punishment. Therefore, Walter S. was entitled to no compensation. Walter S. protested, but the thin bureaucratic response in his file indicates that he lost his appeal. Justice and compensation for so-called *Mischlinge* after World War II were not easy goals to achieve, especially if the victims were poor and lacked effective legal counsel. Walter S.'s forlorn attempts at securing restitution are indicative of why many former *Mischlinge* chose anonymity over compensation.[9]

Because Berlin had been home to a large Jewish population before 1933, and because there were many families of mixed Jewish-Christian heritage living in the capital, it was also the hometown to several thousand *Mischlinge*. For the most part, the Berlin *Mischlinge* chose to return from forced-labor camps, prisons, or remote places of refuge to the capital after the war. They did so despite the city's stark devastation, its division into four Allied sectors, and a postwar death rate from malnutrition and disease that approached medieval levels. Pride in Berlin played a role. Even after severe mistreatment by the Nazis, most of Berlin's *Mischling* survivors were determined to resume life in *their* city despite whatever hardships that decision might entail. Hardship was no stranger to them. They had also had personal experience of arbitrary bureaucracies — none could be any more arbitrary than a National Socialist bureaucracy — so that the cumbersome military governments of postwar Germany were unable to intimidate them either. Thus, a modest but unusual wave of returnees (many Germans were exiting the stricken capital at that time), consisting of a few thousand *Mischlinge*, found their way back to the capital.

In the Soviet zone, one of the alarming aspects of their new existence was the fact that Berlin's Jews (this held true for Jews and Jewish-Christian *Mischlinge* throughout the eastern zone) found it almost impossible at first to be heard by the Soviet troops about what they had experienced. Germany's Jews found this indiscriminate postwar treatment appalling, and so did the *Mischlinge*. After a few months of Soviet occupation, the Berliners, *Mischlinge* included, felt that a slight normalization of society had begun to emerge. Various individuals and groups were able to make the Soviet authorities understand that in addition to Jews, thousands of other Germans had also suffered grievously under National Socialism. The half-Jews, singly or in small numbers, explained to the new authorities what had happened to them. Their efforts finally produced results. In the autumn of 1945, various circles of victims of Nazi persecution created with Soviet approval a legally recognized category of formerly persecuted persons who might receive some kind of consideration or support in the Soviet zone. This included persons who had been persecuted for political or racial reasons, such as Communists, Social Democrats, Jews, *Mischlinge*, Gypsies (Roma and Sinti), Jehovah's Witnesses, and several other groups. They called themselves *Opfer des Faschismus* (Victims of Fascism) or OdFs, and were officially recognized by the Soviet authorities as having been victims of Nazi discrimination. Although the OdFs were a somewhat loosely defined and amorphous group, the persons who won such status found their paths to advancement eased somewhat in postwar society. For example, many *Mischlinge* had come from middle-class, professional families that set great store by education. The Nazis had disrupted that education, and the *Mischlinge* were determined to redeem it.

Meanwhile in postwar Berlin, the Soviet authorities had set about reopening the famed Friedrich-Wilhelms-University (present-day Humboldt University). The admissions committees looked more favorably upon a person's application if he or she had attained OdF status. Thus, a number of former *Mischlinge* discovered to their joy in that cheerless postwar autumn that they had been admitted to "Berlin University," which reopened under exclusive Soviet authority in January 1946. Unremarkable though it was, that seemingly mundane development was to have profound consequences for a number of Victims of Fascism several years later. Among those few hundred

OdFs admitted to study in a student body of three thousand persons were a few dozen former *Mischlinge*. One of them was Otto Hess.

Berliner Hess knew he was lucky to have survived National Socialism and the war. A veteran of the 1940 French campaign, he had been dishonorably discharged, forced into menial jobs, and then placed in the OT labor camp at Zerbst until it dissolved in April 1945. Now at age thirty-four, partly because of his OdF status but also because he was highly qualified, he was admitted to medical studies. Hess had seen much suffering and wanted a profession in which he could alleviate some of it. Hess's postwar experiences are described elsewhere.[10] Suffice it to say, he completed his university studies and became an acclaimed professional. Yet, his career did not evolve as he had envisaged it in 1945. Although a beneficiary of Soviet largess because of his OdF status, Hess soon became disillusioned when the Soviets and the Socialist Unity Party (SED), the East German Communist party, sought to turn Berlin University into a Communist institution. Showing rare civic courage, he, along with a core group of thirty or forty other students, protested ideological restraints, starting in May 1946. Recognized as a gifted organizer, Hess led the students' successful three-year drive to create their own Free University, which opened in 1948 with American support. At the same time that he was discovering that he had a talent for leadership, Hess started editing a popular student journal, *Colloquium*. It attracted Soviet ire while at the same time educating the public about higher education issues. It also succeeded in enlisting American support for the students' cause. Subsequently, Hess became a successful publicist and founded his own publishing house, the Colloquium Verlag, which later earned kudos as a scholarly press. Hess abandoned medicine for a career as full-time publisher, and his press continued to issue academic books for four decades thereafter. In 1987, U.S. president Ronald Reagan personally decorated Otto Hess for his many years of service to Berlin and to the Free University, which he, its leading student, had done so much to create. Otto Hess died in 1995, respected by all who knew him — by all except the Nazis and later the Communists. However, ostracism by extreme ideologues had long ceased to bother him. After all, Otto Hess's professional accomplishments had earned him the respect of his nation.[11]

Fellow ex-*Mischling* Eva Heilmann, daughter of Prussian Landtag deputy Ernst Heilmann, whom the Nazis had murdered, also survived. She and her brother, Peter, and two younger siblings had endured persecution for twelve years. While all of the Heilmann children survived the war, they admitted afterward that they still carried emotional scars. Eva, too, had been granted OdF status and gained admittance to Berlin University. However, she, like Hess, was one of the students who created the Free University in 1948. Hauling a typewriter to its hastily improvised admissions office in Dahlem in June 1948, she became that soon-to-be-famous university's first administrative assistant and later was elected its first student spokesperson, a rare accomplishment for a young woman of the late 1940s. Eva Heilmann soon married, changing her name to Furth. She raised a family, thus abrogating her professional career. However, many years later in the late 1980s she returned to her studies, and as an older citizen was recognized repeatedly in public ceremonies as one of those courageous students of 1948 who had founded a major university despite Soviet threats. She still lives in Berlin and enjoys her status as a prominent Berliner. Besides, as a doting grandmother (and widely noted for her supreme wit), she has long outlived the system that had tried to destroy her and other *Mischlinge*.[12]

Peter Heilmann was less fortunate in some ways than his older sister. A convinced Socialist like his father, Peter aligned himself in 1946 with the militant SED, a merger of the old German Communist Party (KPD) and the Social Democratic Party (SPD) in the Soviet zone. First, he won election as a young deputy mayor in an eastern district of Berlin. Then he became involved in the SED's youth movement, the Free German Youth (FDJ) along with another soon-to-be-prominent SED member, Erich Honecker. However, in the rough-and-tumble of SED power struggles, Heilmann lost out to the ruthless Honecker. The latter trumped up charges that Peter, the son of a prominent German Social Democrat, was an "English spy," and he was sentenced to five years in prison. The experience sobered him, and upon his release, Peter moved back to West Berlin where he became an academic assistant at the Free University. Then he joined Berlin's Protestant Evangelische Akademie. One stark fact emerged from his experiences in East and West German politics. During a lifetime as an outsider, Peter Heilmann realized that his former *Mischling* status was no guarantor of respect or sympathy from either the SED or any other political group; rather it was a burden. Abandoned by childhood friends during the Hitler years, he reestablished ties with virtually none of the schoolmates and associates of his youth. After all, they had deserted him, especially in wartime, when Germany's *Mischlinge* suffered a persecution that was leading them, too, toward the Final Solution.[13]

Berlin native Meta Alexander recalled that it was impossible to talk with others after the war about her experiences as a former *Mischling*. The memories were simply too painful. She, like several other *Mischlinge* such as Thekla Brandt, decided to study medicine and, given her excellent qualifications, she earned her doctorate in medicine at the new Free University. Eschewing private practice, Alexander compiled a distinguished medical career at the Free University as a professor of internal medicine and infectious diseases. Yet, for decades she never talked to others about her wartime experiences. Then, in 1979, her mother died. It was a traumatic experience, and Meta Alexander realized that she had cast aside not only her own past but also her family's past. At a reunion of her high school class later that year, she decided to reveal the ugly experiences that had befallen her and her family. Meta told her prewar classmates candidly for the first time what it had been like to be a *Mischling*. She explained how she had learned that beloved family members were being murdered because they were Jewish. She explained how she and other family members had barely survived. Her classmates were shocked. They did not realize the kind of trauma she and her family had experienced. She also told them that because of that terrible twelve-year experience, she had refused to reveal her true background to acquaintances and friends ever since 1945. She told how those experiences had conditioned her to be suspicious of others, especially strangers. She never married. She had learned to avoid talking about herself or about family members to anyone outside her family (i.e., she compartmentalized her life). She had also learned under the Nazis how to avoid political topics, a habit she found she could not break after the war. Classmate Meta Alexander stunned her fellow classmates.[14]

Having caught their attention, Meta elaborated. As a university student in the postwar years, she realized during conversations with other "normal" students who related their experiences under National Socialism that she and they had led utterly different lives for twelve years. They had been part of society's mainstream, whereas she had become an outsider. Then, one day she realized with a shock that her status as an outsider was continuing and would probably continue for the rest of her life. In those postwar discussions she found herself listening in silence as young male students talked freely about their recent military service. Young women in the group spoke positively about their experiences in the BDM, in the Reichsarbeitsdienst (RAD), or as wartime auxiliaries. Meta had been banned from participation in each and every one of those organizations and could add nothing to such conversations. She found she was still being excluded in many ways from her postwar society (i.e., her *Mischling* experience was continuing).[15]

Later, Meta admitted that she had found a silver lining to her tribulations as a *Mischling*. It was her fate to have been born into a prosperous family, an existence that normally would have isolated her from anyone except the middle class. Because of Nazi persecution and her family's subsequent impoverishment, she had had to associate on a daily basis with people from many nationalities, ethnic groups, social classes, and walks of life. She had learned in a tough school that there was evil and brutality in the world. Yet, she also learned that there were many good people in society. No matter what class or what race they represented, she found many of them to be caring people, whose virtues had shown through despite the evils propagated by the Nazis. Finally, Meta Alexander stated that she felt motivated to persevere with her medical career, and it was that accomplishment especially that had brought her some consolation later in life. She died in 1999, respected by all her colleagues, who finally knew what she had once endured and what she had had to overcome in order to achieve her distinguished career.[16]

Thekla Brandt and her sister, having helped their parents run their medical practice in Neukölln in the final year of the war when persecution of Jews and *Mischlinge* had increased alarmingly, decided in peacetime that they, too, would like to study medicine. Both received OdF status, and the Soviet authorities admitted them to Berlin University. Thekla and her sister joined the group of breakaway students who founded the Free University in 1948. They studied fervently in those postwar years, determined to make up for their lost years when the Nazis had cast them aside from society. For Thekla, too, the effects of persecution did not disappear quickly. She, her sister, and her two brothers found it difficult to overcome strong feelings of inferiority vis-à-vis the rest of society even after 1945. All four Brandt siblings were loath to open up to others, especially to strangers, after the war. Yet, they also knew that they had been lucky. Their family had survived intact, a piece of good fortune they did not underestimate, especially after their mother's narrow escape from transport to a death camp in 1945. Moreover, they were able to form their own modest support group, since each of them as a former *Mischling* first degree knew exactly what the others had endured. Each was also acquainted with other former *Mischlinge,* who suffered on in isolation, still surrounded by the invisible walls that society had erected earlier. Those individuals had no support groups. Therefore, Thekla and her three siblings considered themselves fortunate. They got on with their lives and gradually overcame the demons of earlier times.[17]

Fellow Berliner Helmut Coper knew that he was lucky to have survived physically unharmed after harrowing experiences with his OT Hundertschaft in Jena and elsewhere during the last year of the war. He recalled many years later that he had left Berlin in the autumn of 1944 with a group of 256 largely healthy men. Only 106 emaciated survivors shuffled back into the capital in April 1945.[18] He also knew what it was like to be a hunted fugitive in a city filled with marauding troops and Nazi death squads. By 1945, he was an orphan in every sense, since his Aryan mother had died in an air raid in 1944, and the Nazis had murdered his Jewish father at Auschwitz a few weeks later. Therefore, his first "family" in Berlin during the final battles of the war consisted of an impromptu group of deserters hiding out from the Nazis in those wild times. Helmut had known genuine fear. He carries those ghosts to this day. For many years he, like Meta Alexander, Thekla Brandt, and many other *Mischlinge,* refused to talk to others about his experiences. "It all seemed so surreal afterwards," he explained to this author, "and what I have explained now is only half of the truth, actually less than half of the truth."[19]

Helmut Coper also admitted that recounting the events of 1933–45 even fifty years later still made him uneasy. He hastened to add that his experiences were not particularly unusual among *Mischlinge* of his acquaintance. Conversations with fellow survivors convinced him that all of them had felt mounting anxiety and a fear of the future, emotions that intensified when the Nazis accelerated the pace of persecution in the late-war period. Like several other survivors mentioned in this account, Helmut Coper decided to study medicine after the war. Given his youth, he had to complete his *Abitur* first. Then, he, too, gained Soviet recognition as an OdF and entered Berlin University. In 1948, along with other students, he joined in the move to create the Free University in the American sector. He and fellow FU applicant Karol Kubicki tossed a coin to decide who would be the first matriculated student at the student-inspired university. Helmut lost, and so became the Free University's second entering student with matriculation number two. Thus began a distinguished medical career in which Coper specialized in neuropsychopharmacology, pioneering in the development of specialized medications for persons with emotional disorders, a subject with which he was already familiar. Broad public recognition of his many accomplishments, first as a founding student of the FU, and then as an outstanding medical researcher, have made him a famous citizen of Berlin, too. And yet, to this day Helmut Coper starts violently when there is a knock at the door or when the telephone rings.[20]

Former secondary school pupils Horst Hartwich and Hanns-Peter Herz had had the dubious distinction of being expelled in the spring of 1942 from their Berlin secondary schools. Both got by on menial jobs for two years, and both entered the OT camp at Zerbst. Both returned to Berlin and survived the final battles in the dying capital. Following the war, they, like Helmut Coper, finished the *Abitur* that the Nazis had denied them and became founding members of the Free University. Hartwich studied medicine, Herz journalism and mass communications. By a curious twist, both developed careers that put them in the public view.

As almost a sideline from his medical studies, Hartwich had helped create and then lead the Free University's Aussenamt, its Office of International Affairs. He was so successful as an international ambassador for the FU that even though he completed his medical degree, Hartwich never practiced medicine. He continued to direct the FU's international programs instead, using his diplomatic and linguistic skills to attract famed scholars from all over the world to Dahlem, thereby turning the fledgling university into one of the leading institutions of higher learning in the German-speaking world. It was Hartwich who placed a medallion around the neck of President John F. Kennedy in 1963, making him an honorary member of the Free University. Hartwich continued to direct the FU's Aussenamt until his retirement in 1989, aiding the giant university's transition into the post–Cold War era. He seldom mentioned his earlier status as a *Mischling*. Neither did he try to hide it. In common with other Berliners who had suffered similar persecution, Hartwich got on with his life and found other challenges. Thus, in later decades his university, his city, and his nation benefited from his emotional resilience and his generous nature. At Horst Hartwich's funeral in July 2000, thousands turned out to pay their last respects.[21]

Like Hartwich and all other Berliners, Hanns-Peter Herz acquired intense, firsthand experience of the Cold War. At an early stage in that strange conflict he was already serving in the "front lines" as an employee of RIAS (Radio in the American Sector) of Berlin. This was western Berlin's leading radio station in the postwar years, reporting such events as the Soviet blockade and subsequent Berlin airlift of 1948–49. RIAS continued to play a prominent role in a war of the airwaves when propaganda and counterpropaganda dominated telecasts, and Herz was intensely involved in those media duels. In succeeding years, he helped inform the rest of the world of mounting East–West tensions, culminating in the building of the Berlin Wall in August 1961. Then, in the turbulent 1960s and 1970s, Herz worked in Berlin city hall, but in 1985 he returned to RIAS where he completed his distinguished career in electronic journalism. Like Hartwich, Herz put his *Mischling* status behind him after 1945, concentrating instead on building a career and in rebuilding his hometown into a great metropolis.[22]

Hans-Joachim Boehm and Ernst Benda had both been designated *Mischlinge* second degree under the Nazis (i.e., they were one-quarter Jewish). Both were quick to affirm that they had suffered significantly less persecution than half-Jews. Yet, their experiences were also illuminating about the ways in which National Socialism discriminated against persons possessing any Jewish heritage. Boehm had had to leave school early to help his widowed mother and siblings. Under National Socialism, social welfare was not forthcoming for *Mischlinge* second degree. Therefore, Boehm had begun a business apprenticeship, but no sooner had he finished it than the Nazis conscripted him into the Wehrmacht in 1939. Even then, his *Mischling* status continued to hound him. Despite five years of distinguished, frontline service, four of them on the eastern front where he suffered two grievous wounds, Boehm never rose above the rank of private. His middle name of Samuel and what the Nazis claimed as "Jewish" physical traits continued to plague him. After the war Hans-Joachim completed his *Abitur* at his old school, Berlin's Friedenau Gymnasium. He refrained from telling others about his former status as a *Mischling* second degree, since he knew so many others who had suffered far worse. Hans-Joachim also became one of the founding students of the Free University. Then, he launched a long and distinguished career in Berlin politics, rising to *Senatsdirektor* and member of the Berlin Assembly.[23]

Ernst Benda held opinions similar to those of Hans-Joachim Boehm about the less onerous status of *Mischlinge* second degree. Slightly younger than Boehm, he had finished his *Notabitur* in 1943 and after passing demanding technical examinations had served in the German navy as a radioman/cryptographer. For him, too, as a *Mischling* second degree, advancement was out of the question. Sailor Benda ended the war in Norway as a prisoner of war, returning to Berlin in 1946. To his relief he found his family still alive, including his father who had suffered worse persecution as a *Mischling* first degree. Denied university studies under the Nazis, he applied for law school, but Benda never mentioned his *Mischling* status, nor did he try to become an OdF. Sheer talent and determination were enough. Like most survivors, he concentrated on the present and on acquiring the skills needed to start a career that had been too long delayed.

Benda, too, became a founding student of the Free University. He passionately debated current politics with other students, discussing ways to help shape a new society. Naturally drawn to politics, Benda joined the new Christian Democratic Party's (CDU) youth organization, the Jung Union. It was there that he emerged as a talented personality likely to rise to a position of leadership in the new society. Word spread to the Americans. Accordingly, Benda became one of the first German students to participate in a cultural exchange to the United States where he studied law at the University of Wisconsin. Upon his return to Berlin, Benda entered politics as a regular member of the CDU. As a native son, he won election to Berlin's Abgeordnetenhaus, its city assembly. Then, he won a seat from Berlin to the Bundestag in Bonn. Simultaneously, he continued to learn law as an academic discipline and became a distinguished law professor. In 1968–69 Benda served as interior minister to the Federal Republic, and after that became president of the Federal Republic's Constitutional Court in Karlsruhe. Later, he became a senior commissioner in the European Union. In short, Ernst Benda built one of the most distinguished careers imaginable for a citizen of Germany — or any other European nation. Benda credited his good fortune in good part to careful nurturing within his tight-knit family, bonds that had held together despite Nazi persecution.[24] It was just as well that Ernst Benda and Hans-Joachim Boehm made their careers in a Germany freed of Nazis. Had the latter remained in power, they would have seen to it that neither of the two *Mischlinge* second degree rose above the level of a common laborer. Furthermore, the

Nazis intended that the forty thousand *Mischlinge* second degree be forcibly sterilized in order to ensure that they would never "Mendel out" progeny exhibiting "Jewish" characteristics.[25]

Berliner Hans Haurwitz, a *Mischling* but also a *Geltungsjude* in Nazi parlance, realized that he and his Jewish father had survived in good part because Frau Haurwitz, Aryan wife and mother, had saved her men. She had intervened repeatedly to rescue Hans and his father from deportation and annihilation by the Nazis. Frau Haurwitz was one of the largely female protesters at the Rosenstrasse in February 1943 whose courageous actions had prevented the transport of their Jewish husbands to the camps.[26]

The Haurwitz family had ended the war in their cramped apartment in Charlottenburg. They had survived numerous Allied bombings as well as continuing humiliation for Hans and his father, whose Star of David armbands marked them for frequent public abuse by diehard Nazis until the bitter end. Not least, all three Haurwitzes were terribly malnourished because of the severely limited rations both men had endured for years, combined with an end-of-war lowering of Frau Haurwitz's Aryan ration that she had shared with them. Soviet soldiers occupied their district in late April, and while the frontline troops were decent, all three Haurwitzes feared the rear-echelon forces. Try as they would, they could not seem to make the Russians understand what they, as victims, had endured under the Nazis. Now they were just Germans again and were despised for it, and they endured the same hardships and dangers all of their neighbors faced. Then, in early July 1945, the Soviets departed, and British forces entered Charlottenburg to begin their occupation. However, it was not a Briton but rather an American who rang the doorbell of the Haurwitz apartment one day in July 1945.[27]

Before the war, Hans had been friends with two brothers from a neighborhood family. All three had received religious instruction together. Then, the two brothers had emigrated to the United States in 1936. Now, nine years later, Hans spotted an army jeep pulling into the curb in front of his building. To his surprise, the soldier who emerged promptly made his way to the Haurwitz family's door. The soldier was one of the two brothers who had emigrated before the war and was now attached to the U.S. Second Armored Division. Remembering the Haurwitz address, he decided to see if anyone had survived. The two young men hugged each other and exchanged information about how each had pulled through the harrowing times. The soldier then asked

Hans how he could help them. Hans did not hesitate. The family desperately needed food, he admitted. Glancing at his painfully thin boyhood friend, the soldier, who was now a general's aide, put Hans in his jeep and drove him to headquarters. The Americans made him a waiter in the general's mess. Hans learned to be an efficient scrounger and server, and he ate well for the first time in his adult life. He also provided for his parents. Thus the Haurwitzes survived the lean postwar years.[28]

No longer ostracized, Hans began to socialize. He met a young woman who was similarly employed by the American forces in Berlin, and soon they married. Then it was time to decide what they should do with their lives together. Feeling no great attachment to the place where he had been a slave worker, Haurwitz and his new bride decided, with help from the Jewish Joint Distribution Committee, to move to the United States. In 1949 they settled in Erie, Pennsylvania, made their careers, raised their family, and now live in retirement. For many years Hans suffered recurring nightmares and flashbacks from his privations as a *Geltungsjude*. However, his wife helped him to cope with post-traumatic stress, and over time the nightmares occurred less frequently. He and his family attend a nearby reform synagogue, and to his satisfaction, Erie's Temple Anshe Hesed reminds him of the synagogue he attended in Berlin. Having put his personal anxieties to rest, Hans Haurwitz can now make occasional public addresses and enlighten audiences of what Jews and Jewish *Mischlinge* once endured in Germany from 1933 to 1945.[29]

Hans Haurwitz was hardly alone in experiencing difficult adjustments after the war. Klaus Muehlfelder had survived OT camps in northern France in 1944 and had returned to Berlin surreptitiously after Germany's defeat in the West. The Gestapo had rounded him up again that October, but he had feigned ill health and was permitted to remain at home with his parents while working as a common laborer. Fearful that the authorities would come for him a third time, Klaus had obtained a rare handgun and ammunition (illegal for civilians) from a fellow *Mischling*. If the Gestapo tried to seize him, he was determined to resist. Fortunately, the authorities never reappeared. He was lucky in another way in that he lived in rural Lübars, an area of Berlin that was out of the path of the invading armies. As soon as he saw his first Russian soldiers, Klaus sighed with relief and wisely threw the handgun and ammunition into a nearby pond.

At first he and his family were happy to see the Soviet troops. Officers used the Muehlfelders' house as their quarters for some weeks, and Klaus's mother prepared meals for them. Nevertheless, tensions and cultural differences soon surfaced. None of Klaus's family spoke Russian. Newly arriving Russian personnel, most of whom spoke no German, indicated disbelief that any Jews had survived. Klaus's family tried to describe the persecution they had suffered, but the language barrier stumped them. Then, one night a new group of officers locked themselves into his parents' bedroom, and the next morning Klaus's father found that they had removed all of the contents from the room and its closets, wrapped them in bedsheets, and were preparing to depart. In desperation, he ran to a Czech neighbor who knew some Russian, then returned to the departing Russians. He announced that he, too, had once been a medical officer in 1914–18 and knew that officers were not supposed to loot. Surprised at his boldness, the officers summoned a senior colleague who then informed the Czech that if this insolent German (Herr Muehlfelder) uttered another word, he would arrest him and put the house to the torch. A strained silence ensued while the Soviet officers stalked off. The family retrieved their belongings, but tensions with their eastern liberators continued.[30]

Amid postwar hardships, Klaus finished his *Abitur* in 1946, then applied to Berlin University. He was nonplussed when the authorities turned him down. He came from bourgeois origins and was inadmissable, they said. After inquiring among friends, Klaus learned of OdF status and as a former *Mischling* finally received it. After further delay, Klaus finally obtained admission to the university, but that experience, combined with the perils he and his family had faced with the Soviet army, caused much resentment. Furthermore, he and other students quickly grew disillusioned when they witnessed the Soviet authorities transforming Berlin University into a Marxist–Leninist institution.

By contrast, Klaus had enjoyed positive experiences with American occupation forces. Spurred on by informal contacts with Americans, he immersed himself in American literature, history, and culture. Thus, in April 1948, when Berlin students began calling for a Free University, Klaus joined them. Along with other students he began — at no little risk — collecting English-language books from sources in the Soviet sector and hauling them to the nascent FU Library. It was, he recounted many years later, an exhilarating experience. After several semesters at the FU, Klaus Muehlfelder achieved a dream that he had nurtured during his years as a *Mischling*. He emigrated to the United States in 1950. Upon reaching New York, he changed his name to Charles Milford and started a new life, distancing himself from the world he had known as a *Mischling*.[31]

Given his aptitude and exemplary scholarly record, Charles was accepted to Columbia University's School of Library Science and became an academic librarian. Then suddenly life changed. In the midst of the Korean War, Charles Milford, refugee from Hitler's militarism, suddenly found himself wearing a U.S. Army uniform even though he was not yet a citizen. Nevertheless, Charles dutifully served as an enlisted man, survived that war, and upon discharge in 1953 stumbled upon a cruel irony. Not yet naturalized, he encountered great difficulty in finding a job. Swallowing his frustration, Charles took humble entry positions in city libraries in the Pacific Northwest towns of Tacoma and Salem. His patience was rewarded when he won appointment to Stanford University where he served as a librarian for thirty years until retirement. This author can attest that he remains an exemplary bibliographer. Milford admits that his experiences as a *Mischling* still haunt him. He remains cautious around strangers because of the anti-Semitism he faced. He still feels the need to wait a considerable time before telling anyone that once upon a time he, too, was a so-called *Mischling*.[32]

While Charles Milford had ended his odyssey outside Germany, Helmut Langer began his odyssey abroad and ended it in the Federal Republic. Helmut and his brother, Eckard, both Sudeten Germans from a village near Gablonz, spent the last year of the war working in a Czech factory on the Polish border. There they found steady employment producing, of all things, Iron Crosses and other military decorations for the Wehrmacht. Their uncle by marriage, Herr Goldbach, was a member of the Sturm Abteilung (SA), who used his Party connections to win wartime contracts. Then the boys' aunt convinced her husband to employ Helmut and Eckard despite their *Mischling* status. For years the Langers had supplied the Goldbachs with eggs and dairy products, and with the boys' father serving in the Wehrmacht, it seemed appropriate — as well as good business — to hire two reliable, industrious youths. The Langers worked in welcome anonymity alongside *Ostarbeiter* (eastern laborers) until war's end. In the aftermath of the German retreat, Helmut and Eckard provided a kind of guardianship for Herr Goldbach and their aunt.

Those were wild times, during which the *Ostarbeiter* celebrated liberation, looting German-owned houses and having nightly revels. They even discussed hanging the SA man and his wife. Reasoning with the workers in Czech, the brothers calmed them, mentioning at the same time that they were *Mischlinge* and that their aunt and uncle had given them refuge at a time when Nazi authorities were rounding up all Jews and half-Jews.

Then the newly constituted Czech authorities arrived. Two police investigators, backed by armed guards, produced a list of all Germans employed in the area. They promptly ordered Herr Goldbach and his wife into an internment camp. At first, the police assumed that the Langer boys were SA members, too, but their list showed that Helmut and Eckard were not on any employment roll. Herr Goldbach had omitted their names so that Nazi authorities would be kept unaware. The boys tried their best to explain to the police what it meant to have been *Mischlinge* in the notoriously anti-Semitic Sudetenland. In the end, it made no difference. The chief investigator ordered Germans Helmut and Eckard Langer out of Czechoslovakia forthwith.[33]

The Langer brothers soon discovered that obeying Czech police orders was not easy. The boys had no money and no place to stay. They found temporary lodging with a kindly Czech family, then made plans to leave their wartime safe haven. First, Helmut borrowed a rusty bicycle and made a clandestine delivery of foodstuffs to his starving aunt and uncle in the harsh internment camp. Since Germans were banned from using railroads, Helmut gathered a few more provisions and set out on foot for Germany (his older brother, Eckard, who knew the Czech language better, returned home to Gablonz). Fifteen-year-old Helmut hiked for weeks, begging food wherever he could. Ultimately, he was reduced to eating the occasional raw potato he gleaned from already harvested fields. Finally he tottered into Weimar in the Soviet zone of occupation, emaciated and discouraged. His only reward was the fact that he had gained reentry into the society to which he was entitled by birth to live.[34]

To be sure, Helmut was just one of thousands of refugees crowding in from the East. Subsisting on meager rations and eager for work, Helmut became an apprentice in a small grocery store, where he earned a pittance but at least got by. By chance, he encountered another aunt in Weimar and explained the misadventures that had befallen him as a *Mischling*. His aunt listened with great interest, then took him to the city authorities where she explained that as a half-Jew, Helmut had barely survived a concentration camp and should now be given a much better ration card. Helmut listened to her explanation dumbfounded. True, he had suffered as a *Mischling*, but that experience had not included incarceration in one of the dreaded camps. The rationing authorities were unimpressed anyway, and ordered them out. Stubbornly, the aunt, with Helmut in tow, tried other offices, each time offering her version of Helmut's persecuted past. He tried to correct her in private, but she would not listen. Finally it dawned on the teenager that his aunt was simply using him as a ticket to obtain better rations. Ashamed, Langer concluded that he would never reveal his *Mischling* past to anyone again.[35]

Alas, he also discovered that being a refugee in the Soviet zone without connections, skills, or rights as a persecuted person carried severe disadvantages. Langer knew nothing of the new OdF status that other *Mischlinge*, usually of middle-class origin, were using. None of his family had ever attended a university. Upon completing his grocery store "apprenticeship" in 1948, Helmut learned that his name had been entered on a list of single persons who were to be sent to mine uranium nearby. In short, he would become a forced laborer. That was the last straw. Helmut promptly purchased a train ticket to a city near the zonal border, not even daring to pack a bag. From there, he made a nighttime trek into the American zone, settling in a refugee camp near Marburg.

Life in the western zones in the late 1940s was not easy either. Even so, Helmut stuck by his decision never to reveal his former *Mischling* status again and accepted any available work. Aged eighteen by now, he labored nights in a textile mill where he shared a barracks with eight other men, sometimes having to wait for a bed to come free before he could sleep. Helmut had excelled in athletics as a boy, and even now he found pleasure when playing for a soccer club on Sunday afternoons. During one match, a teammate announced proudly that he had just been made a policeman and suggested lightheartedly that Helmut should apply. "Why not?" he asked himself and turned in his application the very next morning. Much to his surprise, Helmut was accepted and graduated from the police academy with ease. Thus, in 1950 Langer became a policeman, the first genuine career — as opposed to casual labor — he had ever held.[36]

Although life improved, Constable Langer (and former *Mischling*) discovered that anti-Semitism was hardly dead in the Federal Republic. When sent out on patrols with more senior policemen, he experienced the usual routines where two cops converse in their vehicle (usually the night shift for a newcomer like him). As is usual anywhere, the two officers might chat about family and personal experiences. Since it was still the postwar period, Helmut's older partners often described their wartime experiences as the night wore on. "Some of my fellow officers explained to me in vivid detail how they had served as Kettenhunde [Feldgendarmerie or military policemen]," he recalled. Those unofficial and official titles sounded innocuous. However, some of the same police officers then added that they had participated in *Sondereinsätze* (i.e., special Einsatzgruppen actions), and had hunted down Jews and anyone else of Jewish ancestry throughout Eastern Europe, *Mischlinge* included. In short, just a few years earlier, Helmut's current partners had been hunting down people just like him. Helmut maintained silence.

Despite those hair-raising encounters, Langer discovered that he had a natural talent for his new job. A survivor, he combined street smarts with compassion, plus humor and toughness when those attributes were necessary. Privately, however, he suffered from his past. Ever since 1945, Helmut had experienced severe headaches, and they became more severe with time. Moreover, he endured periodic bouts of depression, although he did his best to hide those maladies from everyone. The result of his efforts was both gratifying and terrifying. Over time, Langer achieved the reputation of being the jovial, beloved local cop in his small Hessian town. Neighbors and acquaintances came to him for advice, not only for legal or police reasons, but also for any number of personal or family problems. He provided answers to myriad questions about law and the legal system. Given his reputation, people even consulted him when buying a used car or deciding on a future job. Everyone knew that he would offer sound advice with unfailing good cheer. With time he became a father figure and informal spiritual adviser, much like a priest, rabbi, or pastor.

Of course, Helmut was none of these. He was a "mere" policeman and formerly a despised *Mischling*. Try as he might, the latter was a status he could never forget. Helmut continued to suffer from severe headaches, and in middle age, his bouts of depression grew stronger. When acquaintances gathered around him at the local pub, asking advice and sharing in a friendly drink, he noticed that as inhibitions let down, his acquaintances not infrequently indulged in anti-Semitic remarks or jokes. Outwardly, Helmut would not respond, but inwardly old anxieties and tensions came flooding back. Yet, he continued to mask his emotions, and none of his acquaintances ever suspected his past. Even his wife of many years was unaware of what he had endured as a *Mischling*. After several decades, including occasional gatherings with Helmut's immediate family (his brother, Eckard, had also fled to the West), she finally elicited the truth from her husband. Even then they made a pact never to reveal his past to anyone. The Langers raised three children, all of whom led normal, happy childhoods. The children were blessed with intelligence and keen athletic prowess, and they all developed excellent work habits, benefits of a loving family relationship. Therefore, except for Frau Langer and his brother, Eckard, Helmut continues to carry alone the burden of what happened to him as a *Mischling* in Hitler's Greater German Reich. He broke his silence only once, agreeing to meet with this interviewer. Toward the end of his sometimes tearful recounting of his past, Helmut squared his shoulders, comforted this interviewer (who in the meantime had also been overtaken by emotion), and splendid human being that he is, brought both participants back to the business of sober reflection. He stated that he had given his account in order that American readers, especially, would know what it was like to have been a *Mischling* in those faraway places and distant times.[37] In this respect, Helmut Langer has become a spokesman for the thousands of former *Mischlinge* who were not highly educated, not well connected in society, and who had no protective group or organization after the war to help them. Therefore, he truly represents the majority of German citizens of Jewish-Christian descent who survived — or did not survive — Hitler's Germany.

Geographically, Martha Rohr was as far removed from Helmut Langer as a *Mischling* could get and still be within the German-speaking world. A Berlin orphan born in 1918, she had grown to adulthood with an adoptive family in tiny Wintersdorf on the Luxembourg border, so exotic a child that she had scarcely encountered any prejudice — until 1933. Then, Ortsgruppenleiter Hans Dokter arrived and focused his malevolent attentions upon Martha. Among many incidents, she successfully endured a humiliating physical examination of her *Mischling* characteristics by Nazi public health officials in 1940, then warded off male suitors including her future husband thereafter because her fellow Wintersdorf citizens, aping the Nazi official, had begun monitoring her every activity. Following the German army's retreat out of Luxembourg in February 1945, Martha accompanied her fellow villagers to a neighboring hamlet. Then, one evening she emerged from a house crowded with fellow refugees to use the nearby toilet, a primitive shed. From that vantage point she clearly heard the Wintersdorf men, neighbors who had known her since infancy, uttering her name and stating loudly: "We'll deal with her! We'll put her into a concentration camp!" Other villagers chorused their assent, and for the first time in her life Martha Rohr felt real fear. Those were her neighbors. They had been kindly to her — until 1933.

Fortunately for Martha, the American armies swept through the region within days, so that the local Nazis were no longer putting anyone into camps. It was her old nemesis instead, Ortsgruppenleiter Hans Dokter, who landed in an American camp for Nazi war criminals, never to be seen in Wintersdorf again. Martha returned home, and with the family's two cows, she traded dairy produce for rations from the American soldiers in Wintersdorf. She also shared what she could with her neighbors and tried to forget the past. Even so, Martha could not help but notice that the same Wintersdorf neighbors who, months earlier, had wanted to place her in a camp wanted to be friends now. She also noted with amusement that church attendance among Wintersdorf's former Nazi sympathizers had risen dramatically. Martha married the village youth whom she had not dared to date earlier, raised a family, and remained in Wintersdorf ever after.[38]

Some *Mischlinge* who had been incarcerated in the smaller forced-labor camps during the war discovered that they were at a disadvantage when seeking compensation in the postwar period. Their "camps" had been small, hastily erected work sites, and few outsiders knew of their existence. Trying to convince restitution authorities of their plight was even more difficult than was the case with larger camps like Caserne Mortier, Zerbst, or Rochau. The experiences of inmates in tiny Camp Bähr or in Witzenhausen outside Kassel bear recounting because they show what happened to former inmates trying to assemble proofs after 1945 for compensation. One of the survivors of the Kassel roundup, Georg B., explained how the smaller camps contrasted to the larger camps. "Two heavily armed French OT . . . guards [!] were supposed to accompany us," he recalled. "However, following our protest, the armed guards were dropped and we made our way to the camp on our own. There we met *Mischlinge* from Berlin, Westphalia, and the Sudetenland."[39] To be sure, Camp Bähr was no joy, even without guards. Georg B. emphasized that their rations were totally inadequate for men engaged in heavy labor. Yet, there were ameliorating circumstances. The authorities simply read the inmates the camp rules and expected them to obey them. They warned the prisoners not to frequent local businesses, restaurants, or other public establishments, nor were they to talk to townsfolk. Family members might visit them, but only on Sundays and only then with written permission. Technically speaking, the laborers were working for a Kassel-based construction firm, Gerdum and Breuer, and the latter actually paid them wages according to a formula established by the OT. Those wages were laughably low: 73 pfennigs per hour for heavy labor (but with 1.5 Reichsmarks deducted per day for food and shelter, inadequate though it was). Thus, the forced laborers earned roughly 60 Reichsmarks per month.[40]

Georg B. also chronicled the Kassel women's late-war experiences. "The female *Mischlinge* were not assigned to camps," he observed. "Instead, they were ordered to take up heavy manual labor. In Kassel, for example, they were assigned to Spinnfaser [textiles] and to Karl Anton Henschel [aircraft components]. They had to give up any current occupations and were required to report for work at the above-mentioned firms. However, they could continue to live at home."[41]

Georg B. also observed that dread of the future hung over the *Mischlinge* at his small Lager. The camp overseers gave them ominous warnings periodically that their current work site was only temporary. "We were told repeatedly that we were going to be transferred away from Kassel to the East," he recalled. "At the beginning of March 1945 we were told to put down our tools one Thursday afternoon and were informed that we would be placed on a transport the following Monday. However, several heavy air raids took place on Kassel over that weekend, during which the offices of the local Gestapo were destroyed. This had the effect of eliminating the intended result." The Kassel camp inmates knew they were extremely lucky. Georg B. spoke for all of the *Mischling* survivors: "Looming over all of us was, of course, the constant threat of being transported to the East. And since all of us were perfectly aware by this time of what had happened in Auschwitz, our mood matched the situation."[42]

Postwar restitution claims indicate that there were even smaller camps for *Mischlinge* than modest Camp Bähr in Kassel. Erich G., who lived in the village of Witzenhausen outside Kassel, decided to apply for compensation for what he had endured in the tiny forced-labor camp there. To his amazement the Hessian restitution authorities expressed disbelief that such a camp had ever existed. Erich G. wrote a blunt letter to the senior responsible official, the Regierungspräsident in Kassel. "I regret that you force me to write down on paper the misdeeds that took place in our camp because I would have preferred to erase them from my memory," he began. Erich G. then described in excruciating detail the miserable conditions in which he and fourteen other detainees had lived. Their diminutive "camp" was formed in July 1944 to build underground, bombproof facilities. Some of the prisoners delivered by the Gestapo to Witzenhausen's miniature labor camp were *Mischlinge*. Others were Aryan men still married to Jewish women. A few were *Ostarbeiter* or foreign laborers. The "camp" consisted of an aged, low-ceilinged clay house with four cramped rooms. The structure lacked heat, electricity, toilets, basins, running water, or amenities of any kind, and the inmates slept on straw sacks on the dirt floor. Their rations consisted of thin soup and bread and very little of either, considering the heavy labor they were expected to perform. The Gestapo was in overall charge of the camp, which the hostile villagers universally referred to as the *Judenlager* (camp for Jews). Like the inmates in Kassel's Camp Bähr, the fourteen Witzenhausen detainees were warned not to visit any businesses or public establishments; nor were they to join public gatherings or speak to the town citizens. Since it was a small town where secrets were few, the camp inmates obeyed, soon falling into complete social isolation. They felt like beasts of burden, plodding silently past villagers who ignored them. Their job was to dig deep bombproof galleries for a city hospital, an overflow facility for the city of Kassel. Erich G. explained to the postwar Regierungspräsident that the restitution authorities were posing naive questions about whether or not there was censorship of mail for prisoners or whether or not the forced laborers had received pay for their work. There was no mail, he explained, adding that after the Americans liberated Witzenhausen in April 1945, they saw to it that the emaciated ex-prisoners were given extra food and paid a hundred Reichsmarks each in order to see them through the end-of-war hardships. Pay? None of the inmates had received any pay at Witzenhausen![43]

Yet, for postwar officials, few of whom had ever seen any forced-labor camps, the situation was often confusing. City and regional officials offered contradictory evidence. For example, soon after Erich G. filed his report, the Landrat for the District of Witzenhausen also wrote to Kassel's new Regierungspräsident. He corroborated Erich G.'s account and even added some details about the unpleasant conditions at the tiny Lager.[44] However, Witzenhausen's postwar Bürgermeister claimed otherwise: the Lager consisted of "one small, older 'Wohnhaus' [livable house] in the city center," he wrote. "It was not guarded and had no security wire or armed guards around it." The mayor noted that the forced laborers had no armed escort to or from the underground gallery. "After work the inmates could move about freely, and in no way were they cut off from the outside world," he emphasized. The mayor also noted that in some instances, wives of inmates could pay visits to their husbands and that there was neither mail censorship nor a *Prügelstrafe* (corporal punishment). There was even a cook for midday meals, initially, who helped to clean the inmates' clothing.[45] In short, conditions at the camp were benign according to Witzenhausen's mayor. Yet, a careful reading of the mayor's letter reveals a disturbing vagueness. Using the term *Wohnhaus* for their hovel was disingenuous at best. Besides, former inmate Erich G. had never claimed that the inmates were beaten or that they were surrounded by armed guards. Neither had he stated that mail was censored. There had been no mail, and the prisoners' food, no matter who prepared it, was totally inadequate. Thus, it came down to a decision by a restitution official in a distant state capital as to whether or not he or she believed a citizen who claimed after the war to have been persecuted as a *Mischling*. Since Nazi officials had either kept no camp records or else destroyed them, it was difficult for postwar claimants to produce proofs. To be sure, many applicants noted that after conducting their own searches, they discovered that the necessary proofs were no longer extant.[46]

Almost all the *Mischlinge* in Kassel and, for that matter, in tiny Witzenhausen had survived Nazi persecution by the spring of 1945. In that respect their experiences, traumatic though they had been, were not completely typical of conditions that large numbers of *Mischlinge* had experienced in brutally run big camps such as Rochau, or Helmut Coper's Jena-based OT Hundertschaften. Furthermore, they fared better, comparatively speaking, than the hundreds of individuals who had run afoul of the Gestapo. An unfortunate consequence of so many different types of incarceration was the fact that after the German defeat, postwar authorities would have a difficult time trying to differentiate among the various camps and types of forced labor for

Mischlinge. It was part of the price that Germany's half-Jews paid for remaining in their own country.

Sometimes persistence — and indisputable proofs — paid off for a postwar claimant, although compensation to most victims in the postwar period was modest at best. Gustav K. was born into more fortunate circumstances than many other citizens, a fate that also carried its share of danger, since Nazi officialdom became ever more corrupt in the waning years of the Third Reich. Born in 1907 in Biebrich to a Jewish father and Christian mother, Gustav K. followed his father's trade and became a master watchmaker and optician in Wiesbaden. Gustav's father had died young, but his son was able, and the business prospered. Word spread among the Wiesbadeners that they could obtain excellent products and reliable service. Gustav K. and his widowed mother prospered, even in wartime. Thus, it may have been simple avarice that motivated the Gestapo on 5 May 1943 to raid his business and the apartment he and his mother shared with a sickly orphan whom they had adopted the previous year. While arresting him, agents stole thousands of Reichsmarks worth of watches, eyeglasses, and jewelry. They also stole more cash from the family apartment as Gustav's mother and the orphan looked on. At Gestapo headquarters he was stripped of his clothing, given a humiliating body search, and, as a last insult, relieved of the ring on his finger, which the agent promptly pocketed. Gustav K. was made to disappear into the night and fog.

Two years passed. In April 1945, American forces located Gustav K. and thousands of others like him at Buchenwald, most of them more dead than alive. With difficulty, Gustav K. related his grim tale. The Gestapo had kept him in their local jail in Wiesbaden for half a year, then shipped him to Buchenwald. By war's end he had seen several "generations" of arrestees enter the camp, only to weaken and die within months. Yet, somehow, he and a few others had found the strength to survive. For several weeks following liberation, the emaciated survivors were treated by U.S. Army medical teams. Then the Americans returned Gustav to Wiesbaden. They also provided him with his Nazi-issued *Häftlings-Personal-Karte* (prisoner's identification card), showing a gaunt Gustav K. and listing all of his particulars including the date of his transfer to Buchenwald (30 November 1943). The Americans issued a certificate showing that they had found him there and that the Supreme Headquarters, Allied Expeditionary Force (SHAEF), was now releasing him from the notorious camp. The certificate contained Gustav K.'s personal identification information, including fingerprints, plus the signatures and stamps of U.S. Army officials. His liberators wanted any and all bureaucracies to know beyond a shadow of a doubt that Gustav K. had been liberated from hell.

Armed with this unassailable proof, Gustav K. returned to Wiesbaden and to his aged mother on 30 May 1945. He applied to the local Wiesbaden government's "Office for Racially and Religiously Persecuted Persons" and received a few hundred Reichsmarks of compensation. It did not amount to much, but it helped emaciated Gustav K. and his mother to survive the immediate postwar shortages. Despite his horrible experiences under the Nazis, Gustav K. never thought to emigrate. He remained in Wiesbaden and reopened his watch-repair and optical store, albeit under decidedly reduced circumstances. After several years of scraping by, Gustav K. finally submitted a second request for compensation in 1950. He listed the many items the Gestapo had stolen from him in 1943, plus the hardship it had caused his elderly mother to survive alone with an ailing orphan while her son was in Buchenwald. He included the grim concentration camp identity card and the Americans' certificate of liberation. Gustav K. then asked for two thousand of the new Deutschmarks in order to pay for replacement repair and diagnostic equipment. The authorities granted him a thousand marks at first. Then, after seeing him use it exactly as he said he would, they granted him the other thousand marks for the purchase of additional urgently needed watch and optical repair tools. With his minimum livelihood restored, Gustav K. returned to the business of providing fine timepieces, precision optical aids, and excellent service to the good citizens of Wiesbaden. The postwar record shows that he never asked for another pfennig of public money.[47]

No one doubted the nightmarish conditions that existed at places like Auschwitz, but few persons had ever heard of Lager Rochau. However, Adalbert Levy, a Frankfurt *Mischling*, had known it intimately. A master butcher, he carried a "Jewish-sounding" family name and found it impossible to continue his trade after the Nazis seized power. In 1940 the Nazis assigned Levy to a Wehrmacht supply depot as a common laborer. Then, in October 1944 the Gestapo arrested him and transferred him to Lager Rochau, located outside Berlin in Delitsch. Over five thousand men were working there when Levy arrived. Their job was to load bombs and munitions into heavy trucks for distribution to the front. It was heavy, dangerous work with the crews constantly exposed to Allied air raids. Their camp was decidedly unpleasant, being surrounded by rings of barbed wire and hostile guards. Levy felt vast relief when American forces liberated him and other *Mischlinge* in April 1945.[48]

Following liberation, Levy returned to Frankfurt intending to resume life as a butcher. Alas, the immediate postwar years were hardly propitious for a butcher, since meat was scarce and few could afford it. No stranger to hard work, Levy shrugged off his unhappy past, and volunteered in building a shelter for refugees and victims in nearby Wiesbaden. Then, exactly ten years after the war, a thought struck him. The Nazis had robbed him of the ten most productive years of his life, preventing him from exercising his skills as a butcher. Adalbert Levy decided in the midst of West Germany's economic upswing that he, too, was entitled to restitution. With the help of an attorney, he presented his claim. Alas, Levy came to realize that obtaining compensation was not easy. Far from accepting his claims, the restitution authorities in Wiesbaden wanted to know what kind of a facility Lager Rochau really had been. Their questions indicated that the bureaucrats had no idea what it was like to have been incarcerated in an OT camp in 1944 and 1945. Was the camp secured or guarded? Had the "inmates" received compensation for their work? Was their mail censored? Did they receive food parcels from home? Perplexed by the naïveté of such questions, Levy nevertheless gave measured responses. As to camp security, he replied that in his section the SS guards and their bristling coils of barbed wire had demonstrated unequivocally to everyone what kind of a camp Lager Rochau really was. Any prisoner caught venturing outside the perimeter wire did so on pain of death. No, they did not receive compensation (what a thought!). No, there was no censorship of mail for the simple reason that no inmate was permitted to communicate in any way with the outside world. Thus, the question referring to inmates receiving outside food parcels was patently ridiculous. Unfortunately, the record does not disclose the final outcome of Adalbert Levy's application for restitution. Nevertheless, his experience with the insensitivity of the process demonstrates why former *Mischlinge* often concluded that no amount of compensation was worth the humiliation and emotional cost involved in responding to such insensitive and often infuriating questions.[49]

Not everyone despaired. Those *Mischlinge* who were born in 1929 and 1930 were among the youngest unfortunates rounded up by the Nazis for forced labor, and they were also resilient enough to start over in 1945 without dwelling unduly on the past. Perhaps youthfulness also aided them in demanding compensation without exhibiting the kind of fear that stalked their older siblings or parents. The case of Gerhard S. from Wiesbaden is also instructive. Born to Jakob and Emma S. in December 1929, he grew up in Wiesbaden where his father ran a successful painting business. The Nazis, angry that Aryan Jakob would not divorce his Jewish wife, put him out of business and made him a manual laborer at the beginning of the war. In March 1943, the Wiesbaden Gestapo, ignoring the couple's "privileged mixed marriage" status, arrested Emma S. and transported her to Auschwitz where she died on 13 July 1943. Her son had been a bright and conscientious pupil with a gift for mathematics, but in April 1944, the Nazis dismissed him from school. Gerhard S. had just begun an apprenticeship with a camera firm in Wiesbaden when, in October 1944, the Gestapo took him to their headquarters. He remained in their custody until 5 January 1945. Then, without explanation, he was released and returned home to his widower father. Jakob and Gerhard did not have much time to celebrate. Two weeks later, having just turned fifteen, Gerhard S. found himself in the company of twenty other *Mischlinge,* plus a contingent of heavily armed SS guards, on their way to Derenburg. Gerhard S. recounted the prisoners' routine there. "The work consisted of building railroad spurs and digging deep pits. We were guarded by SD men and were led off to work at 5:30 every morning. Then we were marched back to the camp at 6:30 in the evening." They maintained that routine every day of their confinement until the Americans arrived on 11 April 1945. Then they rested and received better rations for two weeks. The Americans arranged for their return. Gerhard S. resumed the schooling the Nazis had denied him and finished his *Abitur* in 1947. He became an official in the Hessian Civil Service, rising to the rank of Landesinspektor, overseeing public welfare services. When economic conditions improved, he finally applied for restitution and in 1956 received a few hundred marks as compensation for the forced labor he had performed. For Gerhard S. money was not the issue. The point was that the authorities recognize the wrongs that had been committed against his family and him.[50]

In contrast to the fortunes of Gerhard S., a few (very few) *Mischlinge* obtained far more generous compensation from postwar authorities. Familiarity with the legal system played a crucial role here. In the Weimar years,

Heinz-Gustav W. had earned a solid Abitur and then obtained an excellent law degree at the Friedrich-Wilhelms University in Berlin. In May 1933, he passed his state law examinations at the top of his class, intending to enter the Prussian Ministry of Justice, where he expected eventually to become a judge. However, the Nazis had other ideas. They had just enacted their Law for the Restoration of a Professional Civil Service, and on 8 June 1933 the Prussian minister of justice dismissed *Mischling* Heinz-Gustav W. from the Prussian Civil Service and from the practice of law.[51]

From June 1933 until the day Germany capitulated, Heinz-Gustav W. worked as a salesman in a small provincial town. Yet, his humble position and low profile helped deflect Nazi attention. He and his wife raised two children, born in 1939 and 1944 respectively, and the family scraped by. Then, in May 1945, his fortunes were completely reversed. It was not easy to find qualified legal staff at a time of denazification because so many law professionals had been politically compromised. In October 1945, Heinz-Gustav W. became legal counsel to the Hessian Ministry of Justice. By 1949, he had advanced to senior legal counsel for Frankfurt am Main. Then, with the onset of West Germany's economic miracle, Heinz-Gustav W. decided that it was time to obtain restitution for the twelve years the Nazis had stolen from his law career.

Because he was intimately acquainted with the legal system, Heinz-Gustav W. was prepared for any obstacles that other bureaucrats might raise. Thus, when skeptics noted that legally speaking, he had never been a prewar *Beamter* (civil servant), he countered that in 1933 he really had qualified for entry and would have risen to the status of judge. After all, his distinguished postwar career in the Hessian Ministry of Justice demonstrated his competence. Furthermore, restitution should consider the fact that Heinz-Gustav had not suffered alone. His wife and children had suffered, too. Ergo, restitution should not only include compensation for him as a senior civil servant; it should also provide for salary supplements for dependents, as would have been provided had he actually risen to the rank of judge. His case was a strong one. After all, he was intimately acquainted with his country's legal system and so received generous restitution. Thus, the case of Heinz-Gustav W. demonstrated a fundamental fact about postwar justice. *Mischlinge* who expected restitution needed either to understand the legal system well or else hire expert legal representation. That representation did not come free as he, a legal expert, was well aware. To be sure, his case and his ability to use it expertly within the German legal system were uncommon.[52]

Bavarian Emil Steiner was one of those who discovered that *Mischlinge* should not assume the postwar legal system would function in benign fashion. Like most other victims, he encountered infuriating obstacles among the restitution authorities. Emil had survived ulcers and dangerous abdominal surgery in August 1944, only to be transported to Theresienstadt a couple of weeks later. Miraculously, he had survived nine months of incarceration, returning to his native Kempten in the summer of 1945. Before the Nazi Seizure of Power, Emil had worked in the petroleum business as an accountant for the giant Aral firm. After 1933, he had continued in the same line of work, albeit as the lowest of low-paid laborers — until his arrest. After regaining his health in 1945, Emil assembled enough capital to open his own modest gasoline station in Kempten. By dint of his hard labor and sacrifice, Emil's service station became known for its reliability and fair prices.[53]

In those same postwar years when denazification had become a prominent issue, Emil received numerous special requests for help from townsfolk — namely, former fellow employees in Aral, and from owners of local coal and oil firms to which he had been consigned during the Nazi years. Then there were the city bureaucrats to whom he had once reported as a despised half-Jew to obtain his pitiful ration card, seek his restricted travel permits, or renew his residence permit. All of those persons had a Nazi past, and now they came calling on Emil. They needed affidavits attesting to the fact they had never been true or fanatical Party members, and Emil had become their *Mischling* of choice. By nature a genial man, Emil Steiner mostly complied with their urgent requests (hard-core Nazis like former Kreisleiter Brändle did not inquire). As he explained privately to his family, he simply wanted to put the past behind him. As a result, his "friends" received their *Persilscheine* (i.e., certificates of exoneration from the local denazification courts — "Persil" referred to a household detergent known to be a particularly effective deodorizer).[54] However, when Emil applied to restitution authorities for compensation for what he had endured, official reactions were utterly different. Suspicious of his claims, the local authorities demanded that he present iron-clad proofs that he had suffered loss of income or other financial injury under National Socialism. Emil soon discovered that such documentation was not easy to obtain. Businesses had closed, employers had departed, and records had disappeared. For a time he got nowhere. Eventually, when his business produced enough profits, Emil hired a lawyer to thread his claim through the involved restitution process. Finally, in the mid-1950s, Steiner received a modest sum, compensating him for eleven years of ridiculously low wages followed by a year's incarceration in Theresienstadt. Nothing could compensate him for such miseries as substandard diet, life-threatening illness, and years of separation from loved ones.[55]

Geographically even farther south than Emil Steiner was fellow *Mischling* Rudolf Klein from Vienna. Klein's odyssey had led him as a music student from Vienna to Brussels in 1938 until the Nazi invasion of 1940. Then, Rudolf endured three years of internment and forced labor in Vichy France while trying four times to escape to Switzerland. He succeeded on his fifth try only after his Catholic mother had placed his name on a crucial Vatican refugee list. Even then, he had to endure a monthlong police grilling before officials in Geneva accepted him. However, persons in his category did not simply take up Swiss residence, find jobs, and start over. It was, after all, wartime. Instead, Rudolf was transferred to a Swiss work camp, helping local farmers in planting and harvesting. It was hard labor, but Rudolf Klein observed that compared with conditions in the Vichy camps, the Swiss camps "were like heaven on earth."[56]

An indication of the vast qualitative difference in the Swiss labor camp system was the fact that after six months of farm work, Klein received something unheard-of for a *Mischling* in Nazi-occupied Europe: the right to study. He had informed the authorities that he had been a student of music — first at the University of Vienna, then at the Belgian Conservatoire Royale — before the Nazis arrived. A Studentenwerk, a central bureau for Swiss students in Geneva, acknowledged his status, and so Rudolf Klein, recipient of Swiss scholarships, dropped his agricultural tools at the end of each growing season and became a student. In the autumn of 1943 he entered the University at Fribourg where he received excellent instruction in the organ plus advanced musicology studies for three years. True, every spring he donned overalls again and worked on farms. However, other than some wear and tear on his hands (not kindly to an organ specialist, he admitted), he had no regrets about wielding pitchfork and hoe in the Swiss variant of a work camp. In fact, he met many fascinating people among his fellow refugees, including

Alphonse Müller, destined to become a prominent Austrian statesman after the war.

Within the local Swiss refugee center to which he reported was an adjoining office that aided Jewish girls. One of its officials was a vivacious young Swiss whom Rudolf met during routine visits. The two young people fell in love and married. In due course, he obtained his university degree, and courtesy of the Swiss, the Kleins were reunited with his parents in Vienna. Against all odds, Rudolf's Austrian-Jewish father and Czech-Catholic mother had survived. Medical professionals (he was a physician, she a nurse), they had been relegated to a tiny attic room of their residence/clinic ever since 1938. Upon his return in 1946, Klein learned that a childhood friend, former classmate, and fellow refugee, Kurt Schell, had already reached his family in May 1945. Known as Lieutenant Kurt Shell, U.S. Army, by that time, Rudolf's high school chum (and a full Jew) had undergone his own odyssey. Teenager Schell had reached the United States in 1939, then volunteered for the army. Kurt had risen through the ranks and become an infantry officer serving in Italy in the war. In May 1945, as part of the spearhead of the U.S. Fifth Army, he and his driver entered Vienna in a jeep. Thereupon, Rudolf's boyhood chum had raced up the steps of the Klein residence, embraced the couple, and treated them to a celebratory ride around the liberated city. Then he saw to it that they got better rations. A grateful Rudolf followed up his reunion with his parents with an equally joyful reunion with Kurt. They remained close friends ever after.[57]

Rudolf Klein discovered that rebuilding his life in Austria after the war was not easy. "Austria is a small country," he observed, "and careers are made on the basis of a person's school. You meet others in school; on that basis you become a member of a social organization, perhaps a student fraternity, and you grow into your profession. You get to know people through school ties." Thus, despite utterly divergent experiences from his Aryan classmates after 1938, Rudolf, a *Mischling* but also a fellow graduate of a prestigious Vienna Gymnasium, received help from former classmates at critical times in postwar Austria. Besides, it was not in his nature to hold grudges against those who might have acquiesced in the Nazi takeover but who had not actively supported it. For a time, Rudolf worked as a music critic for an American-licensed newspaper that benefited from employing a professional with impeccable anti-Nazi credentials. Then, in 1955, when Austria became a sovereign nation again, he discovered quickly that he, a former *Mischling*, had to hustle. After all, old school ties only went only so far, and anti-Semitism was by no means dead in Vienna. Fortunately, Klein's standing as an expert musicologist had grown considerably in that decade after the war. Consequently, he became a featured writer and commentator in Viennese journals and magazines. Klein's voice also became a familiar feature on Viennese public radio. In short, he developed into a renowned music critic and media celebrity. Reminders of his former status as a *Mischling* occurred less often. And yet, they occurred, as his experiences at high school reunions demonstrated.

Klein's 1938 *Matura* (Class of '38) was also the last to have Jews and half-Jews who had completed their high school diploma. Six of his classmates had been Jewish, and only two of them, Kurt Schell (now Shell) and Franz Neumann, had survived. As memories of the war receded, class reunions became more common, and in the 1970s and 1980s attendees began to view the past through rosier prisms as their youthful, "golden," or at least more adventuresome years. Franz Neumann (not the famed political scientist), a fellow survivor with Rudolf of the brutal French camps, had moved to Israel after 1945, and Judaism had become a central focus in his life. He had returned several times to Class-of-'38 reunions but was put off by traditional functions that were largely religious in character. Besides, those years had not been so "golden" as far as he was concerned. Therefore, Neumann stopped attending. By contrast, Kurt Shell, also a full Jew, but one who had remained secular in outlook, continued to attend the 1938 *Matura* gatherings. Shell had become a political scientist of international fame, building a career that had placed him in leading British, American, and German universities. Klein, a keen observer of events, found Shell's attendance at gatherings of the 1938 *Matura* riveting because the political scientist was so detached and so analytical. Not least, he was fearless. "He was interested in the psychology of the situation," Klein recalled. "He would pose extremely direct, blunt questions to the group. [He asked them] to write down how they had comported themselves with the Nazis. He wanted to know how they thought about it now." To be sure, Kurt Shell's candor was unappreciated by many of those aging men, many of whom had become senior civil servants in Austria. They had grown used to imparting their own ethos to class gatherings. Hitherto, reunions had called for mandatory attendance at solemn Catholic masses. After Neumann's departure, Klein, Shell, and others began to question this aspect of their gatherings. Reluctantly, their classmates got the point and began to show greater sensitivity. A person of emotional resilience, professionally attained, and happy in his personal life with a lifelong loving spouse and attained children, Rudolf Klein was able to shrug off the old furies that had accompanied him on his life as a hunted man in Nazi-occupied France. He is pleased that readers can learn what happened to him and others and is optimistic that revelation of his *Mischling* experience (as a corollary to the Jewish experience) will help show what racial bigotry can do to seemingly normal, decent people.[58]

Ursula Kühn also overcame extreme adversity to become a celebrity in her hometown. In her case it was not Vienna but Hamburg. Like Rudolf Klein, Ursula Kühn had endured a string of persecutions that extended through her school years down to the last days of the war. For her, the persecution accompanied her on her escape from firebombed Hamburg into the soon-to-be-firebombed Giessen. Then she had led the life of a threadbare refugee, often on the move through various Hessian villages during the last half-year of the war. Even so, the chaos provided protection of a sort for her as a *Mischling,* since Nazi authority was breaking down. Besides, it was in one of those humble villages that she finally found release. In April 1945, Ursula was standing alongside a road among a crowd of Germans, all of them observing American troops walking by. "They looked like men from another galaxy," she thought. "They were well fed and well clothed too." Ursula was secretly delighted and later proclaimed that moment to be one of the happiest in her life. However, knowing that she was still surrounded by relatives, she, of course, hid her emotions. Her *Mischling* experience had taught her to be circumspect. Thus, even at that moment of liberation, she dared not show her glee. Yet, she had survived, and Nazism, judging by what she was now witnessing, had not.[59]

Following the cessation of hostilities, Ursula Kühn returned to her mother in Hamburg. At the very least, peace had brought an end to the family separations she had suffered so long. However, that hardly meant that her family's standard of living improved. In fact, the opposite occurred. Virtually all residents of Germany's large cities had to endure sharply reduced rations after the war, and unlike citizens in rural areas, they had few means to supplement their diet. Kühn recalled years of acute hunger and abject poverty in postwar Hamburg. In addition to hunger, everyone had to accept crowded living conditions — three occupants per room was the norm. It was only in the 1950s that the Kühn family's living standard began to rise slowly, along with that of the rest of the population. Her former status of persecuted *Mischling* had counted for little for Ursula after the war, and her mother, the doughty Frau Kühn, never remarried.

With time, Ursula finished her formal education. Meanwhile, she married, and bore two sons. Like most former *Mischlinge*, she chose to remain silent about her former status. Then, in the early 1980s, and not knowing entirely why, Ursula finally began to tell friends about her experiences and those of her family under the Nazis. She was surprised that fellow Germans were so ignorant about what she had suffered. It was then that she realized that the public knew nothing about the persecution that had befallen Germany's *Mischlinge*. This was unacceptable to her. As an older adult, Ursula entered the University of Hamburg where she received a doctorate in history. Thereupon, Dr. Kühn (but under her married name of Randt) began to educate succeeding generations of Hamburg citizens about the brutal treatment citizens of Jewish heritage had endured. She published a detailed study about the role that a Jewish girls' school had once played in improving the quality of education in Hamburg from its founding in 1884 until the Nazis disbanded it in 1942. To this day, Ursula Randt greets visiting groups of foreign guests to Hamburg to enlighten them of the city's history, including that of its citizens of Jewish heritage. She also speaks at public forums about what it meant to be a *Mischling* from 1933 to 1945 and has raised consciousness among the citizens of her Hanseatic town about what racial persecution can do to people. She continues her campaign of enlightenment even now.[60]

CONCLUSION

Germany's *Mischlinge* led abnormal lives, lives that were profoundly altered by National Socialist persecution. The longer Hitler's regime lasted, the more harshly Germany's citizens of Jewish-Christian ancestry had been treated. It is no exaggeration to say that, like their fully Jewish relatives before them, they had become hunted people, and it was only a matter of time before an acquaintance betrayed them, a faceless bureaucrat identified them, a Gestapo agent apprehended them, or an order arrived turning them into forced laborers. Yet, after the guns fell silent in May 1945, many *Mischlinge* discovered that the forces of liberation scarcely understood their predicament. Field troops, be they Soviet infantrymen closing in from the East, or Anglo-American soldiers advancing from the West, often failed to comprehend what the term *Mischling* meant. Lacking the necessary background information or language skills, they often assumed the hapless victims were Germans like any other. That explains why Werner Jentsch and the other *Mischlinge* from his OT contingent were confined by American troops in a high-security prisoner-of-war camp among SS during the last months of the war. It also explains why many *Mischlinge* in Berlin such as Charles Milford were unable to explain to their Soviet liberators the persecution they had endured for years. It explains why Helmut Langer and his brother were unceremoniously ejected along with all other Germans from Czechoslovakia in 1945.

In Germany itself, the immediate postwar years were "hunger years," so that *Mischlinge* suffered the same malnutrition and hardships that all Germans faced. While it was true that the Allied occupation authorities banned anti-Semitism in parallel with their campaign of denazification, the lingering effects of discrimination were all too obvious to former victims who knew that many Germans covertly maintained their prejudices. True, under Allied prodding, the various land authorities in the three western zones set up boards of restitution to aid victims. The Soviet authorities also established an official zonewide category of *Opfer des Faschismus* or "Victims of Fascism," which included persons who could demonstrate that they had been persecuted for racial, religious, or political reasons. These OdFs received some forms of aid such as higher priority in finishing secondary education, gaining admittance to a university, or qualifying for some civil service positions. However, outright compensation for lost incomes, endangered health, or expropriation of properties or goods was rare to nonexistent in the threadbare Soviet zone. Furthermore, the Soviets and their SED allies expected unquestioned allegiance to their ideology, *Mischlinge* included.

In the three western zones, the former *Mischlinge* discovered that the process of obtaining restitution for their persecution was as arduous as it was uncertain. The responsible bureaucracies were grossly understaffed, and their officials were burdened with heavy caseloads. Furthermore, those same officials were often unsympathetic or soon became callous. Unsurprisingly in those hard times, they were suspicious of all claims. Therefore, victims had to provide extensive proofs of persecution. They had to provide concrete documentation of incarceration in a labor camp, denial of education, loss of income, expropriation of family property, damaged health directly attributable to incarceration, or other tangible injustices perpetrated by the Nazis. In those chaotic postwar years, when postal, telegraph, and telephone systems as well as most other forms of communication and transportation were fragile, obtaining such proofs proved to be exceedingly difficult. Furthermore, much of the population was in flux, old governmental offices and institutions were defunct, and many bureaucrats of the defeated regime were either dismissed, missing, in hiding, or in jail. Even when former victims finally did obtain proofs of persecution, the shaky postwar governments could offer only what amounted to token sums of compensation. Appeals to Allied occupation authorities were often futile. Many *Mischlinge* discovered that the latter expected them to provide occupation authorities with additional proofs that they had been officially listed as members of a Jewish community during the Hitler years. Since most *Mischlinge* could not do so — the *Geltungsjuden* were a sometime exception — their requests for outside assistance such as CARE packages, were usually unsuccessful. Thus, they hungered along with the rest of Germany in the postwar period. In this respect they held one dubious advantage: most *Mischlinge* already knew what hunger really meant. Finally, the former *Mischlinge* saw with foreboding that the emerging bureaucratic system, indifferent to their fate, was inclined after the occupation authorities departed to allow former Nazis, even members of sinister organizations like the Gestapo, to reintegrate rapidly into the mainstream of society.[61]

If the experience of Germany's *Mischlinge* teaches us anything about National Socialism, it is that that violent ideology only became more dangerous over time. After all, it was the most fanatical elements in that movement that had seized control of the state and that by 1944–45 were exercising complete control over all aspects of German society. Meanwhile those same elements had lost any inhibitions about shedding the blood of anyone not to their liking. They had also insinuated their beliefs in enough citizens that victims still integrated to some extent in society, *Mischlinge* being the most obvious example, had to reckon with a proliferation of informers among acquaintances, neighbors, employers, and coworkers. The telling proof of the Nazis' intentions toward full Jews had come with their implementation of the Final Solution in 1942. The experience of the *Mischlinge* demonstrates to what fur-

ther extent the Nazis were willing to go in order to rid themselves of any remaining vestiges of Judaism. Germany's half-Jews had good reason to be
traumatized for a lifetime by persecutors who held the entire power apparatus of a modern state in their hands, one which, now that the Jews were gone,
they were eager to turn toward the killing of surviving "undesirables" such
as *Mischlinge* in their crazed determination to make Germany *judenfrei*. Thus,
in the final analysis, Germany's *Mischlinge* had to reckon with the stark fact
that it was non-Germans who had made it possible for them to remain alive
and to resume their status as German citizens.

CONCLUSION

More than half a century has elapsed since Germany's surviving *Mischlinge* returned from detention camps, prisons, involuntary work sites, and places of hiding during the final phase of Nazi persecution. They knew they were lucky to have survived so terrible an ordeal — most of their Jewish family members had not. Thus, unlike many other Germans, the former *Mischlinge* were already on intimate terms with the Holocaust and needed no revelations or reminders after the war about the genocide that had just taken place. Therein lay a dilemma for Germany's Jewish-Christian citizens, especially its half-Jews. Should they emigrate? Or should they remain in Germany? Obviously, a few had already chosen the first option from 1933 to 1939 when emigration by Germany's full Jews had become an urgent necessity. Nevertheless, the great majority of Germany's *Mischlinge* were in the country when the war began, and they were still there six years later when the guns fell silent.

Germany's former *Mischlinge* faced a cruel dilemma in 1945. Because of their mixed cultural heritage, most Jewish-Christian Germans were from urban backgrounds. Their family lives had been largely secular — religion had not played a central role in most mixed marriages, neither for the parents nor for their children, although approximately nine-tenths of the former *Mischlinge* had been baptized in the Protestant and Catholic churches. Their language, customs, associations, and identity were German. Therefore, from 1933 until the end of World War II, the large cohort of *Mischlinge* who had come of age under the Nazis still identified themselves as Germans. True, ever-increasing discrimination had given them pause to consider their identity. However, because of the crucial time lapse between the Nazis' decision to murder the full Jews in approximately 1942, and their rounding up of *Mischlinge* for forced labor in 1944 and whatever other fate they had in store thereafter, Germany's *Mischlinge* were saved by Allied victory. It had been a narrow race with death, and the survivors lived with an awful truth. They knew that, in the final analysis, German society had not protected them. True, some individuals besides family members had aided them. Most citizens were indifferent. By contrast, other citizens, neighbors or acquaintances, had proved only too eager to denounce them. The sharp point in their painful existence came when they realized toward the end of the war amid mass roundups into forced-labor camps, followed by concerted actions by the Gestapo to snare the rest, that they were indeed the next intended victims of the Holocaust. Historian Raul Hilberg summed up their intolerable situation succinctly. "The 'Mischling' controversy illustrates as no other issue does bureaucracy's tremendous urge to make the 'final solution' really final . . . the mere fact that they existed was disturbing; they were living proof of a task unfinished, for they were carriers of 'Jewish blood' and Jewish characteristics in the German community."[1] Hence the question: Should citizens of partial Jewish ancestry leave Germany as Jewish survivors were doing, or should they remain at home?

It may seem baffling to some readers, but most *Mischlinge* chose to remain in Germany. It was the country of their birth, their language, and their culture. They were, for the most part, urbane, secular, and well educated (at least up to the moment when they had been forced out of schools and higher education). They knew, too, that not all Germans had wished them ill even if, in the final analysis, individual acts of kindness had failed to protect them. Allied victory had saved them. That, after all, was why some survivors found ways to emigrate to places like North or South America, Palestine, later Israel, the United Kingdom, or elsewhere. Those mostly young emigrants were, however, the exception. Most *Mischlinge* remained at home, identifying with certain, undeniably attractive aspects of German society.

By remaining in Germany and resuming their lives as Germans, the *Mischling* victims of Nazi persecution also made a second decision: they would largely repress what had happened to them from 1933 to 1945. Neither would they speak about, nor would they, if at all possible, think about the injustices, indignities, or terrors they had so recently experienced. They understood only too well in the postwar world that for many Germans, anti-Semitism had not died with the defeat of the Nazis. They saw firsthand that former Nazis quickly reemerged into mainstream society after Allied denazification programs had run their course and that the civil service and such professions as law and medicine were once again under the sway of former Nazis. Former *Mischlinge* also observed that the German public had quickly developed a guilty conscience about the Holocaust, toward both its victims and its survivors. In short, half-Jews and quarter-Jews found that their prior *Mischling* status, if revealed, only served to complicate their lives in the two Germanys that

emerged after World War II. Expunging their past seemed to be the best re-
course. Therefore, as much as possible, they became fully conventional Germans once again. In this they received their society's encouragement. As other
researchers have pointed out, the former victims were often able to reknit
social ties to superiors in places of work, to neighbors, teachers, and other
acquaintances who were no longer driven by state-sponsored policies of discrimination and who were eager to forget about the past.[2]

Although it brought rewards, this practical decision by former *Mischlinge*
to remain at home came at a heavy price. In essence, it required on one level
that they deny their past. For many, this strategy worked for years and years.
For some it still does. However, for many former *Mischlinge* that price has
exacted a heavy toll. Feelings of guilt plague many former *Mischlinge* because
they had survived the Holocaust when many of their Jewish relatives had not.
Historians who have interviewed surviving *Mischlinge* frequently encounter
eyewitnesses who try to minimize the discrimination and hardships they faced
because of that crucial difference. This is a peculiar *Mischling* variation of
"survivor guilt."[3] Furthermore, research by experts in psychoanalysis in the
last decade indicates that generational reverberations continue to emanate
from the traumatic effects of discrimination upon the former *Mischlinge* who
involuntarily passed along their anxieties to the next generation. This phenomenon includes the effects of personal and professional setbacks relative
to their own generational cohort that often led former victims to hold attitudes
of low personal esteem, sometimes bordering on self-loathing. Unsurprisingly,
such attitudes could and often did produce negative consequences for the
victims as they tried to build or rebuild lives and careers after the war. Inevitably, it also produced negative effects in personal relationships for the former
victims, either with spouses or others. Inevitably, such emotional disorders
also had an impact upon the children and other close relatives of Jewish-
Christian Germans persecuted under the Nazis. Historian Beate Meyer has
pointed out another negative effect that emerged specifically among the
youngest of the former *Mischlinge* (i.e., those persons who had been born in
the late 1930s or in wartime). It was especially their age group that had to confront the possibility as they grew to adulthood that they had been conceived,
consciously or unconsciously, as a kind of protective shield by parents whose
marriages automatically moved from "mixed marriage" to "privileged mixed

marriage" status under the Nazis once half-Aryan children were born, even though, in the end, there was nothing "privileged" about such marriages as far as the Nazi fanatics were concerned.[4]

Faced with such harsh memories and ongoing consequences, it is little wonder that many former *Mischlinge* tried to erase the events of 1933–45 from their memories. Nevertheless, as their generation comes to the end of its natural life span, many victims cannot help but recall the travails of their earlier lives and ask anew: Why was it that such injustices had ever come to pass? The world of today is not like that. Public opinion regularly condemns racial prejudice. Therefore, what befell them then is as unacceptable as the persecution that had befallen Europe's Jews, Gypsies (Roma and Sinti), homosexuals, ideological victims, mentally or physically handicapped persons, or other persecuted persons during the war years. Like so many other Holocaust survivors, they yearn to be remembered, even if remembrance imperils the very anonymity that they had sought so long to maintain. Recognition of what they endured is their right.

It is because of the desire for recognition of suffering over anonymity that a few former *Mischlinge* have finally come forward in the last years of their lives to give testimony despite the personal anguish that such recollections cause them. Memoirs by half-Jewish survivors are appearing more frequently now, and other investigators are finding success in locating persons who are willing to speak out. Former German chancellor Helmut Schmidt is only the most prominent example.[5] As this author can attest, oral histories with eyewitnesses are a valuable, even if imperfect, contribution to the historical record. They offer a dimension that no archival research can match. Even so, they need whenever possible corroboration by written records or by other eyewitnesses' accounts. Fortunately, some German archives are opening oncesensitive collections of documents to researchers, too. Postwar restitution files are rich sources of information. The more limited Gestapo files with their sinister contents leave an unforgettable record. This study depended heavily upon those original documents, and they corroborated to a large extent the levels of persecution that the survivors had described in their interviews. In fact, by comparison to those files, the eyewitnesses may, if anything, have understated what had befallen them. A few, when questioned, conceded that this was so. One caveat about such archival sources needs mentioning. Since the process for seeking restitution was, especially in the postwar years, so arduous, demeaning, and — for those times — expensive, many victims refused to engage in it at all, preferring anonymity and getting on with their lives. Therefore, the written record is also skewed. Probably many more *Mischlinge* eschewed restitution than ever sought to win it. That is hardly a problem with the extant Gestapo files. The surviving collections in Düsseldorf (plus a smaller collection in Würzburg) offer an unvarnished historical record of what the Nazi true believers thought about *Mischlinge,* to say nothing of what they had in store for Germany's full Jews.

Since the German-Jewish *Mischlinge* of 1933–45 are reaching the end of their natural life spans, this researcher decided to proceed with this study in order to utilize the oral histories that only such eyewitnesses can provide. By volunteering such information, they have bequeathed to future generations further proofs of the human costs of the Holocaust. The record they have compiled serves, along with other studies, to warn of the consequences that ensue when societies succumb to racial bigotry against innocents. After all, most of Germany's *Mischlinge* had been mere children when persecution by unknown adults altered their lives irrevocably. At least now, the racially repugnant terminology that had been applied to them for so long no longer exists. No one in the German-speaking world today speaks of *Mischlinge.* For that matter no one uses terms like "half-Jew" or "quarter-Jew" either. To do so would consign the user to the ranks of racial bigotry, a status that is anathema to virtually all citizens of the Germany of today.

To their credit most *Mischling* survivors shrugged off twelve years of racial discrimination at the hands of the Nazis and went on to lead productive lives — after all, they mostly came from hardworking, law-abiding families. But are the persons of Jewish heritage cited in this study, especially those who granted interviews, truly representative of those whose lives had been skewed by Nazi persecution? There is no concrete statistical evidence. Researchers who seek information about Germany's seventy-two thousand former *Mischlinge* first degree and forty thousand *Mischlinge* second degree quickly discover that survivors are still loath to come forward even now. In old age most of them continue to fear repercussions for themselves and for family members should they reveal their once-reviled status. Therefore, they remain silent. For most, that silence has become a lifelong habit.

It is for this very reason that succeeding generations should recognize what persons of partial Jewish ancestry endured under Hitler and the Nazis. Like their Jewish mothers or Jewish fathers, they, too, had arrived at that critical point when, solely for reasons of race, they confronted imminent death. Yet, unlike most of Europe's Jews, they had survived — along with their ghosts. Thus, it was their very reassimilation into the nation of their birth that adds special poignancy to the lives and fates of Germany's Jewish-Christian citizens. It should be remembered that most former *Mischlinge* had, out of sheer necessity, adopted a survival strategy after 1945 that was nearly identical to the one they were forced to choose under National Socialism: obscurity. They chose to remain in the nation of their birth and to resume life as German citizens. Monstrous though their treatment had been under the Nazis, National Socialism was now dead, and they had survived. Thus, as survivors they, or at least most of them, retreated into their society's background and resumed the low-profile existences to which they had already become accustomed. Like the characters in the final scene of Bertolt Brecht and Kurt Weill's *Threepenny Opera*, Germany's *Mischlinge* filed from darkness back into society in 1945 — and from there promptly back into obscurity. Of them and of their former persecutors (many of whom soon reacquired social prominence) an imaginary commentator might have said in a paraphrase of Brecht: We see those who walk in sunlight. Those in shadows don't exist.

NOTES

INTRODUCTION

1. See Ian Kershaw, *The Nazi Dictatorship: Problems and Perspectives of Interpretation*, 4th ed. (New York, 2000), chap. 5.

2. For an excellent overview of the many persecuted groups under National Socialism, see the recent compilation of scholarship by Robert Gellately and Nathan Stoltzfus, eds., *Social Outsiders in Nazi Germany* (Princeton, 2001).

3. Scholars generally refer to the German census issued on 17 May 1939 for statistics on "non-Aryan" Germans. See Jeremy Noakes, "The Development of Nazi Policy towards the German-Jewish 'Mischlinge,' 1933–1945," in *Leo Baeck Institute Yearbook 34* (1989) (New York, 1989), pp. 292–94.

4. See Reiner Pommerin, *"Sterilisierung der Rheinlandbastarde": Das Schicksal einer farbigen deutschen Minderheit, 1911–1937* (Düsseldorf, 1979).

5. See Adolf Hitler, *Mein Kampf*, ed. and trans. John Chamberlain et al. (New York, 1941), pp. 603–4. This is the translation of the unabridged version using the two volumes published in the original German in 1925 and 1927; see also pp. 448–49.

6. See Raul Hilberg, *Destruction of the European Jews* (New York, 1973), p. 47.

7. See Hilberg, *Destruction of the European Jews;* see also Noakes, "Development of Nazi Policy," pp. 291–354.

8. See Beate Meyer, *"Jüdische Mischlinge": Rassenpolitik und Verfolgungserfahrung, 1933–1945* (Hamburg, 1999). She has also published numerous articles in German journals and has made many contributions to edited works on the Holocaust.

9. See Nathan Stoltzfus, *Resistance of the Heart: Intermarriage and the Rosenstrasse Protest in Nazi Germany* (New York, 1996).

10. See Bryan Mark Rigg's recent book, *Hitler's Jewish Soldiers: The Untold Story of Nazi Racial Laws and Men of Jewish Descent in the German Military* (Lawrence, Kans., 2002). Rigg had already released some results of his research to the press. See London *Daily Telegraph* of 2 December 1996 and *Times* of London, 6 December 1996. Rigg revealed to the *Daily Telegraph* that a list prepared by German army personnel in January 1944 revealed seventy-seven "high-ranking officers of mixed Jewish race or married to a Jew" serving in the Wehrmacht. Most of them were apparently one-quarter Jewish.

11. See Gerhard Lindemann, *"Typisch jüdisch": Die Stellung der Ev.-luth. Landeskirche Hannovers zu Antijudaismus, Judenfeindschaft und Antisemitismus, 1919–1949* (Berlin, 1998); see also Aleksandar-Saša Vuletić, *Christen jüdischer Herkunft im Dritten Reich: Verfolgung und organisierte Selbsthilfe, 1933–1939* (Mainz, 1999).

12. Unfortunately, the acronym "KDF" usually referred to a relatively benign Nazi travel and entertainment organization known as Kraft durch Freude (Strength through Joy). Hitler's Chancellery was not benign.

13. For an authoritative overview of Hitler's connection to the decision making that led to the Final Solution, see Kershaw, *Nazi Dictatorship*, chap. 5.

14. See Noakes, "Development of Nazi Policy," p. 310.

15. For a useful overview of how the Nazis generated the appearance of an anti-Semitic groundswell among the people as an emotional backdrop for promulgation of the Nuremberg decrees, and for an equally useful description of the arbitrary ways in which they arrived at those decrees, see Stoltzfus, *Resistance of the Heart,* pp. 65–75.

16. See Noakes, "Development of Nazi Policy," pp. 315–19.

17. For a thorough treatment of this self-help organization, see Vuletić, *Christen Jüdischer Herkunft,* chaps. 3 and 5.

18. See Hans A. Schmitt, *Quakers and Nazis: Inner Light in Outer Darkness* (Columbia, Mo., 1997), pp. 54–74, 111–22, 176–84.

19. See Noakes, "Development of Nazi Policy," pp. 295–96. He gives a statistical breakdown from the 1939 census of births of half-Jewish and quarter-Jewish citizens in five-year brackets, starting with under six years of age up to age sixty-five and older.

CHAPTER 1: INNOCENTS IN CLASSROOMS

1. See Hilberg, *Destruction of the European Jews,* p. 43.

2. See Noakes, "Development of Nazi Policy," pp. 298–99, 325–27.

3. For a general treatment of educators and National Socialism, see Richard Grunberger, *The Twelve-Year Reich: A Social History of Nazi Germany, 1933–1945* (New York, 1971), pp. 286–89. For an authoritative analytical and statistical treatment on teachers and other professionals, see Konrad Jarausch, *The Unfree Professions: German Lawyers, Teachers, and Engineers, 1900–1950* (New York, 1990), pp. 100–103, 149–50, 152–53, 194–95.

4. Eva Furth, née Heilmann, interview by author, Berlin, 13 December 1994; Peter Heilmann, interview by author, Berlin, 10 January 1996.

5. Peter Heilmann, interview.

6. Eva Furth, interview.

7. Eva Furth and Peter Heilmann, interviews.

8. Eva Furth, interview.

9. Peter Heilmann, interview.

10. See Eric A. Johnson, *Nazi Terror: The Gestapo, Jews, and Ordinary Germans* (New York, 1999), pp. 84–85.

11. Hans-Joachim Boehm, interview by author, Berlin, 28 June 1994.

12. Ibid.

13. Ibid.

14. Ibid.

15. Ernst Benda, interview by author, Karlsruhe, 8 December 1994.

16. Ibid.

17. Ibid.

18. Ibid.

19. Ibid.

20. Horst Hartwich, unpublished memoir of his youth, p. 25, cited with permission of author.

21. Ibid., pp. 30–31.

22. Hessisches Hauptstaatsarchiv Wiesbaden (hereafter cited as HHStA), Abt. 518, no. 4432, Margit W.

23. Ursula Kühn (not her real name), interview by author, Hamburg, 6 December 1994.
24. Ibid.
25. Ibid.
26. Ibid.
27. Ibid.
28. Ibid.
29. Dr. Meta Alexander, interview by author, Berlin, 29 June 1994.
30. Ibid.
31. Ibid.
32. Ibid.
33. Hans Haurwitz, telephone interview by author, Erie, Pa., 6 November 1994.
34. Helmut Langer, interview by author, Rhine–Main region, 23 June 1994.
35. Hanns-Peter Herz, interview by author, Berlin, 30 June 1994.
36. Ibid. Other contemporaries and friends of Hanns-Peter Herz, such as Horst Hart-wich and Stanislaw Karol Kubicki, hastened to confirm to this author the claim that Herr Paschowski, although nominally a member of the NSDAP, was in reality anti-Nazi.
37. Hanns-Peter Herz, interview.
38. HHStA, Abt. 518, no. 5930, files concerning H. Kranz.
39. Ibid.
40. See Noakes, "Development of Nazi Policy," p. 339.
41. Landesarchiv Berlin, Record Group 38 Kammergericht Berlin, Decimal File 3915, no. 40/I, file for Edith W., formerly Edith G.
42. Charles Milford (who formally changed his name from Klaus Muehlfelder when he emigrated after the war to the United States), telephone interview by author, Palo Alto, Calif., 10 July 1994. Horst Hartwich confirmed the incident in his unpublished memoirs, p. 31. Copy in author's possession.
43. Rudolf Klein, interview by author, Vienna, 15 June 1996.
44. Martha Rohr, interview by author, Wintersdorf near Trier, 9 December 1994.
45. See Grunberger, *Twelve-Year Reich*, p. 286.
46. Dr. Thekla Schwarz, née Brandt, interview by author, Berlin, 29 June 1994.
47. Ibid.
48. Bernd Rebensburg, letter to author, 2 September 2000, in author's possession. Having demonstrated leadership skills at an early age, Rebensburg became a naval officer during the war, entered a prisoner-of-war camp in the British zone in 1945–46, and became an agriculturist and part-time consultant to the Federal German Navy once the FRG entered NATO. See James F. Tent, *E-Boat Alert: Defending the Normandy Invasion Fleet* (Annapolis, 1996), passim. For another African-German youth's detailed account of growing up in Nazi Germany, see Hans J. Massaquoi, *Destined to Witness* (New York, 1999).
49. Rebensburg, letter to author, 23 November 2000. Following receipt of that letter, the author conducted a detailed conversation on 25 January 2001 with Klaus Otto Kühne, formerly the director of the evangelisches Pädagogium (now the Otto-Kühne-Schule), grandson of its founder, and son of its second director. He confirmed in great detail the statements made by Bernd Rebensburg about multiethnic

pupils of his acquaintance in Bad Godesberg in the early 1930s (Rebensburg and Kühne were fellow schoolmates, although Herr Kühne is several years younger). Herr Kühne provided detailed information from school records about those and other pupils in a fax forwarded to the author on 3 October 2000, plus further details in a follow-up letter dated 5 April 2001.

50. Rebensburg, letter to author, 2 September 2000. For an account of the fate of African-German children born during the post–World War I Rhineland occupation, see Pommerin, *"Sterilisierung der Rheinlandbastarde."* Pommerin shows that Hitler's personal preoccupation with the so-called Rhineland bastards, as mentioned in *Mein Kampf,* ensured their mass sterilization within a few years after the Nazis seized power (i.e., in 1937).

CHAPTER 2: *MISCHLINGE* NEED NOT APPLY

1. See Noakes, "Development of Nazi Policy," pp. 298–99, 327–28.

2. Ibid., pp. 328–36.

3. Ibid., p. 350.

4. The authoritative account of non-Aryans serving in the German armed forces has been compiled by Bryan Mark Rigg, whose recently completed dissertation reveals that hundreds of Jews and thousands of *Mischlinge* rendered military service. See Rigg, *Hitler's Jewish Soldiers.* See especially chapters 4 and 5 on Nazi policy toward Jews and *Mischlinge* in the Wehrmacht from 1933 to 1943.

5. Werner Jentsch, conversation with author in a train compartment en route in the German Democratic Republic, August 1978.

6. Otto Hess, interview by author, Berlin, 12 December 1994.

7. Ibid., pp. 4–5.

8. Nordrhein-Westfälisches Haupstaatsarchiv Düsseldorf, Gestapo Files (RW58), RW58/45874, internal memorandum of Gestapo regional office in Duisburg, concerning Hermann D. and dated 23 March 1943; hereafter cited as NWHD with appropriate file designation. The word used by the Gestapo official concerning the cancellation of her removal to a concentration camp was *zurückgestellt.* The word also implies "delay" or "deferral."

9. Hans-Joachim Boehm, interview.

10. Ibid.

11. Eva Heilmann, interview.

12. Ibid., pp. 6–7.

13. Peter Heilmann, interview.

14. Dr. Meta Alexander, interview.

15. Ibid., pp. 10–11.

16. Dr. Thekla Schwarz, née Brandt, interview.

17. Ibid., p. 4.

18. Hessisches Hauptstaatsarchiv Wiesbaden, 518/3106, file concerning Hilde B. The file includes a letter from a former associate in the Reichsvereinigung Eisen in Berlin, dated 12 February 1957, attesting to her persecution; a memorandum from the Regierungspräsident in Wiesbaden, dated 16 April 1958, granting compensation; and a personal statement from Hilde B. detailing her many educational and vocational

experiences at the hands of the Nazis; hereafter cited as HHStA with appropriate file classification.

19. Erika Waldegger, daughter of Emil Steiner, interview by author, Memmingen, Bavaria, 17 December 1994.

20. NWHD, RW58/45352, file for Elsa R. This includes a brief memorandum of 9 July 1936 listing the accusations against her; a lengthy letter by RMK official Gräwe to the state police in Essen, accusing Elsa R., dated 26 June 1936; and a copy of the newspaper insert, announcing the performance, as well as handwritten accusations by Herr Gräwe, dated 24 June 1936. For an authoritative account of Nazi control of the arts including their expulsion of Jews and other non-Aryans from the arts, see Alan Steinweis, *Art, Ideology, and Economics in Nazi Germany: The Reich Chambers of Music, Theater, and the Visual Arts* (Chapel Hill, 1993). Steinweis reveals that the Reich Chamber permitted a few exceptions for non-Aryans, mostly *Mischlinge*, to remain professionally active, but it kept that information away from the public; see pp. 116–20.

21. HHStA, Abt. 518, no. 4189, files for Ernesta V., including written testimony from the Protestant vicar's office in Wiesbaden, dated 1 March 1948, and the applicant's sworn statement dated 24 March 1950.

22. Hans Haurwitz, interview.

23. Ibid., p. 4.

24. Ibid., pp. 4–5.

25. Ibid., p. 6.

26. Hanns-Peter Herz, interview.

27. Ibid., p. 8.

28. Landesarchiv Berlin, Record Group 38 Kammergericht Berlin, Decimal File 3915, no. 39, file for businessman Martin F.

29. NWHD, RW58/57764, file for Karl R., including a three-page memorandum to the Gestapo in Düsseldorf concerning his status and appeals, dated 17 September 1936, letter from the Reichskammer der bildenden Künste to the Gestapo in Düsseldorf, dated 16 June 1937, and Karl R.'s further appeal (no date indicated).

30. NWHD, RW58/47071. This includes a dossier for Max S., a list of charges against him, plus his personal statement with signature. Also included is a police report from Essen about the incident with the tobacconist, dated 4 November 1943; statements by the tobacconist and by Marta; a letter by a police official from the prison in Essen on behalf of Max S., dated 1 June 1944; and movement orders from the Gestapo confirming his transport to Auschwitz on 31 July 1944.

31. Dietrich Goldschmidt, interview by author, Max Planck Institut für Bildungsforschung in Berlin, 12 December 1994. Tragically, Hans Goldschmidt, who was profoundly deaf, had been released from detention by the British authorities, only to die in his apartment in Wimbledon during a German air raid on London in the autumn of 1940. He never heard the sirens and therefore had not taken cover.

32. Dietrich Goldschmidt, interview.

33. NWHD, RW58/11136, concerning Adolf G., including his employer's report of 7 July 1942, his interrogation report, a follow-up report of 14 August 1942, and a concluding report of 28 August 1942.

34. NWHD, RW58/11196, report of 7 July 1942 concerning sabotage from Adolf Gersonsohn's former employer to the Industrie und Handelskammer, Düsseldorf, with transmission to the Abwehrstelle in Münster, plus two interrogation transcripts, the second of which was dated 14 August 1942, and a concluding report dated 28 August 1942.
35. HHStA, Abt. 461, no. 7664, Strafprozeßakten gegen den Metzger Siegfried G. This includes a memorandum from the prosecuting attorney of Frankfurt am Main to the Reichsminister for justice, dated 28 December 1936, plus a list of statements by eyewitnesses dated 22 October 1936, and a statement by Siegfried G. while in prison, dated 30 November 1936.
36. NWHD, RW58/29938, including Personalbogen for Rolf H., his police photograph and suggested sentence by Krefeld Gestapo, dated 15 March 1944; excerpts from police reports and interrogations of 29 November and 26 December 1943; a letter of support for Rolf by Heinrich Pöllen, dated 22 March 1944; and an unsigned denunciation report about Rolf, stamped 20 June 1944.
37. Ibid.
38. Martha Rohr, interview. Additional details added by Martha Rohr's daughter, Dr. Elisabeth Rohr, in a letter to the author dated 8 March 1995.
39. Gerda Leuchtenberg, interview by author, Rhine–Main region, 28 June 1994.
40. NWHD, RW58/3470, including a letter of denunciation by W. Zons of 16 February 1943; a memorandum announcing the dismissal of Alfred F. from the Landrat of Rhein-Wupper Kreis to the Gestapo in Düsseldorf; and an internal memorandum by the Gestapo in Cologne concerning Alfred F., dated 14 September 1942.
41. Helmut Langer, interview.
42. HHStA, Abt. 518, no. 199, copy of indictment, Generalstaatsanwalt, Kassel, dated 5 June 1944, copy submitted 30 April 1951.
43. Ibid., p. 2.
44. Ibid.
45. Ibid., p. 3; memorandum to Hessian minister of the interior, 11 September 1968.
46. HHStA, Abt. 518, no. 4712, file of Friedl Goldschmidt with his statement forwarded from the Katholiek Comité voor Slachtoffers van Geloofsverfolging to Hessian Restitution Authority in Wiesbaden, no date but probably late 1958 or early 1959.

CHAPTER 3: DRAWING THE LINE
1. See Hitler, *Mein Kampf*, p. 448.
2. See Noakes, "Development of Nazi Policy," pp. 306–15.
3. See Johnson, *Nazi Terror*, pp. 362–74, also his annotated notes on pp. 571–72. See also Robert Gellately, *The Gestapo and German Society: Enforcing Racial Policy, 1933–1945* (New York, 1990). It was a former persecution victim, Ingeborg Hecht, who used the term "invisible walls" in her autobiographical account, *Als unsichtbare Mauern wuchsen: Eine deutsche Familie unter den Nürnberger Rassengesetzen* (When Invisible Walls Arose . . .) (Hamburg, 1984).
4. Eva Heilmann, interview.
5. Cited in Erwin Leiser, *Gott hat kein Kleingeld: Erinnerungen* (Cologne, 1993), p. 49.
6. Hessisches Hauptstaatsarchiv, Wiesbaden, Abt. 468, No. 501, 5a KW 1/1938 Heintz . . . Hereafter cited as HHStA with appropriate file classification.

7. HHStA, Abt. 468, no. 501, 5a KW 1/1938, appeal decision, 1 D 851/1937; and Bescheinigung of Oberstaatsanwalt Kurtzwig, dated 6 February 1958.

8. See Noakes, "Development of Nazi Policy," p. 310.

9. HHStA, Abt. 461, no. 11133, Sammelakten über Bestrafung der Verbrechen und Vergehen im Allgemeinen, memorandum from Dr. Amrhein to Generalstaatsanwalt concerning Harlem Klub and OK Gang Club, June 1940.

10. Ibid., memorandum from Staatsanwalt Schlaeger to Generalstaatsanwalt concerning Harlem Klub, 9 February 1942. For an authoritative treatment of Nazi attitudes toward popular music, see Michael H. Kater, *Different Drummers: Jazz in the Culture of Nazi Germany* (New York, 1992). On dissident youth, see Detlev J. K. Peukert, *Inside Nazi Germany: Conformity, Opposition, and Racism in Everyday Life* (New Haven, 1987), pp. 145–74.

11. HHStA, Abt. 461, no. 17910, Handakten, Leichensache, H. Ullmann, dated 14 December 1942.

12. Gerda Leuchtenberg, interview by author, 28 June 1994.

13. HHStA, Abt. 6262, concerning Karl Metzger, undated.

14. Johnson, *Nazi Terror,* p. 323.

15. HHStA, Abt. 461, no. 8672, sentencing for Hermann C. This includes a memorandum from the Gestapo in Wiesbaden to the chief prosecuting attorney in Frankfurt am Main, dated 19 October 1943.

16. HHstA, Abt. 461, no. 8753, File, Strafsache, Margarete W. This includes her husband's letter to the Gestapo of 10 September 1943; the judgment, dated 17 December 1943; and the decision of the prosecuting attorney of Frankfurt of 20 March 1945.

17. Nordrhein-Westfälisches Hauptstaatsarchiv, Düsseldorf, RW58/21813 and RW58/29393 concerning Anna H.; hereafter cited as NWHD with appropriate file classification.

18. NWHD, RW58/55375, memorandum from Oberbürgermeister in Krefeld-Uerdingen to Gestapo in Krefeld, dated 25 July 1938.

19. NWHD, RW58/33926, file for Wilhelm S. (but including extensive information about the Family G.), from Gestapo Krefeld to Gestapo Düsseldorf, 4 May 1942.

20. Ibid. Viktor Lutze, head of the SA, was a prominent Nazi leader.

21. Ibid.

22. Ibid., copy of letter sent by Hubertus at Hotel Metropole in Wiesbaden to Magdalene G., with postmark of Luftgaukommando IX, dated 20 November 1942.

23. Ibid., memorandum, strictly confidential, from Höhere SS und Polizeiführer to Gestapo Leitstelle, attn. Regierungsrat Breder, subject, removal of citizenship of the Jewish *Mischlinge*, dated 29 September 1942.

24. Ibid., memorandum, Gestapo Krefeld to Gestapo Düsseldorf, concerning radio singer Wilhelm S., dated 16 February 1943.

25. NWHD, RW58/152, files concerning Rolf B., including arrest report of 21 December 1942; denunciation reports by neighbors such as Aurelie S. and Frieda M. of 3 December 1942; confession by Hilda S., also of 3 December 1942; Gestapo order transferring Rolf B. to Auschwitz as of 1 February 1943; and memorandum with prisoner's photograph and typewritten statement confirming his death as of 17 April 1943.

26. NWHD, RW58/21100, concerning Erna and Moritz M., 19 April 1943, 5 May 1943, and sentencing of 24 August 1944.

27. Martha Rohr, interview.

28. See Johnson, *Nazi Terror*, pp. 289–93; see also Harry Oosterhuis, "Medicine, Male Bonding, and Homosexuality in Nazi Germany," *Journal of Contemporary History* 32 (1997): 187–205.

29. NWHD, RW58/21755, concerning Günther O., including his personnel file; Wehrmacht memorandum concerning Heinz K. of 6 March 1943; and Essen prosecuting attorney's sentence concerning Günther O. of 4 May 1943.

30. See Johnson, *Nazi Terror*, pp. 287–88.

31. NWHD, RW58/52666, deposition by Hans E. to Criminal Inspector K. in Essen, 16 April 1943, accompanied by depositions of Friedl E. and Edna S.

32. NWHD, RW58/12511, memorandum from Ortsgruppenleiter, Düsseldorf, to Geheime Staatspolizei, Düsseldorf, dated 5 April 1941, relating charges by PG Heinrich Johannes against Hanni B.; also the interrogation report signed by Hanni B. and Putz.

33. NWHD, RW 58/41885, copy of report of Kreisleitung Wuppertal to Kriminalrat Hufenstuhl dated 30 July 1942; three denunciation reports by housewives dated 4 August 1942; deposition by Erna B. of 6 August 1942; statement by Karl M. of 6 August 1942; memorandum from Wuppetal Gestapo of 3 October 1942 recommending the transfer of Karl M. to a concentration camp; a telegram ordering his transfer to Buchenwald, dated 28 October 1942; and a telegram from Commandant Höss at Auschwitz to Gestapo headquarters in Düsseldorf announcing the time, place, and cause of Karl M.'s death.

CHAPTER 4: THE PENULTIMATE STEP

1. See Noakes, "Development of Nazi Policy," p. 337.

2. See Kershaw, *Nazi Dictatorship*, pp. 93–133.

3. See Noakes, "Development of Nazi Policy," p. 338.

4. For a detailed treatment of Hitler's 1939 "prophecy" that a second world war would lead to the destruction of Europe's Jews, see the second volume of Ian Kershaw's biography, *Hitler: 1936–1945, Nemesis* (New York, 2000), pp. 461–95.

5. See Christian Gerlach, "The Wannsee Conference, the Fate of German Jews, and Hitler's Decision in Principle to Exterminate all European Jews," in *The Holocaust: Origins, Implementations, Aftermath*, ed. Omer Bartov (New York, 2000), pp. 111–15. The Wannsee Protocol, both in its original German and in English translation, can be found in John Mendelsohn, ed., *The Holocaust*, vol. 11, *The Wannsee Protocol and a 1944 Report on Auschwitz by the Office of Strategic Services* (New York, 1982).

6. See Noakes, "Development of Nazi Policy," pp. 339–41.

7. Ibid., p. 341.

8. Gerlach, "Wannsee Conference," pp. 128–29.

9. See Stoltzfus, *Resistance of the Heart*, pp. 243–57.

10. Noakes, "Development of Nazi Policy," pp. 341–52; see also Meyer, *"Jüdische Mischlinge*, pp. 237–38.

11. See Kershaw, *Hitler: 1936–1945, Nemesis*, pp. 784–86.

12. Dr. Rudolf Klein, interview.

13. Ibid., p. 9.

14. Ibid., p. 11.

15. Ibid., p. 12.
16. Ibid., p. 14.
17. Ibid., p. 17.
18. Ibid., p. 18.
19. See Noakes, "Development of Nazi Policy," p. 337.
20. Werner Jentsch, conversation with author, on a train in GDR, August 1978.
21. Ibid.
22. Ibid.; also correspondence, author with Jentsch family, 9 March 1995.
23. Charles Milford, interview. He officially changed his name from Klaus Muehlfelder to Charles Milford when he became an American citizen.
24. Ibid.
25. Hessisches Hauptstaatsarchiv, Wiesbaden, Abt. 659, no. 936, Beiakte, Entschädigung, Rüdesheim am Rhein, sworn statement of Horst R., 14 September 1950; hereafter cited as HHStA with appropriate file classification.
26. Charles Milford, formerly Klaus Muehlfelder, interview.
27. Ibid.
28. HHStA, Abt. 659, no. 936, p. 2.
29. Charles Milford, interview.
30. Ibid., p. 9.
31. Ibid., pp. 10–11.
32. See David K. Yelton, "Ein Volk Steht auf: The German Volkssturm and Nazi Strategy, 1944–1945," Journal of Military History 64, no. 4 (October 2000): 1061–83.
33. Otto Hess, interview.
34. Personal memoir prepared by Horst Hartwich, presented to the author on 11 December 1994; hereafter cited as Hartwich memoir.
35. Ibid., p. 45.
36. Hanns-Peter Herz, interview.
37. Ibid.
38. Hartwich memoir, pp. 46–47.
39. Ibid., pp. 48–49.
40. Dietrich Goldschmidt, interview by author, 12 December 1994, pp. 4–5.
41. Ibid., p. 5.
42. Ibid.
43. Otto Hess, interview.
44. Dr. Helmut Coper, interview by author, Berlin, 30 June 1994.
45. Ibid., p. 7.
46. Ibid., pp. 8–9.
47. Ibid., pp. 9–10.
48. Erika Waldegger, daughter of Emil Steiner, interview.
49. Ibid.
50. See Noakes, "Development of Nazi Policy," p. 351.
51. Dr. Meta Alexander, interview, transcript, pp. 11–12.
52. Ibid., p. 12.
53. Dr. Thekla Schwarz, née Brandt, interview.
54. Ibid., p. 7.
55. Ibid. p. 8.

56. Ibid., p. 7.
57. Ibid., p. 8.
58. Ursula Kühn, interview, pp. 15–18.
59. Ibid., p. 20.
60. HHStA, Abt. 461, no. 31,864, files concerning Heinz Karry.
61. Ibid., deposition by Willi K., Frankfurt, 1 March 1946.
62. Ibid., deposition by Heinz Karry, Frankfurt, 26 March 1946.
63. HHStA, Abt. 518, no. 6262, file of Karl J. M. with appendix to application for restitution under Härtefond, no date.
64. HHStA, Abt. 518, no. 4756, K. Josef G. to Regierungspräsident in Kassel, 23 July 1951.
65. Ibid.
66. See Noakes, "Development of Nazi Policy," p. 348.
67. For a treatment on the German medical profession, 1933–1945, see Robert J. Lifton, *The Nazi Doctors: Medical Killing and the Psychology of Genocide* (New York, 1986), pp. 71–75, 100, 515 n. 15. For a study on the euthanasia program as the start of genocide, see Henry Friedlander, *Origins of Nazi Genocide: From Euthanasia to the Final Solution* (Chapel Hill, 1995).
68. HHStA, Abt. 518, no. 3411, files concerning Wolfgang F. , including his lengthy written statement to an official session of the Hessian Wiedergutmachungskammer, dated 20 February 1953. His statement received written corroborative statements from two other eyewitnesses and fellow *Mischlinge*, Kurt H. and Fritz B., both of whom had also been incarcerated in the same camps with Wolfgang F.
69. Ibid.
70. Ibid. Further detail on Hadamar and the Nazi euthanasia program can be found in Patricia L. Heberer, "'Exitus heute in Hadamar': The Hadamar Facility and 'Euthanasia' in Nazi Germany" (Ph.D. diss., University of Maryland, 2001).
71. HHStA, Abt. 518, no. 4493, concerning Ludwig Schmidt, 27 May 1946. Patricia Heberer noted in her dissertation, cited in note 70 above, that in addition to the 10,000 victims gassed at Hadamar during the euthanasia program up to 1941, an additional 4,400 persons were murdered by narcotic overdose or lethal injection from 1942 until the Americans overran Hadamar in late March 1945.
72. HHStA, Abt. 518, no. 3411, files concerning Wolfgang F.
73. HHStA, Abt. 518, no. 3568, letter, Georg B. to Betreungsstelle für ehem. Pol. Häftlinge, Kassel, 30 October 1946.
74. HHStA, Abt. 659, no. 915, letter, Bürgermeister Eskelund in Hattenheim, to Landrat, Rheingaukreis, 3 March 1948, concerning Otto E.
75. HHStA, Abt. 659, no. 915, deposition by Henrika Z. to Landrat, Rheingaukreis, 8 March 1948, concerning Otto E.
76. Ibid.
77. HHStA, Abt. 659, no. 915, deposition by Otto E. to Betreuungsstelle für politisch, rassisch, und religiös Verfolgte, 15 December 1947.

CHAPTER 5: A TIME OF SILENCE

1. Protestants predominated, but there were major exceptions, such as the heavily Catholic Rhineland. Nathan Stoltzfus has observed that in the Weimar Republic, two-thirds to three-quarters of marriages between Jews and Christians were com-

posed of Aryan women married to Jewish men. Although generalizations are dangerous, the men tended to be less attuned to religion, a fact that may help explain why most Jewish-Christian households became secular in outlook and why the children of those marriages were baptized into the two Christian denominations recognized by the state. See Nathan Stoltzfus, "The Limits of Policy: Social Protection of Intermarried German Jews in Nazi Germany," in *Social Outsiders*, ed. Gellately and Stoltzfus, p. 125.

2. See Christian Pross, *Paying for the Past: The Struggle over Reparations for Surviving Victims of the Nazi Terror* (Baltimore, 1998), p. 21.
3. See Johnson, *Nazi Terror*, pp. 29–33, 479–81.
4. Professor Werner Jentsch, conversation with author, East Germany, August 1978, transcript of notes in author's possession. The author conducted further correspondence with Frau Jentsch, who, because of her husband's advanced age and delicate health, kindly replied in his stead on 16 March 1995. However, she also made it clear that no further interviews with her ailing husband were possible, since the topic now caused him great anguish.
5. Professor Werner Jentsch, conversation with author, August 1978.
6. Hessisches Hauptstaatsarchiv, Wiesbaden, Abt. 518, no. 2109, files of Ruth S., born Ruth W. This includes a letter of 13 March 1958 from her attorney to the Entschädigungsbehörde in Wiesbaden (hereafter cited as HHStA Wiesbaden, with appropriate file classification).
7. See Pross, *Paying for the Past*, p. 171.
8. Hessisches Hauptstaatsarchiv, Wiesbaden (HHStA), Abt. 518, no. 3147, files of Walter S., decision by Hessian Regierungspräsident concerning Walter S., dated 6 September 1950.
9. HHStA, Abt. 518, no. 3147, files concerning Walter S. The files include a letter of corroboration of his claims by his former high school teacher, Rudolf H., dated 3 January 1950; an application of restitution by Walter S., dated 6 September 1950; a second declaration by Walter S., dated 4 October 1950; and a much more detailed declaration by Walter S., dated 19 March 1951.
10. See James F. Tent, *The Free University of Berlin: A Political History* (Bloomington, 1988), pp. 39–49 and passim.
11. Ibid.; also Otto Hess, interview.
12. Eva Furth, née Heilmann, interview.
13. See Leiser, *Gott hat kein Kleingeld*, pp. 49–50; Peter Heilmann, interview.
14. Dr. Meta Alexander, interview.
15. Ibid., p. 13.
16. Ibid.
17. Dr. Thekla Schwarz, née Brandt, interview.
18. Dr. Helmut Coper, interview by author, Berlin, 4 September 1985.
19. Dr. Helmut Coper, interview by author, Berlin, 30 June 1994.
20. Ibid.
21. For Hartwich's role in the Free University, see Tent, *Free University of Berlin*. The author is indebted to Dr. Hartwich for the use of his unpublished postwar account of his experiences under National Socialism.
22. Hanns-Peter Herz, interview.

23. Hans-Joachim Boehm, interview.
24. Ernst Benda, interview.
25. See Noakes, "Development of Nazi Policy," p. 354.
26. For the Rosenstrasse demonstrations, see Stoltzfus, *Resistance of the Heart*, pp. 209–57.
27. Hans Haurwitz, interview, p. 6.
28. Ibid.
29. Ibid.
30. Charles Milford, interview.
31. Ibid., p. 11.
32. Ibid.
33. Helmut Langer, interview, p. 7.
34. Ibid., p. 8.
35. Ibid., p. 9.
36. Ibid.
37. Ibid.
38. Martha Rohr, interview, pp. 7–8.
39. HHStA, Abt. 518, no. 3568, files for Georg B., including his sworn statement to the Kassel Authority for former political detainees, dated 30 October 1946.
40. Ibid.; memorandum attached to Georg B. file, Gerdum and Breuer to Kassel Betreuungsstelle für ehemalige politische Häftlinge, dated 9 December 1946.
41. Ibid.; Georg B.'s sworn statement of 30 October 1946.
42. Ibid.
43. HHStA, Abt. 518, no. 4610, file for Erich G., including his response of 23 July 1951 to a communication from the Regierungspräsident in Kassel to him of 19 July 1951.
44. Ibid.; see letter accompanying Erich G.'s communication, namely a letter from the Landrat des Kreises Witzenhausen to the Regierungspräsident in Kassel, dated 4 August 1951.
45. Ibid.; attachment to Erich G.'s file, letter from Bürgermeister of Witzenhausen to Regierungspräsident in Kassel, dated 22 October 1951.
46. HHStA, Abt. 518, no. 4610, file of Erich G., namely his letter to Regierungspräsident in Kassel, dated 23 July 1951.
47. HHStA, Abt. 518, no. 784. This file contains Gustav K.'s prisoner's identity card from Buchenwald, a SHAEF-issued certification, proving that he had been located as a prisoner at Buchenwald, liberated on 11 April 1945, and listing the particulars of his incarceration plus his fingerprint. The file also contains Gustav K.'s correspondence, listing the items stolen by the Gestapo in 1943, as well as a memorandum from the Wiesbaden Office for Racially and Religiously Persecuted Persons, dated 5 May 1950, acknowledging his arrest and detainment and releasing DM 2000 for the purchase of precision repair equipment.
48. HHStA, Abt. 518, no. 3325, files of Adalbert Levy, including two letters submitted by his attorney to the Hessian Restitution Authority in Wiesbaden, dated 7 June 1955 and 14 May 1957, respectively.
49. Ibid.
50. HHStA, Abt. 518, no. 6679, file of Gerhard S. This includes his initial sworn statement of 1 December 1949 and a second, more detailed sworn statement of 24 May 1956.

51. HHStA, Abt. 518, no. 3250, file concerning Heinz-Gustav W. memorandum from Hilfsdezernent H. to Präsident des Oberlandgerichts, dated 8 May 1951.
52. Erika Waldegger, daughter of Emil Steiner, interview.
53. Ibid.
54. Steiner's "popularity" among ex-Nazis seeking *Persilscheine* was hardly an isolated case. Historian Beate Meyer noted in her research and her many interviews with former *Mischlinge* that the adults among them became favorite targets for ex-Nazis, seeking certificates or proofs of exoneration during the postwar denazification phase. See Meyer, *"Jüdische Mischlinge,"* p. 365.
55. Erika Waldegger, interview.
56. Dr. Rudolf Klein, interview.
57. Ibid.
58. Ibid.
59. Ursula Kühn, interview, p. 19.
60. Ibid., p. 21.
61. See Johnson, *Nazi Terror*, pp. 463–87.

CONCLUSION

1. See Hilberg, *Destruction of the European Jews*, p. 274.
2. See Meyer, *"Jüdische Mischlinge,"* p. 357.
3. Sigrid Lekebusch clearly identifies this phenomenon of survivors' guilt in *Not und Verfolgung der Christen jüdischer Herkunft im Rheinland, 1933–1945: Darstellung und Dokumentation* (Cologne, 1995), pp. 242–44.
4. See Meyer, *"Jüdische Mischlinge,"* pp. 357–58.
5. It was only after decades of silence that former SPD chancellor Helmut Schmidt finally revealed his wartime status as a *Mischling* to his friend and colleague French president Giscard d'Estaing. See Valéry Giscard d'Estaing, *Le Pouvoir et la Vie* (Paris, 1988), pp. 161–62.

BIBLIOGRAPHY

PRIMARY SOURCES

Archival Material
Hessisches Hauptstaatsarchiv Wiesbaden.
Files of Criminal Proceedings of the State Prosecuting Attorney of the District Court of Frankfurt am Main, Abteilung 461.
Files of Criminal Proceedings of the State Prosecuting Attorney of the District Court of Wiesbaden, Abteilung 468.
Postwar Files of the Hessian Office for Compensation and Support of Persecuted Jewish *Mischlinge*, Abteilung 518.
Landesarchiv Berlin.
Berlin Supreme Court, Record Group 38, Decimal File 3915, Documents Concerning Compensation.
Berlin Supreme Court (Civilian Chamber), Decimal File 2933, Documents of the Chamber of Compensation.
Nordrhein-Westfälisches Hauptstaatsarchiv Düsseldorf.
Files of the Former Geheime Staatspolizei, Record Group 58.

Correspondence and Interviews by James F. Tent
Alexander, Meta. Berlin, 29 June 1994.
Benda, Ernst. Karlsruhe, 8 December 1994.
Boehm, Hans-Joachim. Berlin, 28 June 1994.
Coper, Helmut. Berlin, 4 September 1985; Berlin, 30 June 1994.
Furth, Née Heilmann, Eva. Berlin, 13 December 1994.
Goldschmidt, Dietrich. Berlin, 12 December 1994.
Hartwich, Horst W. (including his private manuscript). Berlin.
Haurwitz, Hans. Telephone interview, Erie, Pa., 6 November 1994.
Heilmann, Peter. Berlin, 10 January 1996.
Herz, Hanns-Peter. Berlin, 30 June 1994.
Hess, Otto. Berlin, 12 December 1994.
Jentsch, Werner. Conversation on a train in GDR, August 1978.
Klein, Rudolf. Vienna, 15 June 1996.
Kühn, Ursula (not her real name). Hamburg, 6 December 1994.
Langer, Helmut. Rhine–Main region, 23 June 1994.
Leuchtenberg, Gerda. Rhine–Main region, 28 June 1994.
Milford, Charles. Telephone interview, Palo Alto, Calif., 10 July 1994.
Rohr, Martha. Wintersdorf near Trier, 9 December 1994.
Schwarz, née Brandt, Thekla. Berlin, 29 June 1994.
Waldegger, née Steiner, Erika. Memmingen, Bavaria, 17 December 1994.

SECONDARY SOURCES

Books

Bankier, David. *The Germans and the Final Solution: Public Opinion under Nazism.* Cambridge, 1992.

Bartov, Omer, ed. *The Holocaust: Origins, Implementations, Aftermath.* New York, 2000.

Baumann, Arnulf H., ed. *Ausgegrenzt: Schicksalswege "nichtarischer" Christen in der Hitlerzeit.* Hannover, 1992.

Benz, Wolfgang. *Holocaust: A German Historian Examines the Genocide.* New York, 1999.

Braach, Mile. *Rückblende: Erinnerungen einer Neunzigjährigen.* Frankfurt am Main, 1992.

Büttner, Ursula. *Die Not der Juden teilen: Christlich-jüdische Familien im Dritten Reich: Beispiel und Zeugnis des Schriftstellers Robert Brendel.* Hamburg, 1988.

———. *Die verlassenen Kinder der Kirche: der Umgang mit Christen jüdischer Herkunft im "Dritten Reich."* Göttingen, 1998.

Crane, Cynthia. *Divided Lives: The Untold Stories of Jewish-Christian Women in Nazi Germany.* New York, 2000.

Deutsch, Gitta. *The Red Thread.* Riverside, 1996 (translation from the German *Böcklinstrassenelegie,* Vienna, 1993).

Duve, Freimut. *Vom Krieg in der Seele: Rücksichten eines Deutschen.* Frankfurt am Main, 1994.

Elbe, Joachim von. *Witness to History: A Refugee from the Third Reich Remembers.* Madison, 1988.

Friedlander, Henry. *Origins of Nazi Genocide: From Euthanasia to the Final Solution.* Chapel Hill, 1995.

Gellately, Robert. *The Gestapo and German Society: Enforcing Racial Policy, 1933–1945.* Oxford, 1990.

Gellately, Robert, and Nathan Stoltzfus, eds. *Social Outsiders in Nazi Germany.* Princeton, 2001.

Giscard d'Estaing, Valéry. *Le Pouvoir et la Vie.* Paris, 1988.

Grunberger, Richard. *The Twelve-Year Reich: A Social History of Nazi Germany, 1933–1945.* New York, 1971.

Hecht, Ingeborg. *Als unsichtbare Mauern Wuchsen: Eine deutsche Familie unter den Nürnberger Rassengesetzen.* Hamburg, 1984.

———. *Von der Heilsamkeit des Erinnerns: Opfer der Nürnberger Gesetze Begegnen sich.* Hamburg, 1991.

Hilberg, Raul. *The Destruction of the European Jews.* New York, 1973.

Hitler, Adolf. *Mein Kampf.* Ed. and trans. John Chamberlain et al., New York, 1941.

Jacoby, Susan. *Half-Jew: A Daughter's Search for Her Family's Buried Past.* New York, 2000.

Jarausch, Konrad H. *The Unfree Professions: German Lawyers, Teachers, and Engineers, 1900–1950.* New York, 1990.

Johnson, Eric A. *Nazi Terror: The Gestapo, Jews, and Ordinary Germans.* New York, 1999.

Kater, Michael H. *Different Drummers: Jazz in the Culture of Nazi Germany.* New York, 1992.

Kershaw, Ian. *Hitler, 1889–1936: Hubris.* New York, 1998.

———. *Hitler, 1936–1945: Nemesis.* New York, 2000.

————. *The Nazi Dictatorship: Problems and Perspectives of Interpretation.* 4th ed. New York, 2000.

Koehn, Ilse. *Mischling, Second Degree: My Childhood in Nazi Germany.* New York, 1977.

Krüger, Helmut. *Der halbe Stern: Leben als deutsch-jüdischer "Mischling" im Dritten Reich.* Berlin, 1993.

Kuehn, Heinz R. *Mixed Blessings: An Almost Ordinary Life in Hitler's Germany.* Athens, Ga., 1988.

Leiser, Erwin. *Gott hat kein Kleingeld: Erinnerungen.* Cologne, 1993.

Lekebusch, Sigrid. *Not und Verfolgung der Christen jüdischer Herkunft im Rheinland, 1933–1945: Darstellung und Dokumentation.* Cologne, 1995.

Lifton, Robert J. *The Nazi Doctors: Medical Killing and the Psychology of Genocide.* New York, 1986.

Lindemann, Gerhard. *"Typisch jüdisch": Die Stellung der Ev.-luth. Landeskirche Hannovers zu Antijudaismus, Judenfeindschaft und Antisemitismus, 1919–1949.* Berlin, 1998.

Maier, Karl-Heinz. *Und hört niemals auf zu kämpfen: Lebensbericht des Thomas A. Sharon.* Berlin, 1994.

Mendelsohn, John, ed. *The Holocaust: Selected Documents in Eighteen Volumes.* Vol. 11, *The Wannsee Protocol and a 1944 Report on Auschwitz by the Office of Strategic Services.* New York, 1982.

Meyer, Beate, *"Jüdische Mischlinge": Rassenpolitik und Verfolgungserfahrung, 1933–1945.* Hamburg, 1999.

Pauwels, Jacques R. *Women, Nazis, and Universities: Female University Students in the Third Reich, 1933–1945.* Westport, 1984.

Peukert, Detlev J. K. *Inside Nazi Germany: Conformity, Opposition, and Racism in Everyday Life.* New Haven, 1987.

Pommerin, Reiner. *"Sterilisierung der Rheinlandbastarde": Das Schicksal einer farbigen deutschen Minderheit, 1911–1937.* Düsseldorf, 1979.

Pross, Christian. *Paying for the Past: The Struggle over Reparations for Surviving Victims of the Nazi Terror.* Baltimore, 1998.

Pschorr, Elizabeth. *A Privileged Marriage: The Autobiography of Elizabeth Pschorr.* Sausalito, 1994.

Rigg, Bryan Mark. *Hitler's Jewish Soldiers: The Untold Story of Nazi Racial Laws and Men of Jewish Descent in the German Military.* Lawrence, Kans., 2002.

Schmitt, Hans A. *Lucky Victim: An Ordinary Life in Extraordinary Times, 1933–1946.* Baton Rouge, 1989.

————. *Quakers and Nazis: Inner Light in Outer Darkness.* Columbia, Mo., 1997.

Schweitzer, Christoph E., ed. *The Twelve Grandchildren of Eugen and Algunde Hollaender Schweitzer: The Impact of Nazi Racial Policies on One Family.* Chapel Hill, 1996.

Stein, Oswald. *Abgebaut: Eine Familie erlebt das Dritte Reich.* Frankfurt am Main, 1992.

Steinweis, Alan E. *Art, Ideology, and Economics in Nazi Germany: The Reich Chambers of Music, Theater, and the Visual Arts.* Chapel Hill, 1993.

Stoltzfus, Nathan. *Resistance of the Heart: Intermarriage and the Rosenstrasse Protest in Nazi Germany.* New York, 1996.

Tent, James F. *E-Boat Alert: Defending the Normandy Invasion Fleet.* Annapolis, 1996.

————. *The Free University of Berlin: A Political History.* Bloomington, 1988.

Tuchel, Johannes. *Am Großen Wannsee 56–58: Von der Villa Minoux zum Haus der Wannsee-Konferenz.* Berlin, 1992.

Vuletić, Aleksandar-Saša. *Christen Jüdischer Herkunft im Dritten Reich: Verfolgung und Organisierte Selbsthilfe, 1933–1939.* Mainz, 1999.

Wiedemann, Heinrich. *Unter Denkmalschutz: Sieben Erzählungen aus deutscher Vergangenheit.* Gerlingen, 1995.

Articles, Papers, and Dissertations

Gerlach, Christian. "The Wannsee Conference, the Fate of German Jews, and Hitler's Decision in Principle to Exterminate all European Jews." In *The Holocaust: Origins, Implementation, Aftermath.* Ed. Omer Bartov. New York, 2000.

Heberer, Patricia L. "'Exitus heute in Hadamar': The Hadamar Facility and 'Euthanasia' in Nazi Germany." Ph.D. diss., University of Maryland, 2001.

Liesenberg, Carsten. "Verfolgung und Vernichtung der Juden." In *Nationalsozialismus in Thüringen.* Ed. Detlev Heiden and Günther Mai. Weimar, 1995.

Lösener, Bernhard. "Das Reichsministerium des Innern und die Judengesetzgebung." *Vierteljahrshefte für Zeitgeschichte* 11, no. 3 (July 1961): pp. 262–313.

Meyer, Beate. "Besser ist doch, man taucht unter": Zur Verfolgung der 'Halbjuden' in Hamburg." In *Hamburg in der NS Zeit: Ergebnisse neurerer Forschung.* Ed. Frank Bajohr and Joachim Szodryzynski. Hamburg, 1993, pp. 125–48.

———. "Man nahm so vieles hin ohne Regung." In *Verletzungen: Lebensgeschichtliche Verarbeitung von Kriegserfahrungen.* Ed. Ulrike Jureit and Beate Meyer. Hamburg, 1994, pp. 26–45.

———. "Zwischen allen Stühlen: 'Mischehen und 'Mischlinge.'" In *"Wo Wurzeln Waren...": Juden in Hamburg-Eimsbüttel, 1933–1945.* Ed. Sybille Baumbach et al. Hamburg, 1993, pp. 147–225.

Noakes, Jeremy. "The Development of Nazi Policy towards the German-Jewish 'Mischlinge,' 1933–1945." In *Leo Baeck Institute Yearbook 34.* New York, 1989, pp. 291–354.

Oberlaender, Franklin A. "The Family Dynamics of German Protestants of Jewish Descent, Stigmatized in Nazi Germany and their Offspring Born in Postwar West Germany." *Holocaust and Genocide Studies* 9, no. 3 (winter 1995): 360–77.

Oosterhuis, Harry. "Medicine, Male Bonding, and Homosexuality in Nazi Germany." *Journal of Contemporary History* 32 (1997): 187–205.

Rigg, Bryan Mark. "Jews and Men of Jewish Descent Who Served in the German Armed Forces during World War II." Ph.D. diss., Darwin College, Cambridge University, 2001.

Yelton, David K., "Ein Volk Steht auf: The German Volkssturm and Nazi Strategy, 1944–1945." *Journal of Military History* 64, no. 4 (October 2000).

INDEX

Geltungsjuden (continued)
Hadamar and, 187–188
Jewish upbringing and, 194
postwar experiences of, 211–212
surveillance of, 92, 116
Geneva, Switzerland, 155
Genocide, 237
Georg B., 189, 219–220
Gerdum and Breuer (Company), 220
Gerhard S., 226–227
German blood. *See Deutschblütige*
German Communist Party (KPD), 204
German Labor Front, 64, 119, 147
German people
Mischlinge as, 2, 45
weakening the will of, 97
See also Rassenschande
German Social Democratic Labor Party.
See Social Democrats
Germany
forced-labor camps in, 162–173
postwar (*see* Postwar period)
remaining in, 237, 238
returning to, 159–160, 173, 201–202
Gersonsohn, Adolf, 87–89
Gestapo
children and, 36
civil service and, 197
disobeying, 189–191
documents, xiii, 240–241
influence of, 8
informers, 92, 94, 104, 109, 116, 191–192
legal prosecution of, 196–197
Nuremberg decrees and, 102–103
pensions for, 197
postwar period, 196–197
roundups by, 14, 15 (*see also* Deportation)
senior officials of, 196–197
single women and, 78–79
youth organizations and, 109–110
See also Denunciations; Surveillance
Ghettoization, 12, 103, 141
Giessen, Germany, 178–179, 190, 232
Goebbels, Josef, 6, 13–14, 102, 148

Goethe, Johann Wolfgang von, 35
Goldbach (Herr), 214
Goldschmidt, Dietrich, 86–87, 167–168
Goldschmidt, Hans, 86
Gontard School, 51–52
Göring, Hermann, 12, 144, 148
Göttingen, Germany, 168
Gräwe (Herr), 77–78
Great Britain, 86, 211
Greater Hesse archives, xiii
Greece, 65
Grefrath, Germany, 190
Gross, Walter, 108
Group identity, 59
Grunewald, Germany, 163–164
Guards
in forced-labor camps, 165–166, 167, 168, 171, 185, 197–198
Luftwaffe, 165, 171
SS, 171, 197–198
Guilt, 238, 239
Gustav K., 223–224
Gypsies, 1, 149, 152

Haciendas, 98–99
Hadamar, 186–187, 188, 252n71
Halberstadt, Germany, 182
Halbjuden. See Half-Jews
Half-Africans, 57, 246n50
Half-Aryans, 4
Half-Jews, ix
current terminology and, 241
definition of, 4
education of, 22, 26–29, 35–43, 45–48, 50–53, 55
emigration of, 97–99
employment for, 66–67, 69–75, 77–81, 87–89, 93–97
military service by, 64–69, 76–77
in the Netherlands, 98
vs. quarter-Jews, 23
statistics on, 103, 241
See also Mischlinge
Half-Mexicans, 57–58, 59
Halle an der Saale, Germany, 156, 198
Hamburg, Germany, 178, 232, 233

Social discrimination *(continued)*
 Nuremberg decrees and, 101–103, 108
 postwar period, 195, 196–197, 205–206
 in schools, 23, 28–29, 30
 state-sponsored, 239
 suicide and, 111
 women and, 111–113, 116–121
 in youth organizations, 31, 107–110
Social isolation, 29, 30, 104–105, 110–111
Socialists, 167
Socialist Unity party, 203
Soldiers, sexual relations with, 132–133.
  See also Military service; Military
  veterans
Sondereinsätze, 217
Songs, 41–42, 115, 164
South America, 98–99
Soviet forces, 211, 212–213, 234
Soviet Union, 34, 140, 143
Soviet zone
 compensation in, 234
 education in, xi, 202–203, 202–206,
   207–208, 210, 213–214
 forced labor in, 216
 refugees in, 216
 speaking out in, 202
Spanish Loyalists, 152
SPD. *See* Social Democrats
Speaking out
 to family, 218
 on forced labor, 221
 refusal to, 207, 238, 241–242
 in the Soviet zone, 202
 willingness to, 197, 205, 212, 214, 233
Spinnfaser (Company), 220
Sports, 25
SS (Schutzstaffel), 8, 171, 197–198
Stalingrad defeat, 34
St. Antoine Prison, 155
Star of David label, 85, 91, 136
Steiner, Eleanor, 76, 174–175
Steiner, Emil
 employment for, 76–77
 forced labor by, 173–175
 postwar experiences of, 228–229,
   255n54

Sterilization
 of African-Germans, 246n50
 involuntary, 3, 144, 145, 146, 211
St. Franziskus Oberlyzeum, 42
St. Matthias Gemeinde, 42
Stoltzfus, Nathan, 7–8, 14, 252–253n1
Storm troopers, 37, 46, 214
Streicher, Julius, 9, 102, 125
Stroux, Johannes, 72
St. Tamié Cloister, 154
Stubenältester, 181
Stuckart, Wilhelm
 on Aryan relatives, 13–14, 144–145,
   146
 Himmler and, 146
 in policymaking, 8
 on racial laws, 5, 6, 11
 Wannsee Conference and, 144–145
Sturm Abteilung (SA), 37, 46, 214
Sudetenland, 43–44, 95, 100, 125, 214–
   215
Suicide, 111
Summer teachers camp, 25
Supervisory positions, 95
Surveillance
 of children, 36
 of correspondence, 120, 121
 extent of, 191–192
 of extramarital relations, 132–134
 of *Geltungsjuden,* 92, 116
 of Jewish physicians, 177
 marital status and, 134
 in villages, 127
 See also Denunciations; Informers
Survival
 anonymity and *(see* Anonymity)
 in concentration camps, 185–188
 guilt and, 239
 strategy for, 99–100, 242
Swing music, 109
Switzerland, 154–155, 229–230

Teachers
 attitudes of, 24, 28, 30–31, 35, 47, 60
 as authority figures, 24, 36–37
 emotional damage from, 36–37